PHILIP PULLMAN'S

His Dark Materials

PHILIP PULLMAN'S

His Dark Materials

—A MULTIPLE ALLEGORY—

Attacking Religious Superstition in *The Lion,
the Witch and the Wardrobe* and *Paradise Lost*

LEONARD F. WHEAT

 **Prometheus Books**
59 John Glenn Drive
Amherst, New York 14228–2119

Published 2008 by Prometheus Books

Inquiries should be addressed to
Prometheus Books
59 John Glenn Drive
Amherst, New York 14228–2119
VOICE: 716–691–0133, ext. 210
FAX: 716–691–0137
WWW.PROMETHEUSBOOKS.COM

12 11 10 09 08   5 4 3 2 1

Library of Congress Cataloging-in-Publication Data

Wheat, Leonard F., 1931–
    Philip Pullman's His dark materials—a multiple allegory : attacking religious superstition in The lion, the witch and the wardrobe and Paradise lost / by Leonard F. Wheat.
        p. cm.
    Includes bibliographical references and index.
    ISBN 978–1–59102–589–4 (alk. paper)
    1. Pullman, Philip, 1946– His dark materials. 2. Young adult fiction, English—History and criticism. 3. Fantasy fiction, English—History and criticism. 4. Allegory. I. Title.

PR6066.U44H63 2007
823'.914—dc22   2007027085

Printed in the United States of America on acid-free paper

CONTENTS

CHAPTER 1

INTRODUCTION

Several Internet newsgroup participants have complained about the sad ending in Philip Pullman's *His Dark Materials* trilogy. The ending is really more bittersweet than sad, and it even displays uplifting themes; but the complainers have a point. Until the final pages, the story seems to be moving in the direction of a traditional happily-ever-after ending. Then Pullman drops his pathos bomb: permanent separation of the two lovers, who belong to and must return to different worlds, never to see each other again.

To the disappointed readers, the so-called sad ending seems unnecessary, the result of arbitrary plot rules. One rule decrees that persons going to another world can live there for only about ten years, after which they will sicken and die. Another rule says that the prevailing means of passage between worlds must be destroyed, preventing future travel between worlds and thereby preventing occasional return to a person's home world for rejuvenation when the ten-year deadline approaches. What the readers don't realize is that the rules aren't really arbitrary. They are necessary. They serve a symbolic purpose.

To understand this you must understand that *His Dark Materials* is allegory, that allegory depends on symbolism, and that the permanent separation of the lovers symbolizes one of Pullman's main themes: Heaven doesn't exist. Lyra and Will, the heroine and the hero, come from different worlds and meet in a third world. After adventures in ten worlds, including the land of the dead and its suburbs, they overcome the forces of evil and fall in love. Lyra wants to return with Will to his world, which to her would be a world of bliss. She wants to live in bliss with Will. *She wants to live in bliss in another world.* The other world—Will's world—symbolizes Heaven, or Paradise, and the bliss is what Christians expect to enjoy in the "next world" after they die. Pullman is using those "arbitrary plot rules" to deliver his antireligious message: there is no other world of bliss, no Heaven, no Paradise. We must build our "Republic of Heaven"—the antithesis of Christianity's supernatural "Kingdom of God"—in the only world there is, our own world.

ALLEGORY

Before we proceed, the meaning and nature of allegory must be clarified. In simplest terms, an allegory is a story—prose, poetry, film, or play—that uses symbols to tell another story, which is hidden, or to present a theme or related ideas in disguise. Bernstein puts it this way: "An *allegory* is a metaphorical narrative . . . in which the surface story and characters are intended to be taken as symbols pointing to an underlying, more significant meaning."[1] Fowler offers a similar description: "Having read a tale, and concluded that under its surface meaning another is discernible as the true intent, we say 'This is an allegory.'"[2] These authorities both point out that allegory has a "surface story" or "surface meaning" that points to a hidden or disguised meaning.

To state the point simply, one story tells another, although the hidden story might more nearly resemble a collection of related ideas than an actual narrative. The first story, the surface story, is the story you actually see on the page, the screen, or the stage. The symbols can be just about anything in the surface story—persons, places, objects, events, colors, words, and so on. These represent other persons, places, events, ideas, and the like in the hidden story, the story you don't see directly. The symbols usually but not always represent something of the same nature in the hidden story: a person usually represents another person, the surface story person being the symbolized person in disguise. But a person may represent something else, perhaps a stag or a lamppost or an event or even an abstraction such as wisdom, despair, or sin. And a thing can represent a person, as in the Stanley Kubrick film *2001: A Space Odyssey*, where the spaceship *Discovery* and its computer brain Hal jointly symbolize God.[3]

George Orwell's novel *Animal Farm* is an outstanding example of allegory. The surface story is about some farm animals living on Manor Farm. They overthrow Farmer Jones, take over the farm, rename it Animal Farm, establish an economic system called Animalism, install a farm anthem titled "Beasts of England," and design a flag featuring a white hoof and white horn on a green background. Their objectives are noble. Farmer Jones, a drunkard, has exploited them, taking almost all of what they produce, giving them subsistence rations, and sending many young animals off to be slaughtered. The new regime has high ideals: all animals will be equal, and all output will be divided equally. But they do need leaders. Their leaders are two young boars named Snowball and Napoleon. Snowball remains true to the objectives of the revolution; but Napoleon calls him a traitor, ousts him, and becomes a dictator. Somehow, the farm's pigs and Napoleon's "enforcer" dogs manage to live more comfortable lives than the others. Before long an idealistic set of Seven Commandments has been reduced to one. Originally "All animals are equal," it now reads, "All animals are equal but some animals are more equal than others."[4] The lower animals now do more work for less food than any other animals in the county. Evil has triumphed.

Published in August 1945, Orwell's story is a thinly disguised retelling of Russia's 1917 Bolshevik Revolution and its betrayal by Stalin during the period ending late in World War II. The farm symbolizes Russia: one place symbolizes another. Farmer Jones is Czar Nicholas II, who was overthrown: one hated boss symbolizes another. Animalism symbolizes Communism: one ideology symbolizes another. "Beasts of England" represents "The Internationale," the Soviet Union's national anthem from 1922 to 1944. (Orwell supplies some wonderfully clever lyrics that can be sung to the tune of either "Clementine" or "La Cucaracha.") The animal flag's hoof and horn are the Soviet flag's hammer and sickle; the green background symbolizes the Soviet flag's red background. Snowball symbolizes Leon Trotsky. We know Snowball is good because snow is white, and white is the color traditionally used to symbolize goodness, virtue, and purity. Napoleon symbolizes Joseph Stalin. We know Napoleon is bad because France's Napoleon, like Orwell's, was a dictator and abused his authority. Napoleon's enforcer dogs are Stalin's secret police. The "more equal than others" pigs and dogs are the Communist Party members. The Seven Commandments represent the Communist Manifesto. "Some animals are more equal than others" describes Stalin's dictatorship, wherein special privileges given to Communist Party members made them "more equal" than ordinary citizens. The lower animals, who do all the work, are the proletariat. *Animal Farm* has lots of other symbols, but these suffice to illustrate the nature of allegory and allegorical symbols.

You can see in the above examples that symbols are recognized by analogies between the symbols and whatever is symbolized. (There are exceptions.) One good analogy is all it takes to create a symbol; the symbol and its referent need not have multiple similarities. The farm can symbolize Russia because both are places: the farm need not be as big as Russia or be run by a czar. Sometimes an allegorical symbol rests on more than one analogy, as with the Animal Farm flag. Analogy 1: Both flags display two emblems. Analogy 2: The emblems on both flags are tools. The hammer and sickle on the Soviet flag represent tools of humans; the hoof and horn on the animal flag represent tools of animals. Analogy 3: Both sets of tools are those used by the revolutionists—the exploited working class or proletariat for the Soviet flag, the exploited animals for the animal flag. Analogy 4: Both flags display their two emblems against one solid-color background rather than, say, against the first and third of three differently colored vertical panels like those on the Canadian flag or against a single background speckled with small stars. For Snowball and Napoleon, the analogies are in their names.

Another example of allegory is the C. S. Lewis children's story *The Lion, the Witch and the Wardrobe*, the original book of the seven-book *Narnia* series. The Lewis story is an especially appropriate example, because Pullman's *His Dark Materials* was conceived as an atheist's answer to the *Narnia* books, which flaunt Christian doctrine. (More about this connection shortly.) Not only that, the surface story of *The Lion, the Witch and the Wardrobe* becomes one of three hidden stories buried in the surface story of *His Dark Materials*. C. S. Lewis puts in his story fifty-two allegorical symbols. He has symbols for God, Jesus, Satan, angels, demons, Heaven, Hell, Earth, prophecies, a Christian church as a refuge in times of crisis, a minister, Satan's power, the weakening of Satan's power, temptation, sin, repentance, redemption, Jesus's birthday, the mocking and scourging of Jesus before his crucifixion, the crown of thorns placed on his head, the nails that held him to the cross, the death and resurrection of Jesus, Jesus's stone tomb, the rolling away of the stone, the "harrowing of Hell," the death of Satan, the apocalypse, the Four Horsemen of the Apocalypse, the Lamb of God, the lamp in new Jerusalem, the Kingdom of God, and other things. The lion, a noble beast named Aslan, symbolizes Jesus. We know this because, like the Jesus of Christian mythology, he dies and is then resurrected. He also goes to the witch's palace (Hell) and restores to life other creatures that the evil White Witch (Satan) has turned to stone, just as Jesus supposedly "descended into Hell" and rescued its inmates in "the harrowing of Hell," a related event from Christian mythology.

The Lion, the Witch and the Wardrobe, its symbols, and what they symbolize will be discussed and explained in chapter 3; so will the analogies that allow the meanings of symbols to be deduced. Chapter 4 will show how Pullman's trilogy retells *The Lion, the Witch and the Wardrobe* by symbolizing just about all of the latter's symbols: Pullman's symbols symbolize Lewis's symbols as well as many other nonsymbolic persons and things in the Lewis story. All told, Pullman has over one hundred symbols that retell *The Lion, the Witch and the Wardrobe*. To anticipate, Iorek, the good armored bear from *His Dark*

Materials, symbolizes Aslan, the lion; and Mrs. Coulter and Iofur, the bad armored bear, share (in different scenes) the role of the White Witch. Mrs. Coulter's seducing Tony Makarios with a chocolatl drink symbolizes the witch's seducing Edmund with a hot drink and delicious Turkish Delight candy; Iorek's slaying Iofur symbolizes Aslan's slaying the witch.

One other aspect of allegory demands recognition. Genuine allegory requires continuity in the symbolism; an occasional symbol doesn't do the job. Neither does scattershot symbolism in which a multitude of symbols lack any unifying theme. In *Animal Farm* the unifying theme is the 1917 Bolshevik Revolution and its betrayal by the Communist dictatorship that followed. In *The Lion, the Witch and the Wardrobe* the unifying theme is Christianity, including the Christian myths of sin, repentance, redemption, the dying and rising Christ, the post-crucifixion apocalypse, the Second Coming of Jesus, and the triumphant arrival of the Kingdom of God. Friedman writes, "We have allegory when the events [*elements* would be a better word] of a narrative obviously and continuously refer to another simultaneous structure of events or ideas."[5] Symbols that arise just occasionally yet have the unifying theme of allegory yield what is sometimes called allegorical tendency. If many symbols are present but lack a unifying theme, such as allusion to the same literary work, all we have is scattered metaphor, allusion, or nonallegorical symbolism.

PULLMAN'S VIEW OF C. S. LEWIS

As a result of wide publicity, many people know that Pullman's strong aversion to C. S. Lewis's pro-Christian *Chronicles of Narnia* is what inspired Pullman to write *His Dark Materials*. Lewis was a Christian apologist who wrote nonfiction as well as fiction books advancing conservative Christian themes. (Lewis believed in Hell and Satan.) His seven-book *Narnia* series, so named because the adventures take place in the magical land of Narnia (akin to Oz), are collectively known as *The Chronicles of Narnia*, just as the three books of Pullman's trilogy are collectively known as *His Dark Materials*. The first *Narnia* book to be written and published, and easily the best known and most popular, is *The Lion, the Witch and the Wardrobe* (1950). This book is actually second in chronological order of events; *The Magician's Nephew* (1955) is chronologically the first—but was the sixth to be written. The last book in both event chronology and order of writing is *The Last Battle* (1956).

The Last Battle is essentially an allegorical retelling of the New Testament's apocalyptic book of Revelation. The apocalypse is the horrifying event that, in Christian mythology, will accompany the destruction of the existing world and its kingdoms, clearing the way for the old world's replacement, God's Kingdom on Earth. Think of the apocalypse as the violent razing of an old, run-down, cockroach-infested building to clear the site for a Frank Lloyd Wright creation. In *The Last Battle*, the four beloved siblings from *The Lion, the Witch and the Wardrobe*—Lucy, Edmund, Susan, and Peter—are killed in a train accident, part of Lewis's apocalypse symbolism. Oddly, Lewis previously symbolized Revelation's apocalypse at the end of *The Lion, the Witch and the Wardrobe*, though he did so hastily, gently, and superficially. Apparently he decided, six years later, that he wanted to do the job more thoroughly and gruesomely, possibly to better express what Pullman calls Lewis's "hatred of the physical world."[6]

Pullman exhibits little restraint in his criticism of the *Narnia* books and their Christian themes. Tony Watkins writes, "When I first witnessed Pullman talking about Lewis I was startled at the anger with which he spoke."[7] In his essay on "The Darkside of Narnia," Pullman calls the *Narnia* cycle "one of the most ugly and poisonous things I've ever read."[8] He particularly decries "the misogyny, the racism, the sado-masochistic relish for violence that permeates the whole cycle."[9] Then he elaborates:

One of the most vile moments in the whole of children's literature, to my mind, occurs at the end of *The Last Battle*, when Aslan [the lion who symbolizes the Christ] reveals to the children that "the term is over: the holidays have begun" because "There was a real railway accident. Your father and mother and all of you are . . . dead." To solve a narrative problem by killing one of your characters is something many authors have done at one time or another. To slaughter the whole lot of them, and then claim they're better off [they are going to a better life in the Kingdom of God], is not honest storytelling: it's propaganda in the service of a life-hating ideology [Christianity].[10]

To support his charge that Lewis is prejudiced against women (misogyny), Pullman highlights another event in *The Last Battle*. It involves Susan, the older of the two girls among the four siblings who are the heroines and heros of *The Lion, the Witch and the Wardrobe*. Susan is turned away from the Stable, which is Lewis's symbol for Salvation. Other people, including her brothers and sister, are going to be saved, but Susan doesn't qualify. Implicitly, she will roast in Hell. The reason is that, being a teenage girl, she has a budding interest in nylons and lipstick and invitations. She is—here Pullman quotes one of Lewis's characters—"a jolly sight too keen on being grown-up."[11] Pullman views Lewis's treatment of Susan with disdain:

Susan, like Cinderella, is undergoing a transition from one phase of her life to another. Lewis didn't approve of that. He didn't like women in general, or sexuality at all, at least at the stage in his life when he wrote the Narnia books. He was frightened and appalled at the notion of wanting to grow up. Susan, who did want to grow up, and who might have been the most interesting character in the whole cycle [of *Narnia* books] if she'd been allowed to, is a Cinderella in a story where the Ugly Sisters win.[12]

In a subsequent interview with Susan Roberts, Pullman reiterates his disgust with the Stable scene: "Here's a child whose body is changing and who's naturally responding as everyone has ever done since the history of the world to the changes that are taking place in one's body and one's feelings. She's doing what everyone has to do in order to grow up."[13] In other words, she's being a normal, innocent teenager. And for this Lewis bars her from Heaven.[14]

In *His Dark Materials*, Pullman slaps Lewis in the face by allowing his female protagonist, Lyra, to grow up. Lyra, by the way, happens to symbolize—in different scenes—both Lucy (notice the name resemblance) and Susan in Pullman's allegorization of *The Lion, the Witch and the Wardrobe*. About eleven years old at the start, Lyra eventually reaches puberty and falls in love with Will, the male protagonist who shares her adventures in the last two books of the trilogy. In the process, Lyra is tempted by a metaphorical serpent (Mary) and eats some metaphorical Forbidden Fruit from a metaphorical Tree of Knowledge, then experiences love—blatant symbolization of Christianity's Original Sin, and analogous to Susan's interest in nylons, lipstick, and invitations. Instead of punishing Lyra for being what C. S. Lewis considered sinful, Pullman makes "the Fall" a gloriously uplifting event. The life-destroying spell of the Church is broken, "Dust" (the symbol for knowledge) begins falling on the world, and society's future transforms from dark to radiant.

Although his fiercest criticism of Lewis is directed at events in *The Last Battle*, Pullman chooses *The Lion, the Witch and the Wardrobe* as a sort of symbol (nonallegorical) for the overall Narnia series. This choice undoubtedly stems from the extreme popularity of the original book of Lewis's series: it makes the best symbol. Pullman evidently wanted to symbolize the *Narnia* series in *His Dark Materials* as a way of saying, in veiled language, that *His Dark Materials* is a rebuttal of the *Narnia* books. He implements the symbolism by including in his surface story a procession of allegorical symbols that retell *The Lion, the Witch and the Wardrobe*. Ironically, the hidden story in this first allegory of Pullman's is free of antireligious ideas. Those ideas are reserved for the surface story and for two other hidden stories.

PULLMAN'S ANTIRELIGIOUS PERSPECTIVE

To understand the antireligious messages hidden, and sometimes blatantly displayed, in *His Dark Materials*, you must understand that Pullman is an atheist. In a recorded conversation with Rowan Williams, archbishop of Canterbury, Pullman said, "As an atheist, I'm rather on difficult ground here, but presumably this is what a Christian believes."[15] Referring to the Mel Gibson film *The Passion of the Christ*, he said, "What fascinates me about the phenomenon is that churches apparently are spending thousands of pounds buying . . . tickets and giving them away to *atheists* in the hope that by seeing someone tortured to death *we'll* reform."[16] By saying "we," Pullman places himself with the atheists. In an interview with Tony Watkins, Pullman said this: "There was a time when we all believed in God— very important, a central part of all our lives. Then it became impossible to believe in it. It's as if God has died. That's the feeling I have."[17] Here Pullman says it is "impossible to believe in" God. And in a BBC "Live Chat" question-and-answer session, Pullman began his response to the question "Why do you hate God so much?" by saying, "Well, it is not that I hate God, it is just [that] I don't believe in God . . ."[18]

Pullman has admittedly hedged about his atheism in a couple of places. On his Web site he says this: "I don't know whether there's a God or not. Nobody does, no matter what they say. I think it's perfectly possible to explain how the universe came about without bringing God into it, but I don't know everything, and there may well be a God somewhere, hiding away."[19] Likewise, in his interview with Susan Roberts he described himself as "caught between the words 'atheistic' and 'agnostic.'" On the one hand: "I can see no evidence in that circle of things I do know, in history, or in science or anywhere else, no evidence of the existence of God." On the other hand: "I know that all the things I do know are very small compared with all the things that I don't know. So maybe there is a God out there. All I know is that if there is, he hasn't shown himself on earth."[20]

In the light of Pullman's several statements affirming his atheism, the additional qualified statements come across as misconceived attempts to avoid the appearance of dogmatic certainty in the absence of proof. Pullman is making the common mistake of assuming "God exists" and "God doesn't exist" are comparable statements, both requiring proof. But whereas proof of God's existence could materialize if God existed, there is no way to disprove the existence of an invisible, nonmaterial (spiritual) entity having no detectable physical properties and capable of hiding not just in a remote corner of the universe or in the earth's core but even in the same room with us—or, as panentheism would have it, hiding as an invisible spiritual "essence" that permeates everything physical in the universe yet has a metaphysical mind that somehow transcends the universe. It seems highly improbable that Pullman would acknowledge the slightest bit of agnosticism about the existence of (1) Zeus or Aphrodite, (2) a Hell of fire, tucked away in a parallel universe where no telescope or other scientific instrument can detect it, and presided over by a red devil with moose-style antlers protruding from each shoulder blade and three serpent's-head-tipped tails attached to his left kneecap, and (3) a supernatural cause-and-effect mechanism that shaves thirteen days off a person's life every time that person sleeps in a hotel room on the thirteenth floor. Yet none of these entities can be disproved or ever will be disproved. All of us nonetheless can and should confidently assert, despite the absence of proof, that they—and elves—don't exist: the burden of proof is on whoever asserts that any one of the entities *does* exist.

Whatever Pullman has said about the hypothetical possibility of God's existence, he has made it perfectly clear that he means it when he says "I don't believe in God." Lest any doubt remain on this point, we need only consult his short essay on "Religion" that appears on the "About the Worlds: Religion" page of his Web site. There he refers to things done "in the name of some invisible god" and then adds, "and they're *all* invisible, because they don't exist" (emphasis added).[21] There you have it. *All* of the gods—that includes God—"don't exist." Pullman has also said, quite bluntly, "I'm an atheist."[22]

Pullman's disbelief in God leaves him free from normal Judeo-Christian inhibitions when it comes to criticizing religion for its evils. A more extensive quotation from the above-mentioned "Religion" essay frankly states why Pullman dislikes religion. He distinguishes between (*a*) what he calls "the religious impulse" and (*b*) organized religion, which includes Christianity and all its denominations:

> The religious impulse—which includes the sense of awe and mystery we feel when we look at the universe, the urge to find meaning and a purpose in our lives, our sense of moral kinship with other human beings—is part of being human, and I value it. I'd be a damn fool not to.
>
> But organized religion is quite another thing. The trouble is that all too often in human history, churches and priesthoods have set themselves up to rule people's lives in the name of some invisible god (and they're all invisible, because they don't exist)—and done terrible damage. In the name of their god, they have burned, hanged, tortured, maimed, robbed, violated, and enslaved millions of their fellow-creatures, and done so with the happy conviction that they were doing the will of God, and they would go to Heaven for it.[23]

Pullman has expressed similar opinions elsewhere: "When you look at organized religion of whatever sort—whether it's Christianity in all its variants, or whether it's Islam or some forms of extreme Hinduism—wherever you see organized religion and priesthoods and power, you see cruelty and tyranny and repression. It's almost a universal law."[24] He says his trilogy depicts the ancient struggle against religious tyranny that continues to this day: "The old forces of control and ritual and authority, the forces which have been embodied throughout human history in such phenomena as the Inquisition, the witch-trials, the burning of heretics, and which are still strong today in the regions of the world where religious zealots of any faith have power, are on one side; and the forces that fight against them have as their guiding principle an idea which is summed up in the words The Republic of Heaven."[25]

Pullman keeps returning to the theme of religious persecution and intolerance. Asked in an interview about "the source of the extreme antipathy to the Church in your books," Pullman replied:

> It comes from history. It comes from the record of the Inquisition, persecuting heretics and torturing Jews and all that sort of stuff; and it comes from the other side, too, from the Protestants burning the Catholics. It comes from the insensate pursuit of innocent and crazy old women, and from the Puritans in America burning and hanging the witches—and it comes not only from the Christian church but also from the Taliban.
>
> Every single religion that has a monotheistic god ends up by persecuting other people and killing them because they don't accept him. Wherever you look in history, you find that. It's still going on.[26]

THE *HIS DARK MATERIALS* TRILOGY

His Dark Materials is Pullman's anti-Christian, antireligious challenge to the pro-Christian *Chronicles of Narnia*. In Pullman's own words, his trilogy is "a sort of riposte to the worldview Lewis puts in front of us in *Narnia*."[27] Ostensibly written for the YA (Young Adult) market, the trilogy is increasingly recognized as being equally suitable for adults. The three books of *His Dark Materials* are *The Golden Compass* (1995), *The Subtle Knife* (1997), and *The Amber Spyglass* (2000). The first book of the series has a different title, *Northern Lights*, in the United Kingdom, where the book was originally published.

How did the first book's second title, *The Golden Compass*, materialize? At an early stage in the publication process, Pullman used *The Golden Compasses* (plural) as a working title for the overall trilogy, not for the first book. The words come from Milton's *Paradise Lost*, where Jesus uses "the golden compasses" from "God's eternal store" to draw huge circles defining the limits of Earth and fixing the orbits of Earth's surrounding bodies—moon, sun, planets, stars.[28] Milton's golden compasses are thus the kind you draw circles with, not the kind you use to find which way is north; much less are they truth-telling instruments. Pullman later found the phrase "his dark materials"[29] in *Paradise Lost* and decided this newer phrase would make a better series title: it can be taken as an allusion to Dust, a crucial ingredient in the plot. Meanwhile, *Northern Lights* was firmly established with Pullman's British editor, David Fickling, as the title of the first book. But editors at Pullman's American publisher, Alfred A. Knopf, mistook "golden compasses" as a reference to Lyra's alethiometer, which is not a compass of any sort. The editors insisted on *The Golden Compass* as the first book's title. Through various forms of persuasion, Knopf was able to secure Pullman's assent to using a different title in the United States. Pullman rationalized the new title in *The Golden Compass* by twice describing the alethiometer as resembling a directional compass and in *The Subtle Knife*, the trilogy's second book, by having Mary Malone twice refer to Lyra's alethiometer as a "compass" or "compass thing."[30]

The three books have taken the publishing world by storm. Critics have generally been effusive in their praise, although some Catholic and conservative Protestant critics have condemned the books on religious grounds.[31] *Northern Lights* won the 1995 Carnegie Medal, awarded each year to an outstanding book written in English for children and young adult readers and published first, or concurrently, in the United Kingdom. The book also won the Children's Fiction Award of the *Guardian*, a leading English newspaper. In America, both *The Golden Compass* and *The Subtle Knife* won the *Publishers Weekly* Best Book of the Year award. Then came the big one. In 2001, *The Amber Spyglass* first won the prestigious Whitbread Prize for the Children's Book of the Year, then went on to win the overall Whitbread Book of the Year Prize, chosen from among the winners in five categories. And the awards didn't end there. In 2007, *Northern Lights* won the "Carnegie of Carnegies" award as the best of the annual Carnegie Award winners in the award's seventy-year history. All three books had long runs on the bestseller lists of London's *Sunday Times* and the

New York Times. Pullman's *His Dark Materials* books have sometimes outsold the immensely popular Harry Potter books.

Such is the popularity of *His Dark Materials* that it has been, or is being, adapted for radio, stage, and film. In January 2003 it was presented as a three-part radio drama, one part for each book, on BBC. Later, in December 2003, London's National Theater staged, on consecutive nights, a two-part version; each part was three hours long. As this book is being written, filming of a three-film version of the trilogy has begun. In addition to these dramatizations, *His Dark Materials* has inspired the writing of eight adult books that try to explain or interpret the trilogy, and sometimes to provide a religious rebuttal.[32] On the Web, at SparkNotes.com, is yet another guide: the Barnes and Noble *SparkNotes* for *His Dark Materials*. And the trilogy has a compendious, well-organized Web site, Bridgetothestars.net, as well as some smaller Web sites.

Despite all the hullabaloo, the awards, the many reviews and commentaries, the guides, and the Web sites, nobody seems to have recognized that *His Dark Materials* is allegory. Much less has anyone spotted the presence of not just one but *three* hidden stories, intricately interwoven in the surface story. To be sure, a smattering of the most obvious symbols has been detected. Many readers who have given serious thought to the books or have read about their background know that Pullman is to some extent basing his story on Milton's *Paradise Lost*: Pullman has openly acknowledged this. But "to some extent" fails to grasp how enormous that extent is.

The obvious symbols that have been recognized are chiefly (*a*) the Authority, the trilogy's remote villain, who symbolizes God—he is actually called "God," "Yahweh," "the Lord," "the Almighty," and "the Creator"—and (*b*) Lord Asriel, who is the Authority's adversary and must ipso facto symbolize Satan. It is also widely recognized that a glorified, latter-day version of "the Fall" from Genesis is being metaphorically represented, if not symbolized. After all, the story openly refers to Lyra, the heroine, as "the New Eve" and to Mary Malone, another major character, as "the serpent." Moreover, the red fruit that Lyra and Will eat just before they discover they love each other unmistakably is equivalent to the Forbidden Fruit from the Garden of Eden. One reviewer has also recognized Pullman's symbol for Milton's "Lapland witches."[33] That symbol is—what else?—Lapland witches.

But that's about it. Once you get beyond God, Satan, the Garden of Eden's symbols, and the witches—the symbols that approach literalism—Pullman's symbols have seemingly become invisible to the reviewers, critics, and analysts. Well over two hundred additional allegorical symbols have gone unrecognized, and these don't count symbols that this interpretation of *HDM* has overlooked. Existing commentaries have barely scratched the surface of Pullman's symbolism. The allegories have gone essentially undetected. Yes, a few reviews and analyses have used the word "allegory"—but without any supporting analysis to substantiate the use of that word.[34] Some people apparently think, erroneously, that a few allusions to *Paradise Lost* or the Garden of Eden are all it takes to create an allegory.

Even some of the most obvious symbols have been overlooked. Nobody seems to have noticed the analogical symbolism embodied in the chocolatl drink Mrs. Coulter uses as bait for hooking Tony Makarios. The drink's being essentially a combination of the hot drink and Turkish Delight candy the White Witch uses to ensnare Edmund in *The Lion, the Witch and the Wardrobe* has somehow been missed. Is Mrs. Coulter too scrupulous and kind to be recognized as a symbol for the witch? Is Tony, who is a thief and therefore a sinner, too enigmatic to be recognized as a symbol for the sinner Edmund, who is a liar and a traitor? And what about the analogy between (*a*) the world of Cittàgazze, which must be passed through to get from Lyra's world to Will's, and (*b*) C. S. Lewis's wardrobe, which must be passed through to get from the Professor's house to Narnia and back? How did the fragrant scent of allegory in that symbolism go undetected?

Plainly visible symbols relating to *Paradise Lost* have also gone unnoticed. Pullman's Jesus symbol is an example. In *Paradise Lost* Jesus drives a chariot and uses it to attack Satan and force him out of

Heaven. *His Dark Materials* has three references to a chariot moving across the sky, including one where the driver is attacking Asriel. Given that Asriel symbolizes Satan—many readers and just about all the reviewers and critics know this—the fellow at the chariot's reins must symbolize Jesus: Jesus is using his chariot to attack Satan. But who has recognized this? The Jesus character gets betrayed by another character. Has everyone forgotten the Gospel story where somebody gets thirty pieces of silver to betray Jesus, and have they forgotten who that betrayer is? Asriel builds a "Bridge to the Stars," a bridge from Lyra's world to Cittagàzze's world; it is even featured in a chapter title. Didn't anyone check *Paradise Lost* to learn about the bridge of wondrous length from Hell to Earth that Satan blazes a pilot track for?

So, all we have are about five widely recognized symbols plus the once-recognized Lapland witches. Each of these symbols relates to *Paradise Lost*; no symbols pointing to *The Lion, the Witch and the Wardrobe* have attracted attention. Three of the five recognized "symbols" are really just metaphors, because Pullman makes these three—Lyra as the "new Eve," Mary as "the serpent," and the red "fruit" as the Forbidden Fruit—more or less explicit. A fourth symbol, the Authority as God, is easily recognized, because Pullman explicitly gives the Authority the titles God, the Lord, the Creator, the Father, and Yahweh. Even the fifth symbol, Asriel as a symbol for Satan, has been boldly hinted at by Pullman in his written references to William Blake and to Blake's opinion that Milton really belonged to the devil's party.

But let's nevertheless count all five of the above as symbols. Five symbols don't create an allegory. And the existing guides and books of essays don't regard Pullman's trilogy as allegory. Yet allegory—two thorough allegories and one diminutive hidden story having allegorical tendency but too few symbols to constitute allegory—is what *His Dark Materials* is. The symbolically told hidden stories are the following:

- A straightforward retelling of C. S. Lewis's *The Lion, the Witch and the Wardrobe*. This allegory uses 104 surface story symbols,

41 of which use characters in Pullman's surface story. (One of Pullman's characters, Lyra, symbolizes two Lewis characters, Lucy and Susan; two Pullman characters, Mrs. Coulter and Iofur, symbolize the White Witch in different scenes; and Pullman's four Gallivespians are second symbols for the four *Narnia* siblings when the siblings go horseback riding.) The allegory's presence hints that *His Dark Materials* is a reply to *The Chronicles of Narnia*, but this allegory does not attack religion.

• An upside-down retelling of John Milton's *Paradise Lost*, augmented by additional borrowings from the Bible, Christian theology, and other religious sources. This hidden story is upside down because Satan is on the side of good and God is on the side of evil, and because Satan's side wins, whereas Satan is the loser in *Paradise Lost*. The allegory uses another 108 identified symbols, of which 31 are characters in Pullman's surface story. The *Paradise Lost* allegory is Pullman's main allegory and has a strong anti-Christian flavor.

• A brief original story describing the last 300 years of human history, beginning with sailing-ship-based acceleration of missionary activity and proceeding through the Darwinian revolution to today's relatively common atheism and agnosticism. This hidden story has only 19 symbols, and they lack continuity; hence, the story is semiallegorical rather than fully allegorical. The theme is again anti-Christian.

These three hidden stories and their 231 symbols will be exposed and analyzed in the remaining chapters. Chapter 2 sets the stage for the analyses that follow by summarizing the *His Dark Materials* trilogy. Chapter 3 focuses on *The Lion, the Witch and the Wardrobe*. This chapter summarizes the C. S. Lewis story, identifying Lewis's allegorical symbols, pointing out the various persons and things that Pullman will symbolize, and refuting arguments purporting to demonstrate that the story is not an allegory. Chapter 4 then explains Pullman's first allegory, which depicts *The Lion, the Witch and the Wardrobe*. Chapters 5 and 6 present the *Paradise Lost* allegory. Chapter 5 lays the allegory's foundation by summarizing *Paradise Lost*, showing how Pullman turns Milton's epic upside down, explaining how Pullman uses Dust and Specters to symbolize his broad theme of our society's warfare between knowledge (Dust) and religious superstition (Specters), and then spotlighting Pullman's narrow theme that there is no Heaven, a theme that emphasizes a particular superstition. Chapter 6 erects the allegory's superstructure by explaining the symbolism in the setting, identifying the symbolic characters, also identifying who (sometimes what) they symbolize, further identifying symbolic things and events, and finally examining the symbolism in the book-title instruments—the alethiometer, the subtle knife, and the amber spyglass. Chapter 7 presents the last of the three hidden stories, which describes the clash between the theology of missionaries (superstition) and the science of Darwin (knowledge).

In the following chapters, the second reference and any subsequent references to the books most often mentioned will use the following abbreviations:

- *LWW* — *The Lion, the Witch and the Wardrobe*
- *PL* — *Paradise Lost*
- *HDM* — *His Dark Materials* (the trilogy as a whole)
- *GC* — *The Golden Compass/Northern Lights* (the first book of the trilogy)
- *SK* — *The Subtle Knife* (the second book)
- *AS* — *The Amber Spyglass* (the third book)

CHAPTER 2

PULLMAN'S SURFACE STORY

This study's purpose is to explain the hidden stories and the related symbolism in Pullman's two main allegories—*The Lion, the Witch and the Wardrobe* allegory and the *Paradise Lost* allegory—and in the semiallegorical third story about missionaries and Darwin. This purpose can best be achieved by beginning with a summary of *His Dark Materials*. Although most of my book's readers have presumably read the *HDM* trilogy, some will not have, particularly in situations where this book is being used as a guide or textbook. Other readers will have read *HDM* years ago, in some cases as each book of the trilogy came out—in 1995 (*The Golden Compass*), 1997 (*The Subtle Knife*), and 2000 (*The Amber Spyglass*). Both the persons who are unacquainted with *HDM* and those whose recollection of details has dimmed over time should benefit from this chapter's summary of *HDM*'s plot. Readers who think they already have a strong grasp of the plot will also benefit: the *HDM* summary that follows is guaranteed to provide insights rarely if ever perceived by persons reading for entertainment or even for scholarly analysis.

Many of the *HDM* plot features presented here will perforce need to be repeated in later chapters, sometimes in more detail. This need exists partly because some readers will have skipped this chapter but mainly because repetition is necessary for developing this book's interpretations and their supporting analyses. The evidence supporting my arguments and conclusions—evidence taken from *HDM*—belongs with those arguments and conclusions.

THE GOLDEN COMPASS
(A.K.A. NORTHERN LIGHTS)

The first book of the trilogy begins when the heroine, Lyra (lie-ra) Belacqua, gets into mischief. Lyra is a girl of eleven or twelve at this point in the story. She believes herself to be an orphan; the Master of Jordan, head of Jordan College in her world's Oxford University (very similar to our world's Oxford University in England), is raising her with the help of other Jordan College employees. Lyra and her daemon, Pantalaimon, sneak into the Jordan College Retiring Room, which is off limits. (Every human person in Lyra's world, witches included, has a daemon. A daemon, pronounced "demon," is an external *soul* that (*a*) takes the form of an animal, (*b*) changes form—weasel, raven, leopard, fly, and so on—constantly with children but has a permanent form for adults, (*c*) is usually opposite in sex from its human, (*d*) must remain close to its human, unless the human is a witch, (*e*) talks with its human, and (*f*) vanishes when its human dies.)

Lyra and Pantalaimon (now a moth) hide behind a chair when Lyra hears someone coming. It is the Master. From her hiding place Lyra sees the Master put poison into a decanter of Tokay wine from which he expects Lord Asriel to drink when Asriel arrives. The Master's intentions are good. He is trying to save Lyra from being drawn into a dangerous expedition to the arctic; he has learned of the danger from a rare truth-telling instrument called an alethiometer, which is the "golden compass" of the book's title.

After the Master leaves, Asriel comes into the room. He is Lyra's father, but she thinks Asriel is her uncle. She has been told her parents are dead. Besides being her father, Asriel is an influential figure—he belongs to the Prime Minister's Cabinet Council—and a resourceful one. He has come to Jordan College to raise funds for his expedition.

Lyra comes out of hiding and warns Asriel about the poison. Then, hearing the porter coming, Lyra hides in a wardrobe. Asriel knocks the decanter to the floor, breaking it and spilling the wine. He blames the porter. Other persons enter the room, and a meeting begins. Its purpose is to allow Asriel to make a fund-raising pitch for the expedition. Using a new emulsion, he has photographed in the arctic some mysterious "Dust" that falls from the sky onto adults, but hardly at all onto children. He has also photographed within the aurora borealis (northern lights) a previously invisible city in the sky. The Jordan College representatives at the meeting vote to give Asriel money for an expedition to investigate these two phenomena. The expedition will take Asriel to "the North." (In *Paradise Lost* [*PL*], "the North" is an area in Heaven where Satan goes to plan a rebellion against God, which happens to be what Asriel is also going to do. Can you guess who Asriel symbolizes?)

Events move swiftly. Lyra learns of kidnapings by mysterious people called the Gobblers. In reality they are agents of the Church's General Oblation Board (GOB, as in GOBblers), run by Mrs. Coulter. She is Lyra's mother. Lyra is the child of an affair Coulter had with Asriel while Coulter was married to another man. The Gobblers soon kidnap Billy Costa, a son of Ma Costa, the "gyptian" (gypsy) woman who was Lyra's nanny during Lyra's first two or three years. (Lyra doesn't know this.) Next, the Gobblers kidnap Lyra's best friend, Roger, the Jordan College kitchen boy. And then, with Mrs. Coulter personally doing the dirty work, they kidnap Tony Makarios, a street urchin who must steal to eat because his mother is an alcoholic. (Pullman makes Tony a thief—a sinner—so Tony can symbolize the sinful Edmund, who betrays his three siblings in C. S. Lewis's *The Lion, the Witch and the Wardrobe* [*LWW*].)

Soon afterward, at a special Jordan College dinner, the Master introduces Lyra to Mrs. Coulter. After dinner, the Master takes Lyra aside and tells her she is being sent away to London—her world's London—with Mrs. Coulter, who needs an assistant and who can give Lyra the female guidance she needs as she grows older. The truth is, however, that the Master is motivated primarily by pressure from the Church, pressure that threatens the future of Jordan College. He actually has strong misgivings about Mrs. Coulter.

The Master reveals these misgivings shortly before Lyra departs with Mrs. Coulter. He gives her the alethiometer that he earlier used to learn of the danger Lyra faced. It is one of only six in existence. An alethiometer resembles a large pocket watch and has thirty-six emblems ringing its face. Three watch-style short hands can be adjusted with three knobs to point to chosen emblems, each of which has a huge number of possible meanings. A longer fourth hand moves freely and determines its own setting. Skilled readers, aided by reference manuals, can get truthful answers to questions from the alethiometer, but Lyra will have to use strange powers of intuition to read it. (She soon develops these more or less psychic powers.) The Master warns Lyra not to let Mrs. Coulter know about the instrument.

A zeppelin transports Lyra and Mrs. Coulter to London. There, living in Mrs. Coulter's flat, Lyra eventually finds that Mrs. Coulter has an nasty side to her personality. And then, at a cocktail party that Mrs. Coulter hosts in her flat, Lyra learns something worse: Mrs. Coulter is involved in the kidnapings and intends to use Lyra to help in this work. She also hears a bishop say, with satisfaction, that Asriel is being held prisoner by the armored bears of the north. (We later find out that the bears are being paid for their services by Mrs. Coulter, who wants to ensure that Asriel doesn't interfere with her experiments with the kidnaped children; the children are being held at a northern facility.) Frightened and disillusioned, Lyra gathers a few belongings, sneaks out from the party, and runs away.

That night, wandering the streets of London, Lyra and Pantalaimon are captured by two non-Gobbler men of evil intent. One of Ma Costa's sons and two other gyptians witness the event. They slay Lyra's captors and bring Lyra to Ma Costa. Ma Costa lives on a narrowboat (houseboat) that is presently in London on the Grand Junction Canal.

The police are now searching for Lyra: Mrs. Coulter has influence in many arenas. But Ma Costa and her friends successfully hide Lyra and take her north on the canal to a gyptian "roping." This is a mass gathering at the fens, a watery northern region of swamps, bogs, creeks, channels, and ocean inlets. The gyptians rule the fens; no one else dares enter. John Faa, king of the western gyptians, has called for the roping in order to organize a rescue party for the many gyptian children the Gobblers have kidnaped. (Ma Costa and John Faa are water people. Two important characters in *LWW*—one female, one male—have a home on the water.)

Lyra meets John Faa and from him learns who her real parents are—Asriel and Mrs. Coulter. She also learns that Ma Costa is the woman who nursed her when she was an infant and that gyptian spies have watched over her during her entire life. Meanwhile, the rescue group gets organized. It will go to Norroway, Lyra's world's counterpart of our Norway. Somewhere in the northern part of Norroway is Mrs. Coulter's Experimental Station. The gyptians decide to take Lyra along on the chance that her developing skill at reading the alethiometer will prove useful. Obtaining a ship, they embark for Norroway.

The ship soon docks at Trollesund, the main port of Lapland in the northern part of Norroway. There the gyptian leaders meet with the witch consul, Dr. Lanselius. They hope to get in touch with Serafina Pekkala, queen of a witch clan whose support they wish to gain. Lanselius informs the gyptians that for centuries the witches have talked about Lyra. She has a "great destiny" that can be fulfilled only in another world. If she fails, they will all die. (Unknown to anyone, that destiny happens to be to preserve the Dust—knowledge—which is what makes us human and without which the human race cannot survive. The Church fears Dust because, whatever it is, it somehow undermines faith, faith in religious superstitions, which are Truth to the Church.)

Lanselius also advises the gyptians to obtain the services of an armored bear. He says such a bear, Iorek Brynison, is in town at the moment. Formerly king of the bears, Iorek was recently expelled from bear society for killing another bear. That bear had challenged Iorek while under the influence of a drug surreptitiously given him by the evil bear Iofur Raknison, the new king. In despair, Iorek allowed some humans in Trollesund to get him drunk and steal his armor, which is his soul: an armored bear's armor is *his soul*. The gyptians try to hire Iorek, but he refuses work for money. He will help them only if they get him back his armor. Lyra goes to her cabin on the ship and uses the alethiometer to learn where the armor is hidden. It is in the cellar of the priest's house. Lyra informs Iorek. He strides to the priest's house, rips it up, regains his armor (his soul), and joins the gyptian rescue party. Iorek, here symbolizing the death and resurrection of the *LWW* character Aslan, has now lost and regained his soul.

Another new person also joins the party. Lee Scoresby, a balloonist who is an old friend of both the gyptians and Iorek, shows up at a café where Lyra and some gyptians are snacking. The presence of friends in need of help is all it takes for Lee to sign on.

While this activity is going on, Serafina Pekkala's goose daemon, Kaisa, flies in with important news. The kidnaped children have been taken to Bolvangar, about four days northeast of Trollesund. He explains how to get to Bolvangar. He also tells the gyptians of other "interpenetrating" worlds that exist and that occupy the same space as their world. And he tells them that the Gobblers have paid the armored bears, now led by Iofur Raknison, to imprison Lord Asriel because the Church is afraid of Dust. The Church has heard that Asriel somehow intends to use Dust (knowledge, but not identified as such) to build a bridge from his world to the world he photographed in the northern lights.

The gyptians and their friends set out by dogsled for Bolvangar. At their first meal stop, Lyra consults her alethiometer and learns of a "ghost" that is frightening people at a nearby village. Suspecting that it is the ghost of one of the kidnaped children, Lyra persuades Iorek to carry her on his back—he runs extremely fast—to the village. There they find a boy who is near death: his daemon (soul) is missing, severed from him at the Experimental Station. The boy is Tony Makarios, and he keeps mumbling "Ratter" and "Where's Ratter?" Ratter is his daemon's name. Iorek carries Lyra and Tony back to the gyptians, but Tony dies. Lyra takes a gold coin, uses a knife to scratch "Ratter" into the soft metal, and puts the coin—a proxy for Tony's daemon—in the boy's mouth. (Pullman is symbolizing the restoration of the soul of, and the return to good health of, *LWW*'s dying sinner Edmund, who the thief-sinner Tony symbolizes in the *LWW* allegory.) The gyptians then burn Tony's body.

As the rescue expedition proceeds, Samoyed hunters attack. Iorek and the gyptians drive them off, but the Samoyeds capture Lyra. They sell her to men from the Experimental Station. There Lyra learns from kidnaped children that Mrs. Coulter is running the show, though Coulter is away at the moment. Lyra also learns that the Gobblers— staff members at the station—take children away from time to time and sever them from their daemons. Billy Costa and Roger are among the children present, children not yet separated from their daemons. New arrivals, Lyra included, are all measured for Dust, evidently to see if they are yet contaminated by sin. The Church doesn't know what Dust is—nobody does—yet somehow equates Dust with sin. (And for good reason: when Adam and Eve acquired knowledge by eating the Forbidden Fruit from the Tree of Knowledge, they became contaminated by sin, "original sin." The Dust is knowledge, and acquiring it is therefore sin. Knowledge—sin—is the false Truth that militates against faith, the Church's version of Truth.)

During the commotion caused by a fire drill, Lyra, Billy, and Roger slip away and find a building with a notice on the door: ENTRANCE STRICTLY FORBIDDEN. Just then Serafina Pekkala's goose daemon, Kaisa, shows up; he has followed Lyra to the Experimental Station and has been waiting for her to come out. Employing a little witch magic—beating his wings against the door—Kaisa gets the door open. Inside they find locked glass cages holding the daemons of children who have been severed from their daemons, their souls. More witch magic opens the cages and releases the daemons. Kaisa instructs the three children to sneak back inside. He then instructs the freed daemons to turn into birds (children's daemons, remember, can change form) and follow him into the sky. They will be returned to their humans.

Back inside the Experimental Station, Lyra hatches a mass escape plan. It involves having all the children run outside, outdoor clothes in hand, when Lyra sets off the fire alarm. Later that evening, after bedtime, she climbs up through a ceiling panel in the dormitory and follows a metal channel to the ceiling above a conference room. There a Dr. Cooper is explaining to Mrs. Coulter, who has just arrived, the details of his new silver guillotine, or intercision machine. A child is put in one of two "compartments" (really coops, i.e., designed by Cooper); the daemon is put in the other. A silver blade then comes down and severs the psychic link between the child and its daemon. This procedure will theoretically prevent the daemon from settling into permanent form. That, in turn, will prevent the child from accumulating Dust that falls from the sky. Dust accumulates in significant amounts only on people whose daemons have settled, signifying the arrival of adulthood. In theory, the children will be Dust-free, and therefore sin-free, the rest of their lives.

Edified, Mrs. Coulter leaves. The staff members still in the room then hear Lyra, pull her down from the ceiling, take her to the intercision room, and put her and Pantalaimon into the two compartments of the silver guillotine. As the blade lifts, Mrs. Coulter enters. She recognizes Lyra, reacts with horror, and releases Lyra and Pantalaimon. She then questions Lyra about the alethiometer. Lyra manages to dash out the door and run down the hall, punching fire alarm buttons along the way. The alarms signal the other children to rush out of the building and head for freedom. Tartar guards pursue them, but a sudden onslaught of arrows from the sky slows the Tartars: Serafina Pekkala and her witches have arrived, flying on cloud-pine branches (broom substitutes). And so has Iorek: he charges past Lyra and begins slaughtering Tartars. Lyra and the other escapees soon reach the oncoming gyptians.

When the fighting is over, Lee Scoresby brings Lyra, Roger, and

Iorek into his suspended balloon basket (gondola) and takes off for Svalbard, where Asriel is being held prisoner by the armored bears. Lyra thinks Asriel wants the alethiometer, although he really doesn't: he already has one. Before the travelers can reach Svalbard, the balloon drifts too low and winged cliff-ghasts attack. Iorek's mighty paws and Lee Scoresby's pistol drive them off, but the basket slams against a cliff in the fog, jolting Lyra onto the ground. She is in armored bear territory. Bears soon take her into custody.

The bears bring Lyra to Iofur Raknison's palace and put her in a cell. Pulling out the alethiometer, she learns that Iorek is coming, along with Roger, and intends to rescue her. She knows Iorek doesn't stand a chance in combat if he has to fight the entire bear clan. But if Iofur can be tricked into a one-on-one fight, Iorek might prevail. The trouble is, armored bears can't be tricked. Unless . . . unless they act like humans. Back at Jordan College, Lyra heard that Iofur Raknison wanted to be human: he wanted his own daemon.

Lyra persuades a guard to take her to Iofur. Addressing the bear king, she claims that Iorek has become the first bear to acquire a daemon. She pretends she is Iorek's daemon: humans have animal daemons, so animals should have human daemons. If Iofur (the bad bear) can kill Iorek (the good bear) in a fight, Lyra says, she can become Iofur's daemon. When Iorek reaches the palace, the fight takes place. Iorek kills Iofur: Lyra's friend wins. (If Iorek symbolizes *LWW*'s lion Aslan, who dies and comes back to life—loses and regains his soul—and Aslan later slays *LWW*'s White Witch, who does Iofur symbolize?) The bears then restore Iorek to the throne he previously held.

Still thinking that Asriel wants the alethiometer, Lyra asks to be taken to him. Iorek accommodates her, and she brings Roger along. On reaching Asriel, they find that his being a prisoner is more a matter of form than of substance. His high status, his striking powers of persuasion, and the bears' fear of his knowledge of Dust have combined to allow him to do as he pleases—and to enjoy a spacious building. Asriel tells Lyra he doesn't want her alethiometer. He also tells her that

Dust is what makes the alethiometer work. (She doesn't know why, but in chapter 5 of this book it will be shown that Dust is knowledge: knowledge of the truth is what enables the alethiometer to tell the truth.) Asriel goes on to tell Lyra that the Church has decided that Dust is physical evidence of original sin.

Asriel has something even more important to say. He intends to build a "bridge" from his world to the world he photographed in the aurora borealis. The bridge will require a tremendous flash of energy. Where will this energy come from? Asriel doesn't say, but he intends to get it by killing a daemon: he has learned that killing a daemon, and thereby also killing its human, creates an incredible, instantaneous burst of energy that he intends to harness. Asriel has been waiting for the opportunity. Unknown to Lyra, Roger represents this opportunity.

While Lyra sleeps, Asriel grabs Roger and takes the boy and his daemon to the highest of the nearby peaks. Asriel's manservant, Thorold (Old Thor), awakens Lyra and alerts her to what has happened. Lyra calls to Iorek for help, and he carries her almost to the peak. But a snow bridge blocks further progress by the bear: the bridge isn't strong enough to support his weight. Lyra and Pantalaimon proceed by themselves. They reach Asriel and Roger but are unable to save Roger. Asriel's snow leopard daemon kills Roger's daemon and thereby kills Roger too. The result: a burst of raw energy zips upward along a wire held aloft by a witch who is helping Asriel. The energy rips the universe, creating a terrible roar—and a Bridge to the Stars, a bridge leading across the aurora borealis to the city in the sky.

Mrs. Coulter arrives on the scene; she has come by zeppelin and has followed Lyra's tracks in the snow. Asriel tries to persuade her to join him in the new world, telling her that he intends to destroy the Dust. (In *AS* we learn he is lying; he really wants to preserve the Dust.) Torn between passion and the Church, Coulter chooses the Church: she refuses to go along, and sadly walks away. Asriel then proceeds alone across the bridge to the new world he photographed. Lyra and Pantalaimon, following in his track, walk into the sky. (In chapter 5 we shall see that, in *PL*, two other characters—Sin and Death, as personified by Milton—do essentially the same thing: they follow Satan's track across a chaotic gulf separating Hell and a new world recently created by God.)

THE SUBTLE KNIFE

SK begins in another world, our own Earth. Will Parry, a twelve-year-old English boy, brings his mentally disturbed and confused mother to the home of Mrs. Cooper, his former piano teacher. He asks Mrs. Cooper to care for his mother for a few days—a gross underestimate—while he attends to unspecified business. The teacher reluctantly agrees: Cooper No. 2 (Cooper No. 1 invented the two-coop silver guillotine) is willing to keep Will's mother cooped up for the duration. (Pullman's marvelous yet subtle sense of humor reveals itself in many of the names he assigns to persons and places.)

Will then goes home to search for a packet of letters his long-missing father, John Parry, wrote to his mother when she was mentally healthy. He finds the letters in a room upstairs. At almost the same time, he hears two men enter the house downstairs. They too are searching for the letters. When one comes upstairs, Will dashes out and slams into the man's belly, causing the man to trip over Will's cat and fall backward down the stairs to his death. As Will runs out the front door he sees a tall, blond man—the second intruder—come out of the living room.

Will is now a killer. He flees to the city of Oxford, forty miles away. Coming to a traffic circle, he sees a cat step through an invisible hole in the air and vanish. He follows the cat through a window connecting two worlds and finds himself in a new world. It is the very world Asriel photographed with his special emulsion and later crossed over to on his Bridge to the Stars. Will is in Cittàgazze, a coastal city in the new world.

The city seems empty. Searching for a place to rest, Will enters an abandoned café and goes upstairs. As he enters one of the rooms, a frightened girl his own age—Lyra—attacks him. The two soon realize they can trust each other. Will learns about daemons, and they both learn that an Oxford city with an Oxford University exists in each of their home worlds. Later, Lyra asks her alethiometer if Will is a friend or enemy. It tells her he is a murderer. (This gross exaggeration of the truth is Pullman's way of making Will a symbol for Cain, *murderer* of his brother Abel. According to *PL*, Cain killed Abel by hitting him in the belly—just as Will did to the intruder.)

Meanwhile, in Lyra's world, Serafina Pekkala seeks information about what Asriel is up to. Visiting Thorold, Asriel's left-behind manservant, she learns that Asriel is so anti-Church that he might be plotting to destroy the Authority, the Church's God. Serafina then returns to Lake Enara, her witch clan's home. At a witch assembly there she confers with a visiting witch, Ruta Skadi, queen of the Latvian witches. Ruta stands and inveighs against the Church. She says that a war is coming, that Asriel will lead the fight against the Authority, and that the witch clans must join together and go to the new world and seek out Lyra, who the witches know has a destiny in the struggle against the Church.

Lee Scoresby is also present. He knows of a scholar named Grumman who knows the whereabouts of a mysterious object that protects whoever holds it. He intends to go to Nova Zembla, search for Grumman, and if possible find the object and take it to Lyra. A young witch, Juta Kamainen announces that she hates Grumman because he scorned her love: she will kill him if she ever finds him. (We later learn that Grumman is John Parry, Will's father, and that he accidentally stepped through a window into Cittàgazze's world and then through another window to Lyra's world, where he became a scholar and adopted the name Stanislaus Grumman so as to be eligible to join the Berlin Academy. He scorned Juta's love out of faithfulness to his wife, Will's mother.) The meeting breaks up, and the witches prepare to fly on their cloud-pine branches to the new world.

Back to Lyra and Will: In the apparently abandoned city of Cittàgazze they suddenly encounter two children—a girl and a boy. Will asks where the grown-ups are. Puzzled, the girl asks if the Specters didn't come to Will's city. Specters? Lyra and Will learn that Specters are spirits that prey on adults. They feed on the minds of adults, leaving the adults alive but in zombielike states, incapable of rational thought. (Pullman is implying that this is what happens when the mind is poisoned by religious superstitions.) Specters are invisible to pre-puberty children but visible to adults. They come and go. Cittàgazze is presently occupied by Specters. When they leave in a few days, the adults will return.

Lyra proposes to return through the window to Will's world so she can visit Oxford University and find a scholar, no one in particular, who knows about Dust. Will has his own reason for going back: he wants to dig up information about his father. He takes Lyra back to his world through the traffic circle's window. There they separate, agreeing on where and when to meet later.

Will phones the lawyer who administers a trust fund John Parry established for Will's mother before Parry disappeared. The lawyer tells him that, as a matter of public record, the senior Parry vanished ten or more years ago while leading an expedition in the arctic. Though nobody knows it, John Parry was looking for Dust. Will next seeks information about his father from an archaeologist. He learns that everyone in John Parry's expedition disappeared. He also learns that a tall, blond man matching the description of the intruder who came out of Will's living room has inquired about his father.

While Will attends to his business, Lyra enters a museum. She encounters a man who looks familiar but who she can't place. A momentary flick of a snake's tongue from inside his sleeve reveals to her that he has a daemon: he is someone from her world. He happens to be Lord Boreal, whom she met at Mrs. Coulter's cocktail party, but she doesn't yet remember him. He gives her his card and suggests that she contact him if she wants more information about some skulls she was observing in a glass case when he showed up. The name on the card is Charles Latrom: Boreal has two identities, one for each world. (Try spelling Latrom's name backward.)

The alethiometer tells Lyra where to find a scholar who knows about Dust. Going to a specified building, Lyra locates the scholar. She is Dr. Mary Malone, a woman in her late thirties. Lyra identifies herself as someone from another world and tells Mary what she knows about Dust. Dust sounds to Mary very much like something Mary has been investigating, something Mary's research team calls dark matter. It consists of something they call shadow particles or Shadows, particles of a unique form of elementary matter.

Mary has a computer called the Cave. When she wires it to her head and thinks, Shadows within the computer respond, providing answers, though the answers tend to be fuzzy: Mary has not yet mastered the Cave. Mary and her colleagues have used the Cave to test ancient skulls like those Lyra saw in the museum. Before a cutoff point somewhere between thirty and forty thousand years ago, no Shadows accumulated on the skulls. Then, at about the time modern humans evolved, Shadows—Lyra's Dust—appeared on the skulls.

(Mary doesn't understand this phenomenon, but the explanation isn't hard to deduce. When the modern human brain evolved, knowledge—Dust—began to accumulate in the brain. Knowledge, or the intelligence that permits the acquisition of high levels of knowledge, is what differentiates man from other creatures. Dust is the physical manifestation of knowledge; particles of Dust are particles of knowledge. The Church fears knowledge—for example, knowledge of evolution—because knowledge attacks religious superstitions, such as the superstition that the human race began when God created two humans named Adam and Eve. The Church regards its superstitions as Truth. More than just Truth, they are the very essence of the Church's religion.)

Mary agrees to let Lyra experiment with the Cave if Lyra can demonstrate her ability to use the alethiometer. Lyra must say what Mary did before becoming a scientist. Lyra's answer is correct: Mary was a nun but stopped believing the doctrines of religion. Convinced, Mary hooks Lyra up to the Cave. The computer's screen puts on a display that astonishes Mary, who has never achieved such clear answers. Lyra learns that the Shadows flickering on the screen are Dust and that they can be made to form words on the screen. She must leave to meet Will but promises to return the next day at the same time.

Lyra and Will reconnect and return to Cittàgazze. That night Will finally has a chance to read his father's letters. The last one has the information he has been looking for. John Parry discovered in the arctic "a gap in the air, a sort of window" like the one Will found at the traffic circle. When Will's father vanished, he vanished into another world.

Back in Lyra's world, Lee Scoresby sails in his balloon to Nova Zembla, borne on winds called up by the witches. An old acquaintance tells Lee that Stanislaus Grumman (the identity John Parry assumed in Lee's and Lyra's world) came to Nova Zembla. Grumman became a tribal shaman with strange powers, powers apparently acquired through a process called trepanning—having a hole drilled part way through the skull. (Implicitly, the hole allowed an abnormal amount of Dust—knowledge—to enter the skull, where the brain is housed.) Parry-Grumman also adopted a Tartar name, Jopari (a corruption of "John Parry"). A witch wanted Grumman for her lover, but he scorned her advances. Talking with other people, Lee finds out that Grumman-Jopari might be in Yenisei, where the shaman's adoptive tribe is located. He also finds out, when he inquires about Dust, that the Church will try to kill anyone who asks about Dust. Sure enough, a Church spy tries to kill Lee. The spy loses his life to a bullet from Lee's gun as his reward.

Putting his balloon in storage, Lee goes by boat to the village of Grumman's tribe. He locates Grumman. Grumman reveals that his true name is John Parry and that he has used his shaman powers to summon Scoresby to him. He describes how, in a blizzard, he and two companions walked through a window to another world—this would be Cittàgazze's—and were unable to find their way back. His companions became victims of Specters, but Grumman managed to find another window and escape to Lyra's and Lee's world. There he went to Berlin, called himself Grumman, and earned his doctorate. While studying northern tribes, he submitted to trepanning, which led to his becoming a shaman. He claims to know a great deal about Dust (he doesn't say what) and wants to help Asriel preserve it. He also knows about a subtle knife, how it is used, where it can be found, how to recognize its bearer, and that the knife can help Asriel's cause. Grumman has drawn Lee to him to take Grumman to Cittàgazze's world, where the knife is. Lee agrees to take him. They retrieve Scoresby's balloon and take off for the new world.

While Lee is seeking out Grumman, Serafina Pekkala, the rest of her witch clan, and the Latvian witch queen Ruta Skadi fly to Cittàgazze's world. They soon witness first-hand the horrifying effects of Specter attacks on adult humans. A transparent, mistlike shimmer envelops the victim, who becomes almost inanimate while the Specter dines on his mind. The victim doesn't die but becomes indifferent to surrounding events: a father, caught waist-deep in a river, drops his son and stands idly by while the son drowns. Eyes become vacant, and the victim doesn't react to being pinched. There is no defense. Ruta Skadi shoots an arrow into a Specter with no effect. Why don't the Specters attack children? A surviving human tells Ruta that children have some power that repels Specters. What is this power? Pullman doesn't say, but later in the story he reveals that Specters feast on Dust. (Superstition sometimes overpowers knowledge: lessons taught in Sunday school and parochial school sometimes overpower the findings of science.) Children who have not reached puberty don't accumulate significant amounts of Dust, so children aren't appetizing to Specters.

Seeing a flight of angels, Ruta Skadi decides to join them. These particular angels are answering Asriel's call; other angels, a far greater number, remain loyal to the Authority. Two days later Ruta and the angels pass through an invisible window in the air and leave Cittàgazze's world, entering Lord Asriel's new world (not the one he and Lyra came from).

Meanwhile, Lyra has returned to Will's world for her next-day appointment with Mary. But as Lyra approaches Mary's laboratory, Mary beckons her into the ladies' washroom. The police are in Mary's lab. They somehow know about and are looking for Lyra. Mary helps

Lyra escape. After running a fair distance—between buildings, over a fence, through a garden—she receives a ride in a chauffeur-driven car. Its owner-passenger is the man from the museum, Lord Boreal, who in Will's world is Charles Latrom. When he drops Lyra off, she discovers he has stolen the alethiometer from her rucksack.

Lyra returns to Cittàgazze and tells Will what happened. After discussing the situation, they decide to go to Latrom's house and confront him. Lyra still has his card; it has his address; Will knows how to get there. At Latrom's house, the scoundrel acknowledges that he has the alethiometer, but he will return it only in exchange for something else. He knows about Cittàgazze and that it has a tower, a tower that Lyra and Will have seen. Someone in the tower has a special knife, a knife the Specters fear. If Lyra will get that knife and bring it to Latrom, he will return the alethiometer.

Once more in Cittàgazze, the two children go to the tower. In a room on the third floor they see a young man with a knife. He is jabbing and slicing with it as though fighting some invisible object. On the next floor they find a bruised, battered old man whose hands are tied behind him. Once untied, he identifies himself as "the bearer," he who rightfully holds the subtle knife. The young man downstairs has stolen it from him.

Just then, the young man with the knife enters the room and attacks Will. In a fierce struggle, Will gains the knife but loses the fourth and fifth fingers from his left hand in the process. Defeated and injured, the knife thief retreats from the tower and yields his mind to awaiting Specters. Back inside, the old man tells Will that Will is the knife's new bearer: the knife knows when to change hands. The man shows Will his own left hand. It matches Will's; the same two fingers are missing.

The man, Giacomo Paradisi, dresses Will's wound. Hearing about Latrom, he says he knows the man and warns the children not to let Latrom get his hands on the knife. He then tells them the knife's story. It was invented by the Guild of the Torre degli Angeli to cut windows opening to other worlds. Guild members used it to steal from those

worlds, enriching themselves in the process. What they didn't anticipate is that each time they cut a new window they created a Specter.
Ironically, the knife both creates and kills Specters. It has a double-
edged blade. One edge will cut through anything and will kill
Specters; the other will cut the fabric of space to create windows to
other worlds. Paradisi teaches Will how to create windows. He also
shows Will how to close windows by using one hand. His tutoring finished, Paradisi announces that he intends to take poison, to which he
has access. He will avoid a fate worse than death, the Specters.

That night Lyra and Will make their way to Latrom's house via
Cittàgazze streets. They know the two worlds are geographically similar, and Will makes frequent cuts into his own world to check their
position. Once on the Latrom grounds, Will enters the house via Cittàgazze while Lyra waits outside. To her amazement, Lyra sees Latrom
arrive in his car with Mrs. Coulter. Now Lyra remembers: Charles
Latrom is Lord Boreal!

Lyra joins Will inside, where they overhear a conversation.
Boreal-Latrom has discovered that Asriel's tampering with the aurora
has shifted the destinations of certain windows. Previously, Cittàgazze's world was a crossroads that all windows opened into; now
some windows lead directly to other worlds. Boreal-Latrom used one
of those windows to bring Mrs. Coulter to Will's world. Coulter knows
Boreal-Latrom has obtained the alethiometer and that Lyra must therefore be near. She has heard what the witches say about Lyra's destiny
and is determined to learn what Lyra knows about Dust. But before the
conversation can go much further, Will creates a diversion, grabs the
alethiometer from a table, and escapes with Lyra to Cittàgazze.

The next day Will and Lyra talk about the Specters. Lyra com-
ments that there are no Specters in Will's world. Will precociously
replies that he isn't so sure. Maybe, he says, the Specters are called
something else in his world—our world. And indeed they are. What is
our word for Specters—something that is pervasive in our society,
something that is related to religion, something of which the beliefs in
Satan and Hell's fire and the Virgin Birth are examples, something that

attacks the mind and cripples rational thought? (Our word, like "Specters," begins with *s*.)

The conversation between Lyra and Will is interrupted by a group of forty or fifty children advancing toward the café. One carries a gun. Another, a girl, shouts that Will killed her brother and stole his knife. Lyra and Will flee to the roof of a nearby building but can't escape. They seem doomed. Then Serafina Pekkala arrives in the nick of time with her witch clan and rescues them.

At a safe location Serafina tells Lyra that the witches have come to Cittàgazze's world to guard her and help her in what has become Lyra's task: guiding Will to his father. The alethiometer tells Lyra to travel to some distant mountains. Some time later, a witch scout reports seeing a balloon with two men over the sea; it sounds to Lyra like Lee Scoresby. Still later, Ruta Skadi and her witch clan join Lyra, Will, and Serafina's clan. Ruta describes Asriel's newly built fortress and the preparations Asriel is making for war against the Authority. More important, Ruta has spied on a gathering of cliff-ghasts and heard the words of their eldest of elders. He has said that, without someone or something called Æsahættr, Asriel will be defeated. Æsahættr means "god destroyer." Ruta speculates that, in view of the ancient witch prophecy that Lyra would put an end to destiny, Lyra might be Æsahættr. Ruta then leaves to rally other witch clans to Asriel's cause.

Back at Mary Malone's lab at Oxford, Charles Latrom pays Mary a visit. Her research's funding is up for renewal the next day. Latrom informs Mary that he has influence and that she will receive no more funds except on his terms. She must tell him everything she learned from Lyra. And she must help him find Lyra and Will. Mary scorns Latrom's offer.

That night Mary returns to the lab and hooks herself up to the Cave. Using insights gained from Lyra plus a hastily developed new program, she begins her session. For the first time, the Cave replies to typed questions with printed answers on the screen. It reveals that Shadows, Dust, and dark matter (dark matter is a real scientific concept here on Earth) are the same thing. The Cave next tells Mary to find Lyra and Will. After finding them, Mary must "play the serpent"—an allusion to the Garden of Eden myth's temptation of Eve by the serpent. More instructions follow: Mary must destroy her equipment, gather provisions for a long journey, go to a certain location (the traffic circle), and pass through a window to another world (Cittàgazze's). The Specters, she is told, won't harm her. Mary follows the Cave's instructions. Before long, she is in Cittàgazze.

Elsewhere, Lee Scoresby and John Parry (a.k.a. Stanislaus Grumman) drift past Cittàgazze in Lee's balloon. Asked what he will do when he finds the bearer of the subtle knife, Parry replies that he will tell the bearer what his task is. As they cross a bay thirty or forty miles wide and head toward the distant mountains, Lee surveys the area with his telescope. He sees four pursuing zeppelins. Parry, using his shaman powers, conjures up a storm whose lightning brings one zeppelin down. But the other three are closing fast: they can't be outrun.

To avoid being shot out of the air, Lee crash-lands his balloon in the foothills. The zeppelins circle overhead, looking for Scoresby and Parry. Parry now uses his shaman magic to direct a Specter into the cockpit of a second zeppelin, causing the airship to crash. Two down, two to go. Parry next commands all the birds of the forest to attack and cling to a third zeppelin; their weight brings it down, and it bursts into flames. But Parry's efforts have exhausted his ailing body. He lacks the strength to down the last zeppelin.

Taking his rifle and a knapsack, Lee leads Parry to the mountains and to the entrance of a long, ascending ravine. They are seen. The last zeppelin descends, hovers, and sends soldiers to the ground. Lee instructs Parry to go up the ravine and escape while Lee takes cover and holds off the soldiers with his rifle. Parry escapes to continue his mission; Lee dies in a firefight, but not before directly killing half the soldiers and then, with his last shot, bringing the zeppelin down in flames on the remaining soldiers.

Lyra, Will, and the witches reach the mountains. They pass a lake and begin climbing. After a while, Serafina sends another witch, Lena Feldt, back to spy on any pursuers. On reaching the lake, Lena finds that there indeed are pursuers, camped at the lake. They are Mrs. Coulter, Charles Latrom, and a group of daemonless guards who had their daemons intercised before the soldiers became adults and who are therefore Dust-free. The Specters, who are attracted to the Dust in adult minds, can't feed on the soldiers. Mrs. Coulter displays an ability to command the Specters, so we cannot doubt that they are friends of the Church. Lena overhears Latrom tell Coulter that the subtle knife is called Æsahættr.

Latrom has now outlived his usefulness: Coulter poisons him, and he dies. A moment later, a Specter envelops Lena's snow bunting daemon; Lena is Coulter's captive. Using Specter torture, Coulter finds out where Lyra and the witches are. And she learns that Lyra is destined to be "Eve again"—a figurative new Eve, not the original Eve. Coulter then hands Lena over to an awaiting Specter and directs the other Specters toward Lyra's camp.

At the camp, Will can't sleep, partly because of his throbbing hand. He gets up and climbs to a plateau. An unseen man grasps Will's arms and, after a brief struggle, sees that two fingers are missing from his left hand. Letting go, he declares that Will is the knife bearer. Will is exhausted from the struggle; he doesn't move while the man brings out some shaman salve and spreads it on Will's still-bleeding wound. The salve will cure the wound, the man says.

Then the man gets down to business, the business he came for— telling the knife bearer what the knife is for. The knife is the one weapon in the universe that can defeat the tyrannical Authority. And if Will doesn't use the knife against the Authority in a coming war, those forces will tear the knife from Will's hands and use it against mankind. The man instructs the boy to go with his knife to Lord Asriel.

The moment of truth arrives. The man and the boy gaze into each other's eyes and somehow recognize each other—father and son. An arrow suddenly flashes down from the sky, killing the man instantly. Juta Kamainen, the witch whose love John Parry had scorned, has taken his life. She lands, tells Will why she killed the man, learns from Will that the dead man is Will's father, and then takes her own life.

Will returns to camp, but Lyra is gone. The witches who had been guarding her are sitting or standing listlessly, victims of Mrs. Coulter's Specters. Serafina Pekkala is not among the witch zombies: just before Lee Scoresby died he summoned her with a magic flower she had given him back in his world. And Lyra? We aren't told where she is, but we can easily guess: Mrs. Coulter has taken her prisoner. Two angels stand where Lyra was. They tell Will they have been following "the shaman," hoping Parry-Grumman would lead them to Will. Having found Will, they intend to guide him to Asriel.

THE AMBER SPYGLASS

The opening scene of *AS* is a cave in Lyra's world. Mrs. Coulter has taken Lyra to the cave and is keeping her there, drugged, asleep, and hidden. Coulter is treating the child in motherly fashion—mopping her brow, teasing out the tangles in her hair, snipping off a lock of her hair to put in a locket hanging from Coulter's neck. And Coulter can't understand why she is doing this—or what the Church will do when it finds out. For her part, Lyra is hearing in her sleep a voice calling her name. It is that of Roger, Roger's ghost, that is. He is saying he is in the world of the dead. He hates it. He wants out.

In Cittàgazze's world, Will confronts the two angels. They want him to follow his father's instructions by going with them to Lord Asriel. But Will has other ideas. He must first find Lyra. Only then will he go to Asriel. The angels agree to do things Will's way. Then they introduce themselves. They are Balthamos and Baruch. The three companions go first to the lake where Mrs. Coulter camped. Inexplicably, the alethiometer has been left behind, so Will puts it in his rucksack. Balthamos soon finds a window to Lyra's world and says that Coulter and Lyra used it. Will and the angels stop for the night.

The next day the three enter Lyra's world through the window. Baruch goes ahead—far ahead—and locates Lyra. She is a long ways away, a captive in a cave in a Himalayan valley. Mrs. Coulter is with

her; there are no others. And Mrs. Coulter is hiding. Will can't understand this. Why should Mrs. Coulter be hiding from the Church? As
Will ponders, a powerful angel spies them from high above and
attacks. Balthamos pleads for Will to cut a window into another world.
They barely escape through the window, which Will closes behind
them an instant before a spear from above slams into the space Will
vacated. Balthamos identifies the attacker as Metatron and refers to
Metatron's "Chariot."

Balthamos elaborates: Metatron is the Authority's Regent, his
right-hand angel. The Authority has given himself such names as God,
Yahweh, the Father, the Almighty, and the Creator. He lives in the
Clouded Mountain, sometimes called the Chariot because it moves
around in the sky. Before finding Will, Balthamos and Baruch sneaked
into the Clouded Mountain and spied. They learned that the Authority
has delegated a large measure of power to Metatron. The Authority,
through the Church, tells humans that those who are religious will be
rewarded with a blissful afterlife with him in Heaven when they die.
The truth is, though, that all who die become ghosts and go to a world
of the dead. Balthamos calls it a prison camp, a place of suffering and
despair. Although Will's companions escaped from the Clouded
Mountain, they knew Metatron would pursue them. It is now urgent
that Asriel learn what has happened. The two angels decide that
Baruch will fly to Asriel while Balthamos accompanies and watches
over Will.

Scout angels working for Metatron spot Baruch as he flies toward
Asriel's fortress. They attack and gravely injure him, but he escapes.
Arriving at the fortress, Baruch goes to Asriel. His message has three
items. First, Metatron is now running the Clouded Mountain and plans
to turn it into an "engine of war." The Regent intends to first destroy
Asriel's republic and to then establish a permanent inquisition in every
world. Second, a boy named Will, the son of the shaman Grumman,
has a knife that can cut openings between worlds. Third, Lyra is being
held prisoner in a cave in her world's Himalayas. After delivering his
message, Baruch dies.

Asriel orders a squadron of troop-laden gyrocopters and an accompanying tanker zeppelin to take off and head southwest; more precise directions will be radioed later. He then summons his alethiometer reader, Mr. Basilides, and instructs him to locate the cave. (Six alethiometers exist; Asriel has one of them.)

In Lyra's world, the Church's Consistorial Court of Discipline is meeting. From a captured and tortured witch, the Court has learned that Lyra is the subject of a prophecy. She will be tempted to do something that can devastate the Church, something involving a name that points to a much earlier parallel case. The name is that of Eve, she who was tempted to eat, then ate, the Forbidden Fruit from the Tree of Knowledge and who, in doing so, brought sin into the world. From its own alethiometer, the Court learns that if Lyra's temptation takes place, Dust and sin will be victorious. The Court's youngest member, a zealot named Father Gomez who has done "preemptive penance" (advance penance for uncommitted sin) every day of his life, volunteers to find and kill Lyra. Father MacPhail, the Court's president, gives his okay. And on a ceiling beam a tiny Gallivespian, a spy for Asriel, hears everything.

Mary Malone is now traveling across Cittàgazze's world; the Specters avoid her. Eventually she comes to a window like the one at the traffic circle in Oxford. She steps through it into a second new world. There she finds, befriends, and learns the language of intelligent but primitive wheeled animals, the *mulefa*. The *mulefa* move around on lava-flow roads by grasping huge, round, wheel-like seed pods with claws on two side legs while using a front leg and a back leg for propulsion; the claws function as axles.

The survival of the *mulefa* is threatened by two problems. The first is huge, flightless sailing birds called *tualapi* who periodically attack. These strange birds have front and back wings they hold aloft in positions resembling the positions of sails on two-masted sailing ships. The *tualapi* (symbolizing whom?) sail upriver from the sea, come ashore at *mulefa* villages, kill any *mulefa* they can catch, destroy the seed pods the *mulefa* depend on for mobility, and leave their feces (symbolizing what?) all over the villages. Not a serious problem until about 300 years ago—the time when the subtle knife was invented— the *tualapi* have been increasing rapidly.

The second problem is the gradual disappearance of Dust, which the *mulefa* call *sraf* and on which their survival depends. *Sraf* falls from the sky and enters the *mulefa* indirectly rather than, as is the case with humans, directly. Dust, you will recall, falls directly on adult humans. But with the *mulefa*, *sraf* falls on and fertilizes the upturned blossoms of the wheel-pod trees, migrates to the developing seed pods, enters the pod oil, and gets absorbed by the *mulefa* when the wheeled animals harvest the pods and grasp the pod-wheels with their claws. Starting about 300 years ago, at the same time the *tualapi* began multiplying and the subtle knife was made, the dustfall began to decline. Now the wheel-pod trees are dying, and if they die the *mulefa* will die with them.

Desperate, and knowing Mary is a scientist, the *mulefa* ask Mary for help. She readily agrees. Because the *mulefa* can see the *sraf* moving across the sky whereas Mary can't, she designs an instrument that will enable her to also see *sraf*. The instrument consists of two lenses, not true lenses but round, flat, transparent sheets. Made from layers of amber sap laquer, the lenses are coated with wheel-pod oil and mounted a few inches apart at opposite ends of a short piece of bamboo. Through this telescopelike device, Mary can see the *sraf*, the very Shadows she had been studying in her own world. By observing the *sraf* with her "amber spyglass," Mary learns why the trees are dying. Whereas the *sraf* formerly drifted down from the sky onto upward-facing blossoms, it is now flowing out to sea and entering only an occasional blossom that happens to be facing inland (toward the Dust flow) rather than upward or seaward.

While Mary helps the *mulefa*, Will and Baruch return to Lyra's world. At a village along the way a pedophile priest tries to get Will drunk on vodka. Will psychologically outmaneuvers the priest and manages to gain important information: armored bears are coming up the river by boat. Upstream means toward the water's source, the

Himalayas. Arctic warming caused by Asriel's tampering with the aurora has persuaded the bears to seek a colder climate in the mountains. Will meets the bear's leader, Iorek Brynison, who Will has heard about from Lyra. When Will tells Iorek he is searching for Lyra, Iorek agrees to join forces. They continue upstream. When the boat can go no farther, the bears disembark and go their separate ways to hunt; they will reconvene later at this spot. Only Iorek remains with Will. With the help of a map given to them by the boat's captain, Iorek and Will move on toward the valley where Lyra is.

Three parties approach the valley at once. Iorek and Will advance overland. Asriel's gyrocopters carrying King Ogunwe's African blacks, Asriel's human soldiers, cross through the sky window over Svalbard and approach through the air. And eight zeppelins carrying troops of the Church's Swiss Guard fly in from another direction. The leading zeppelin, commanded by Father MacPhail, carries two stowaways. Their names: Chevalier Tialys and Lady Salmakia. They are Gallivespians, just a hand-span tall and armed with venomous spurs on their heels. Each rides a large dragonfly. Tialys and Salmakia have been instructed by their back-at-the-fortress commander, Lord Roke, to fly to the cave when the zeppelin unloads and help Will defend Lyra.

Will and Iorek are the first to reach the cave. Will goes inside and confronts Mrs. Coulter; Lyra is still asleep, drugged. Will learns from Coulter that she has made an agonizing choice between her daughter and the Church. The Church intends to kill Lyra. Coulter now loves Lyra and has forsaken the Church. Pretending to be satisfied, Will retreats. Later, he sneaks back in, cutting into the cave from another world with his knife. But when Coulter looks at him, he thinks of his mother; the knife shatters. Other forces arrive, and fighting between the Africans and the Swiss Guard breaks out. The two Gallivespians enter the cave and help Will subdue Mrs. Coulter, who has a gun. Will and the Gallivespians get Lyra outside the cave. Iorek then holds off the Swiss Guard while Will cuts a window to another world. Finally, Lyra is safe.

The Africans drive off the Swiss Guard and capture Mrs. Coulter. They transport her to Asriel's fortress in his new world. The next day,

Lyra, Will, and the two Gallivespians return briefly to Lyra's world to seek Iorek's further assistance. Iorek uses his armor-making skills to mend the broken knife. The Gallivespians insist that Lyra and Will return with them to the fortress, but Lyra has other ideas. She has heard Roger's call in her drugged sleep: she is determined to go to the land of the dead. Will, for his part, wants to speak to the ghost of his father. Will cuts a window into the world he and the two angels temporarily escaped to earlier when they fled from Metatron. Lyra, Will, and the Gallivespians enter this world.

After further difficulties, Lyra's party reaches the suburbs of the dead. From there an aged boatman rows the ghosts of dead people across a lake to an island where the gate to the land of the dead is. The boatman initially refuses to take Lyra, because Pantalaimon, her soul, is with her. That means she is still alive. In the most excruciating decision of her life, Lyra agrees to leave Pantalaimon behind. As they leave the shore, Will feels his own daemon, one he didn't know he had, ripped from his heart and left behind with Pantalaimon. Lyra, Will, and the Gallivespians, reach the island and enter the land of the dead. Grotesque, smelly, screeching harpies—half woman, half bird—preside there and make life miserable for the resident ghosts. Lyra searches for and finds Roger's ghost.

Much earlier, while supposedly asleep in Lee Scoresby's balloon, Lyra overheard the witch prophecy that she has a destiny. She thinks her destiny is to release the ghosts from their misery by leading them out of the land of the dead. Will tries to help her by cutting a window to an outside world, but his knife keeps running into solid rock. To cut through, he will have to find a place closer to the surface of an outer world. Then a stroke of luck: he and Lyra accidentally discover that the harpies crave truth. It nourishes them. Tialys takes over and negotiates with the harpies. Every ghost will tell the harpies a story from his or her life. The harpies will sit in judgment. Ghosts, both those now present and those who arrive in the future, who tell true stories will be led out of the world of the dead. Ghosts who lie will remain in the harpies' wasteland. The harpies agree; the exodus begins.

But complications develop. Mrs. Coulter, who is a prisoner of Asriel, steals an intention craft, an aircraft guided by the mind instead of by controls. Before she departs, however, Lord Roke, commander of the Gallivespians, flies into the craft unseen on his blue hawk. Coulter flies to the Church's headquarters in Geneva and foolishly goes to Father MacPhail. He makes her a captive. That night, while she sleeps, MacPhail sends a priest to steal the lock of Lyra's hair from Coulter's locket. MacPhail intends to use the hair as a homing device in an incredibly powerful supernatural bomb. The bomb will be triggered in Lyra's world by electric power, but its explosive force will be felt only where the rest of the lock of Lyra's hair is—on Lyra's head. The bomb's devastating energy will come from essentially the same source as that of the burst of energy Asriel used to build his bridge across the aurora: death. Mrs. Coulter and her daemon will be put in the twin coops of a silver guillotine, and the link between the two will be severed in an unexplained way that kills them rather than merely unlinking them. (Merely unlinking the human and its daemon was the procedure used on the children at the Experimental Station).

MacPhail, priests, engineers, soldiers, and Mrs. Coulter—and the unseen Lord Roke—arrive by zeppelin at a rural power station. There the bomb's triggering device, which requires enormous amounts of power, will be set off. Engineers put Lyra's hair in a bomb chamber. But before they can put Mrs. Coulter and her golden monkey daemon in the silver guillotine, Lord Roke kills two guards and a hostile witch, freeing the two prisoners. Unfortunately, Roke loses his own life when he falls from the air with the witch, whom he has climbed on and stung with one of his venomous heel spurs. So determined is MacPhail to kill Lyra and defeat sin that he decides to sacrifice himself: he will take Mrs. Coulter's place in the silver guillotine. Just then Asriel arrives with a rescue party, but not in time to stop MacPhail. From inside his guillotine cage he brings two wires together, detonating the bomb.

Back in the land of the dead, the harpy No-Name has brought Lyra's party and the truthful ghosts to a point well removed from where they started. Here Will meets his father's ghost. The shaman has used his psychic powers to learn of MacPhail's plot. He instructs Will to find the shortened strands of Lyra's hair, cut them off at their roots with his knife, open a window to another world, put the hair through, and close the window. Will obeys. He uses his knife to carve out a small hollow in the rock on the other side, inserts the hair, and shuts the window. An instant later the ground shudders. A huge, seemingly bottomless abyss opens beside them. The procession cautiously circles the abyss and moves on. The ground begins to slope upward, and they reach a point close enough to the surface for Will to cut a window to the outside.

At Asriel's fortress, other events are taking shape. Mrs. Coulter, no longer treated as a prisoner, is again present. She and Asriel have learned from Asriel's alethiometer reader that Lyra escaped the bomb and is leading the ghosts out of the world of the dead and into, of all places, Asriel's world. They have also learned about the abyss and about cracks in outside worlds at the end of passages leading to and from the abyss. And they have learned that Lyra's daemon and Will's have entered Asriel's world.

Soon Asriel sees the Clouded Mountain, Metatron's Chariot, moving in across the sky to attack the fortress. Hordes of angels form the vanguard of the enemy. Asriel has gathered his own forces—rebel angels, witches, Gallivespians, the armored bears, and a multitude of humans—from all the worlds. He calls his three top commanders together. King Ogunwe and his blacks will defend the fortress. Madam Oxentiel, who has taken over from the dead Lord Roke as the Gallivespian commander, will use her forces to locate the two daemons, guide them to Lyra and Will, and protect the daemons and the children until they can escape to another world, where Lyra can realize her true destiny. And Xaphania, commander of the rebel angels, will initially use her angels to locate a nearby fissure opening to the underworld.

The angels soon find an opening and report its location to Asriel. He tells his commanders that he intends to go down to the abyss and destroy Metatron. As the apocalyptic "battle on the plain"—the Authority's forces fighting Asriel's—begins, Asriel finds his way down to the abyss. Mrs. Coulter, meanwhile, has overheard Asriel and somehow knows she has a role to play. She steals another intention craft, flies to the Clouded Mountain, locates Metatron, and offers herself to the lustful Regent as a bribe for his following a plan to kill Asriel. Coulter tells Metatron where Asriel can be found and, together, they go through the opening and descend to the abyss. Metatron expects to ambush Asriel and hurl him into the abyss, but instead Coulter *betrays* Metatron and helps Asriel ambush Metatron. (What person in actual history betrayed another person who, in *Paradise Lost*'s fiction, drives a chariot and who also, in a widely used religious creed, "descended" into an underworld?) In a fierce struggle that the powerful Metatron nearly wins, all three plunge into the abyss and die.

Just before Lyra's party and the ghosts reach the surface, the ghost of John Parry learns through his psychic power that the two missing daemons are in Asriel's world and that that world is the one they will enter. He also reveals that humans who leave their worlds and don't return become ultra-mortal (just as Adam became mortal when he left Eden), dying within ten years or so. Boreal-Latrom had to return from Will's world to his own periodically to rejuvenate; otherwise he would have died. Parry himself was mortally ill when Juta Kamainen killed him: he had been away from his world for ten years, unable to return to it. Parry then reveals something else. He and Lee Scoresby's ghost have concocted a scheme for helping Asriel's cause. Ghosts have lost their souls and are thus immune to Specters, who are on the Authority's side. Those ghosts who have the experience and temperament for fighting will keep their spiritual substance intact as long as they can and take on the Specters—spirits fighting spirits, as it were.

Lyra's party—all except No-Name, the harpy—leaves the world of the dead and enters a scene of tumult: screams, rockets, thunderous explosions, and whizzing arrows are everywhere. Most of the ghosts dissolve and become part of nature; those with warrior personalities manage to hold themselves together long enough to move on and fight the Specters. Will and Lyra, approaching puberty, can now see the

Specters dimly. Will fights them off with his subtle knife and later uses the knife to drive off cliff-ghasts.

As the surviving ghasts flee from the knife in terror, Lyra sees a litter holding a crystal chamber. The chamber contains an ancient, feeble, demented, cowering, terrified, whimpering angel—the Authority. In preparation for battle, Metatron had ordered the Church's God transferred to a supposedly safe location, away from the fighting. But the cliff-ghasts had found and begun feeding on him when Lyra and Will came along. Not really the mortal being he in better times claimed to be, the Authority is bleeding and near death.

And now the subtle knife, Æsahættr, lives up to its name's meaning—"god destroyer." But it does so indirectly, not in the way you would expect. Will uses the knife to slice open the crystal cage. He and Lyra then reach in and help the Authority out. Their efforts to help him, however, merely accelerate his demise. As soon as he is exposed to the wind, he evanesces and vanishes. (Pullman's message: God never had any real substance.)

Lady Salmakia arrives on the late Lord Roke's blue hawk, now her blue hawk. Hundreds of dragonfly-mounted Gallivespian warriors accompany her. The Gallivespians have located, and take Lyra and Will to, their missing daemons. Along the way the Gallivespians, then Iorek and a regiment of his armored bears, and finally the ghosts and Will's knife, ward off three groups of attackers, more Specters in the last instance. Reuniting with their daemons, the children exit to another world through a window Will cuts open with his knife. When they depart, the warrior ghosts who had protected them relax, allowing their atoms to rejoin nature.

The new world is that of the *mulefa*. Before long Lyra and Will run into Mary and become acquainted with the *mulefa*. Mary has been expecting them: she learned in a dream they were coming. Apparently without realizing what she is doing, Mary proceeds to play the serpent—the role the Cave told her she must play when she finds the girl and the boy. She first tells the children how, some years ago at a conference, she fell in love with a man while still a nun. Then she tells them about the first time she fell in love. It was at a birthday party when Mary was twelve years old. She met a boy who gently put some marzipan, an almond confection, in her mouth and then kissed her. Lyra listens intently, enthralled, trembling, while strange feelings fill her body. She has been tempted, just as Eve was tempted.

In the morning Lyra tells Mary that she (Lyra) and Will must go and look for their daemons, who have run off, still a bit miffed at having been left behind in the suburbs of the land of the dead. Mary packs the coming-of-age children a lunch containing some little red fruits. (In the context of a figurative Eve—Lyra—what do the fruits symbolize? Viewed in the same context, what do they contain? If eaten, what will they give to Lyra and Will?) Lyra and Will depart.

They are watched. Father Gomez, the zealot priest commissioned by the Church to find and kill Lyra, has found her. He has been to Cittàgazze, talked with children there, and learned that Lyra has gone on. (The Specters haven't attacked Gomez, presumably because his mind is so corrupted with superstition that hardly anything rational is left in his mind for them to feed on.) After questioning people almost endlessly and searching resolutely, he has discovered the window Mary used to go from Cittàgazze's world to the *mulefa's* world. In the *mulefa* world he has found he can command the *tualapi*. They have become agents of the Church.

And now Gomez has found Lyra. While she and Will search for their daemons, Gomez follows them stealthily, trying to get close enough for a clear shot with his rifle. As the morning progresses, Gomez notices that Lyra and Will are becoming more and more absorbed in each other and paying little heed to whatever they started out to do: they are clearly moving toward mortal sin. Gomez raises his rifle . . . and suddenly finds himself gasping. Something has clutched his daemon and is pulling her away. The something is Balthamos, Will's guardian angel. A fierce struggle follows. It ends when Gomez slips in a stream, cracks his head on a rock, and drowns as Balthamos holds the stunned priest's head under the water.

Lyra and Will stop for lunch. And Mary's marzipan story enjoys a reprise, somewhat in reverse. The girl, not the boy, takes the initiative. Lyra presses one of the delicious red fruits to Will's lips, then presses her own lips against his. What, if anything, happens next we don't learn.

In the *mulefa* village, Mary's friend Atal cries out with excitement. He is telling her to look—to look up at the sky. She takes out her amber spyglass and gazes upward. The flow of Dust out to the sea has stopped. The Dust is now drifting down like snowflakes, down to the thirsting blossoms of the wheel-pod trees. The trees will survive and renew themselves. The *tualapi* will once more be held in check. And the *mulefa* race will endure. Lyra's destiny, enigmatically foretold by the witches, has been realized.

Atal then points to something else. The former children, now emerging adults, are returning. They are walking slowly, hand in hand, oblivious to the world around them. Mary starts to raise her spyglass but quickly realizes there is no need to. She knows what the spyglass would show her. Lyra and Will, saturated with love, are also saturated with golden, sparkling Dust. Metaphorically speaking, Lyra has become the "new Eve." She has succumbed to the temptation proffered by the metaphorical serpent, Mary. She has metaphorically eaten the Forbidden Fruit from the Tree of Knowledge. She has sinned as Eve sinned—by partaking of knowledge, the thing the Church fears most. She is now saturated with it. Can anyone doubt what the particles of Dust represent?

That night Serafina Pekkala arrives and speaks to the daemons of Lyra and Will. She gives Will's daemon a name, Kirjava, then tells Pantalaimon and Kirjava some sad news they must relay to their humans. Dust is still leaking out of the worlds, and there is only one way to stop it. Throughout the last 300 years, each time the knife opened a new window Dust began flowing out the window—not to the world on the other side but to an in-between "nothingness." Thousands of open windows exist, so Dust will continue leaking out of all the worlds until all windows are closed. Closing them means that Lyra, to avoid death in ten years, cannot do what she longs to do: live in bliss with Will in his world. The lovers must spend the rest of their lives apart, unable to move back and forth between worlds.

The knife is no solution; it can't be used to open temporary windows between Will's world and Lyra's so that Lyra can return periodically to her world (as Boreal did) for rejuvenation. The knife must be destroyed. Otherwise it could eventually fall into the wrong hands and be used to open windows again. Each time a window is opened, a Specter is created. That is why Cittàgazze's world had so many Specters: originally, all windows opened in that world. Just as bad, new windows would let Dust escape, dooming humanity in the long run. Lyra and Will must separate, never to see each other again.

Distraught, Lyra brings out her alethiometer to verify these facts. But she discovers she can no longer read it. The angel Xaphania, the wisest being in the universe, comes. Her arrival verifies what is already apparent from the fulfillment of the witches' prophecy about Lyra and from the return of Dustfall: the apocalypse is over. The forces of religion have been defeated. This is why Xaphania has been able to leave her post as commander of the rebel angels.

Xaphania tells Lyra that Lyra has been reading the alethiometer "by grace." By grace means as an unearned (unlearned in Lyra's case) benefit—here the benefit is a psychic skill—rather than by the normal adult process of learning complex rules and meanings and applying them by effortful thought and reasoning. Now that Lyra has come of age, she must learn to read her alethiometer the adult way: by thinking and reasoning. (Here lies a cryptic meaning: a child receives superstition not by reasoning and drawing logical conclusions but by grace, as an unearned "gift" from authority figures—parents and priests—whereas an adult receives knowledge by observing, experimenting, reasoning, and drawing logical conclusions.)

Xaphania learns from Will how to close windows. She promises that her angels will close all the windows. She also promises to eliminate the remaining Specters.

No sooner has Xaphania left than the two daemons "settle"—assume their permanent forms, signifying that Lyra and Will are now adults. Pantalaimon becomes a pine marten. Kirjava becomes a large cat with dark, lustrous fur. Then the gyptians, guided by Serafina Pekkala, arrive by ship to take Lyra home. (Evidently, though we aren't told this, Serafina learned of a sea window between Lyra's world and the *mulefa* world.)

First, though, the gyptians must take Will and Mary home to their world. The group sails to Cittàgazze (presumably passing through yet another sea window). From there Will and Mary, temporarily accompanied by Lyra and Serafina, go through the traffic circle window back to Will's Oxford. Lyra takes Will to a bench in the Oxford Botanic Garden (a figurative Garden of Eden). Her own world's Oxford has a bench in the same place. The lovers vow to return each year on Midsummer Day to their respective Botanic Garden benches to silently renew their love. Afterward, all four companions return briefly to Cittàgazze; Lyra and Will kiss farewell; Will and Mary return to Oxford, where Will destroys the knife; and Lyra, Serafina, and the gyptians go back home.

For Lyra, "back home" is all the way back home—Jordan College. There she learns that the Church's power grew while she was away but then mysteriously declined precipitously. (Pullman doesn't say why, but we know: a Dust-based renaissance of knowledge is smothering superstition.) The Church is now in disarray, confused and leaderless. The Master of Jordan introduces Lyra to Dame Hannah Relf, head of St. Sofia's, one of the women's colleges at Lyra's Oxford. Dame Hannah will shelter and St. Sofia's will educate Lyra, who will learn how to use the alethiometer the scientific way—rationally, not by grace. In time, Lyra will build her own "Republic of Heaven" in the world she lives in. There is no other world, no "next world" of bliss.

CHAPTER 3

THE LION, THE WITCH AND THE WARDROBE:

C. S. Lewis's Story and His Allegory

Pullman's intent to provide an antireligious fantasy that refutes *The Lion, the Witch and the Wardrobe* (*LWW*) is widely understood. But few people if any have even suspected that Pullman's refutation includes an allegory—a hidden story told by 104 symbols in the surface story—that straightforwardly retells the C. S. Lewis tale. No antireligious content has been added. The symbolized Christ still dies, then rises from the dead. He still defeats the symbolized Satan. And the Four Horsemen of the Apocalypse ride again. To recognize this allegory, Pullman's readers need to be familiar with *LWW*. This chapter therefore begins with a summary of that book, which is itself allegorical: *LWW* uses 52 symbols to present a hidden story based on Christian themes. (View the following summary of *LWW* as an intensive supplement to chapter 1's first illustration of allegory, George Orwell's *Animal Farm*.) In chapter 4 we will look at the setting, the characters, and other *His Dark Materials* (*HDM*) symbolism pointing to things in C. S. Lewis's children's fantasy.

THE C. S. LEWIS STORY

One requirement of allegory is continuity in the symbolism. Observe in the following analysis how Lewis's story is a start-to-finish parade of symbols. Contrary to what other analysts have said, the symbolism is not confined to three death-and-resurrection chapters.

The Professor, His House, His Staff, and the Siblings. During World War II, four siblings—Peter (oldest), Susan (second oldest), Edmund (second youngest), and Lucy (youngest)—have been sent from London to live in the country to escape German air raids. They are temporarily living in the house of a kindly old Professor. He is unmarried but has a housekeeper named Mrs. Macready ("make ready") and three servants—Ivy, Margaret, and Betty. The Professor has shaggy white hair and a white beard covering most of his face. He knows things no ordinary person could possibly know, such as that the children will get back to Narnia someday but not via the wardrobe. The Professor symbolizes God: his white beard fits the standard cartoon caricature of God, and his knowledge of unknowable things suggests God's omniscience.

Symbolism at the end of the story depicts the Bible's apocalypse, from Revelation. In Revelation the apocalypse is followed by the end of human kingdoms (the children leave Narnia, abandoning their thrones) and the arrival of the Kingdom of God, presided over by God. When the children return from Narnia to the Professor's house, they are entering the symbolized Kingdom of God, presided over by the Professor, who symbolizes God.

In *The Magician's Nephew*, the sixth book to be written in the *Narnia* series but the first in chronological order, the Professor's character is radically revised. He becomes Digory Kirke, a very unGodlike boy who grows up to be the Professor. This revisionist Professor bears less resemblance to God than the Professor of the original story, but don't be deceived. The Professor of the original story is analogous to—symbolizes—God.

Ryken and Mead aptly explain the conflict between the two characterizations of the Professor: "Lewis did not anticipate the other six Narnian stories when he wrote his first volume [*LWW*]. As a result, he created this story as a 'stand-alone' narrative, and the development of this first tale was not written to take into account any subsequent books."[1] The authors add that "to read *The Magician's Nephew* first would be to undercut the very fabric by which Lewis so carefully constructed his previous tale."[2] In other words, the Professor of *LWW*—Lewis's God symbol—is not the unGodlike Digory Kirke of *The Magician's Nephew*. He doesn't even have a name.

One other problem with the God symbolism requires attention. *LWW* has two references to the "Emperor-beyond-the-Sea," who incontrovertibly is God.[3] We know this because, just as the Christ is the son of God, Aslan (Lewis's Christ symbol) is the son of the Emperor (the God symbol). But there is no reason why the Professor cannot be the Emperor. Just as the people of Earth have never seen God, the inhabitants of Narnia (Lewis's Earth symbol) have never seen the Emperor (God's title in Narnia). So who is to say the Emperor-beyond-the-Sea isn't the Professor and "beyond the Sea" isn't the Professor's house (heaven)? The Professor could be either God's only form (a form never described but implicitly human) or one of several different manifestations of God. After all, later in *LWW* Aslan becomes the White Stag, and in the subsequent *Narnia* book *The Voyage of the "Dawn Treader"* Aslan becomes a lamb. If Aslan can have three guises, why can't God have at least two? For that matter, even the White Witch—Satan, the god of evil—has two guises: a woman and a stump. If the bad god can have two guises, why can't the good god?

Since the Professor represents God, Mrs. Macready and the three servants must symbolize God's servants—the angels. Why else would Lewis mention the existence of the three servants, give them names, and then leave them entirely out of the story? The answer is that they have just one function: to represent angels. Even Mrs. Macready, whose name is mentioned several times in one scene, is never onstage.

Before we leave the Professor, you might want to try to figure out in advance which Pullman character symbolizes him. Like the Professor, Pullman's symbolic character should be someone who has a housekeeper and three servants—say, a butler, a steward, and a porter—and who is master of the domain where the servants are employed. The Professor first appears in chapter 1 of Lewis's story, so it might be a good idea to look for the Professor's symbol in chapter 1 of *The Golden Compass* (*GC*), the first book of Pullman's trilogy.

Lucy, the Wardrobe, Narnia, and Tumnus. Exploring the house, the children find a room that is empty except for a huge wardrobe (a free-standing, cabinet-style closet). After the others lose interest in the room and depart to explore elsewhere, Lucy stays behind and enters the wardrobe. As she passes through the wardrobe the soft fur of clothing hanging there becomes the rough branches of trees. Snow is suddenly underfoot. As she crunches forward through it she comes to a lamppost, suggestive of an entrance. She is in the magical land of Narnia. Talking animals inhabit Narnia. They are ruled by an evil White Witch, who represents Satan. As long as the witch reigns, it will remain winter in Narnia. Winter—discomfort, bleakness, barren trees—symbolizes Satan's misery-creating power.

Lucy soon meets a faun, Mr. Tumnus. A faun is a man from the waist up and a goat from the waist down. Tumnus takes Lucy to his well-furnished cave home and feeds her. When she tries to excuse herself to return home, Tumnus tearfully confesses that he serves the White Witch, who is responsible for keeping Narnia in the perpetual grip of winter. Tumnus is supposed to catch any humans he meets and hand them over to the witch. But because Lucy is so polite and friendly, he lets her go. She returns through the wardrobe to the Professor's house. No time has passed in the house, because our world and Narnia have different time systems.

Narnia symbolizes Earth. This is easily deduced. Earth is where Jesus died and was resurrected in Christian mythology, and Narnia is where the Jesus symbol (Aslan, coming up shortly) dies and is resurrected. But not all of Narnia is Earth. A castle where the White Witch resides symbolizes Hell, but that's getting ahead of the story.

If Narnia is Earth, the Professor's house must symbolize Heaven.

Just as Heaven contrasts with Earth, the Professor's house contrasts with Narnia. Confirmation that the Professor's house is Heaven is seen in the fact that the symbols for God and his angels—the Professor, Mrs. Macready, and the three servants—live in the house. Heaven is where God and his angels dwell. At the end of the story, the house becomes the Kingdom of God, God's Kingdom on Earth. It will come down from Heaven after apocalyptic suffering and upheavals destroy the kingdoms ruled by human kings, according to the Bible's book of Revelation.

The wardrobe is just a portal between Earth and Narnia. But Freudian interpreters have suggested that the wardrobe is more than that: a womb from which the children are born into Narnia. That interpretation has two flaws. The first is that, after being born, people do not return to the womb; much less do they return two or three times, and still less do they get reborn once or twice. Not even figuratively "born-again" Christians get reborn twice. Yet Lucy returns through the wardrobe to the Professor's house three times, Edmund twice, and Susan and Peter once. After returning, Lucy goes back from the Professor's house to Narnia twice and Edmund once. That isn't the way wombs operate.

Flaw number two in the womb interpretation is that allegorical symbolism must support the allegory's unifying theme. C. S. Lewis's allegory's unifying theme is Christianity, not Freudianism. Freud, by the way, professed atheism, about as far from Christianity as you can get. The wardrobe is simply a story device for getting someone from one world to another—like Alice's rabbit hole, Dorothy's Kansas tornado, science fiction and fantasy "gates," and Pullman's windows. It is not a symbol.

Edmund, the Witch, and the Dwarf. A few days later Edmund follows Lucy into the wardrobe during a game of hide-and-seek. Lucy is gone, and he finds himself alone in Narnia. There he meets the White Witch, Lewis's Satan symbol. She is driving through the woods on a sledge (sleigh) pulled by reindeer, and with her is a dwarf, her servant. The dwarf symbolizes a demon, a servant of Satan. The witch gives Edmund a cup of a hot, sweet, foamy drink and some Turkish Delight candy to coax him into her service. If he will bring his brother and two sisters to her, she will reward him with more Turkish Delight. Here temptation by the devil is being symbolized. Edmund, eager for more Turkish Delight, agrees to help the witch. He is now C. S. Lewis's symbol for a sinner.

In this scene, Lewis might or might not intend some additional symbolism. Edmund, who is tempted, might be symbolizing not only a sinner in the general sense but also Adam. His tempter, the witch, would then be additionally symbolizing the serpent in the Garden of Eden, who the Bible does not identify as Satan. The Turkish Delight would be the Bible's Forbidden Fruit. And Edmund's eating the candy would symbolize the Christian doctrine of the Fall, or man's fall from God's grace. But since the serpent in Genesis tempts Eve rather than Adam, the validity of these four symbols is doubtful. Later in this chapter, they will not be counted when the total number of *LWW* symbols is tallied.

On the way back to the Professor's house, Edmund meets Lucy, who entered Narnia ahead of him. He pretends to know nothing about the witch: he is deceptive, another instance of sin. When the two get back to the Professor's house, Edmund again lies, telling the others that Lucy made up her story about Narnia. Edmund's lies move him deeper into sin.

The Robin and Mr. and Mrs. Beaver. On a still later day, all four children enter the wardrobe to hide from visitors: Mrs. Macready has warned them to keep out of the way when visitors are touring the house. They quickly find themselves in Narnia. Seeing a robin, they follow it. A robin is the proverbial "harbinger of spring" and, in the story, signifies that the witch's wintry grip on the land will soon end: Satan's reign is coming to an end, as foretold in the Bible's book of Revelation. The robin leads the children to Mr. Beaver. He takes the children to his home, which is in the middle of an ice-covered pond.

There they meet Mrs. Beaver, who treats them to a delicious

dinner. After dinner the Beavers tell the children the witch has abducted Tumnus. The witch has probably used her magic wand to turn him into a stone statue, something she does to all who incur her wrath. Considerably later the children find out that Tumnus has indeed been turned to stone.

The children also learn about a magical lion, Aslan; Aslan is the Christ figure. Aslan has been gone for an extremely long time and has just returned to Narnia. He is now at a Stone Table on an open hilltop, about a day's journey away. He somehow knows the children are in Narnia, and he has sent word to the Beavers that the four are to meet him the next day at the Stone Table if they can. The Stone Table is a large gray stone slab supported at its corners by four elongated, upright stones. As we shall see shortly, it is a triple symbol: it has three symbolic referents.

Mr. Beaver also tells of an amazing prophecy: "Down at Cair Paravel—that's the castle on the seacoast . . . which ought to be the capital of the whole country if all was as it should be—down at Cair Paravel there are four thrones and it's a saying in Narnia time out of mind that when two Sons of Adam and two Daughters of Eve sit in those four thrones, then it will be the end not only of the White Witch's reign but of her life."[4] (In Narnia, male and female humans are called Sons of Adam and Daughters of Eve.) Soon thereafter, when the witch has Edmund in her clutches, she too mentions the prophecy. She observes that Cair Paravel has four thrones. Then she ominously concludes: "How if only three were filled [assuming she kills Edmund]? That would not fulfill the prophecy."[5] The Narnia prophecy is easily recognized as a symbol of biblical prophecies, especially the prophecy in the New Testament's book of Revelation that Satan will get his comeuppance.[6]

The Journey, the Hiding Hole, and the Stinging Drink. After hearing about Aslan, but before hearing about the prophecy, Edmund sneaks off from the Beaver house to find the witch. The Beavers and the three siblings discover his absence and realize where he has gone. They also realize that he will tell the witch where they are and that she will come for them that very night. There is no time to lose, so they begin hiking in the dark to the Stone Table. They follow a path along the river.

After several hours, Mr. Beaver leads them aside to a hidden hole in the riverbank. It is the opening to an old hiding place used by beavers "in bad times."[7] They go inside to a snug underground chamber to catch a few hours of sleep. First, though, Mrs. Beaver pulls out a flask and passes it around for everyone to drink from. The drink is alcoholic, for it stings the throats of the children and causes them to cough and sputter. But it makes them feel comfortably warm inside, and they go right to sleep. (Mentally browse back through the plot of *GC* and see if you can find the scene that symbolizes the siblings' drinking an alcoholic beverage from a flask in an underground chamber, the hiding hole.)

The hiding hole undoubtedly symbolizes a church, a shelter from Satan and a place where Christians can find psychological refuge "in bad times." As the person in charge of the hiding hole, and also as the person guiding people to Jesus (Aslan) and protecting them from Satan (the witch), Mr. Beaver symbolizes a Christian priest or minister. Mr. Beaver performed another ministerial duty earlier when he "preached" to the children about the prophecy: ministers like to tell their congregations about biblical prophecies.

Edmund's Betrayal of His Siblings at the Witch's Castle. Back to Edmund. On his previous visit the witch told him how to get to her "house." He finds it without much difficulty. But it is really a small castle with towers that are topped with sharply pointed spires. The castle symbolizes Hell, where Satan (the White Witch) resides. (Lewis may have based his description of the castle on Pandemonium, the capital of Hell in Milton's *Paradise Lost*. Pandemonium is a towered structure resembling a castle.)

In the castle's courtyard are stone statues of all sorts of creatures. Edmund doesn't know it, but these are formerly living creatures that the witch has turned to stone with her magic wand. They symbolize the inmates of Hell that Jesus rescues in the myth about "the harrowing of Hell." Later in the story, they will be rescued—restored to life—by Aslan in a reenactment of "the harrowing of Hell."

Locating the White Witch, Edmund sins again. He tells her where his brother and sisters can be found: he betrays his siblings.[8] Then he tells her about Aslan's return. She is shocked to learn about Aslan. And she is deeply disturbed by the children's presence in Narnia: she knows of the prophecy, and knows that the children will bring an end to her reign if they are not killed or turned to stone. But instead of rewarding Edmund with more Turkish Delight as she had promised, she feeds him stale bread and water. (C. S. Lewis's symbolized Christian moral: Satan doesn't keep his promises.) Then she sends the wolf Maugrim, chief of her Secret Police, to the Beavers' house with orders to kill anyone he finds, after which he is to proceed to the Stone Table. Maugrim and the other Secret Police wolves, agents of the White Witch, symbolize more demons, agents of Satan.

The witch herself sets off on her sledge (sleigh) to intercept the children, who she knows may have already begun hiking to the Stone Table. She intends to catch them and to turn them to stone. The witch takes Edmund with her.

The Little Creatures and Their Tea Party. Along the way the witch spies some small forest creatures seated at a little table, having a merry party. Present are Mr. Squirrel, his wife and children, two satyrs, a dwarf, and an old dog-fox. The food and holly decorations attract her attention. "Where did you get all these things?" Learning that the things are recent gifts from Father Christmas, the witch explodes with anger, waves her wand, and turns the unfortunate partyers into stone statues.

Then, as the witch and the horrified Edmund proceed, more signs of spring (the impending end of the witch's reign) appear: patches of bare ground, then flowers. The ground soon becomes totally bare, bringing the sledge to a halt. Cutting the reindeer loose to find their own way home, the witch proceeds on foot with the dwarf and Edmund. Edmund's hands are tied behind his back, and the nasty dwarf prods him with curses and flicks of a whip. The witch's transportation breakdown gives the Beavers and the children needed time in their race to the Stone Table.

Father Christmas. When the Beavers and the children wake up from their sleep in the hiding hole, they hear bells jingling. Some cautious scouting by Mr. Beaver reveals the presence of Father Christmas (Santa Claus)—yet another sign that spring is approaching. Father Christmas represents Christmas, the birthday of the Christ, which in turn points to the coming of Aslan, the Christ. (Here C. S. Lewis is guilty of mixed metaphor. Christmas, a metaphor for the arrival of the Christ, conflicts with spring, a metaphor for the decay of the witch's power. Christmas is in December; spring begins on the spring equinox, about three months after Christmas. Another flaw is that Aslan, who has already returned, has been "born" ahead of Christmas, the time of the Christ's arrival.) Father Christmas gives the children gifts. These including an ivory horn for Susan to blow for help when in danger, a sword for Peter, and a bottle of cordial, a magical cure-all, for Lucy. The Beavers also receive gifts.

Lewis may or may not be using Father Christmas as an additional symbol for God. The Professor might be in Narnia but in a different guise. Like the Professor and the standard cartoon caricature of God, Father Christmas has a white beard. And Christmas, the birthday of the Christ, brings the Christ into the world, just as God in Christian mythology brought the Christ into the world. Note too that Father Christmas, despite being hated by the witch, moves about with impunity: he doesn't seem to fear the witch, else he wouldn't have jingling, attention-attracting bells. (Because considerable doubt exists about whether Father Christmas is the Professor in another guise, he will not be counted when Lewis's symbols are enumerated later in this chapter.)

Aslan, Susan, Peter, Maugrim, and the Secret Police. The children and the Beavers soon meet Aslan, the mighty lion. He is at the top of a hill where the Stone Table is. With him is a small army of loyal creatures—dryads and naiads (tree women and well women), centaurs (half man, half horse), a minotaur (half man, half bull), a unicorn (a horse with a spiral horn on its forehead), an eagle, a great dog, two leopards, and other creatures.

The Stone Table is inscribed with mysterious lines and figures suggestive of letters from an unfamiliar alphabet. The inscribed table's role as a symbol is not immediately apparent, but C. S. Lewis explained part of its symbolism—it symbolizes three things—in a letter he wrote in 1960. It represents the two stone tables, also called tablets, that Moses brought down from Mount Sinai with the Ten Commandments engraved on them.[9] The Stone Table's lines and figures are the engraving; the unfamiliar alphabet is the Hebrew alphabet. Later, the Stone Table evolves into a symbol for two other things, but these other meanings will have to wait.

Aslan and his followers prepare to rescue Edmund from the witch. But before they can start, the Secret Police wolf Maugrim attacks Susan, who has become separated. She climbs a tree and blows the call-for-help horn Father Christmas gave her. Peter runs to her and slays the wolf with his gift-sword. Indirectly, Father Christmas has rescued Susan from Maugrim. The horn and the sword are proxies for Father Christmas. (This is an important fact when we come to Pullman's symbolism. Can you recall a scene from *GC* where Lyra—here she symbolizes Susan—escapes danger by going up above the ground carrying an object that might symbolize Susan's gift horn?)

Although Maugrim has been slain, another wolf, one of Maugrim's Secret Police, has been overlooked. He has been hiding in a thicket, spying on Aslan and the others. Aslan spots him and calls upon his centaurs and eagles to pursue the spy wolf. But the wolf gets away and rushes to the witch. He tells her that Maugrim has been killed and that the children have reached Aslan at the Stone Table. The wolf urges the witch to flee. But she has other plans. "Call out the giants and the werewolves and the spirits of those trees who are on our side. Call the Ghouls, and the Boggles, the Ogres, and the Minotaurs. Call the Cruels, the Hags, the Specters, and the people of the Toadstools. We will fight."[10]

Edmund's Rescue, Repentance, Forgiveness, and the Deep Magic. As the witch and her newly assembled army prepare to seek and attack Aslan, he finds them first and attacks. Aslan and his followers rescue Edmund, but in the resulting chaos the witch uses her wand to disguise herself and the dwarf as a stump and a boulder; she has escaped. Much of her horde also escapes. Edmund apologizes to the others, saying to each one, "I'm sorry." Edmund is repenting his sins: Lewis is symbolizing repentance. Each of his siblings replies, "That's all right." Lewis is now symbolizing Christian forgiveness, the belief that forgiving is a virtue and perhaps even an obligation, regardless of the offense.

The next day the witch goes to Aslan's camp with a demand sanctified by the Deep Magic installed in Narnia by the Emperor-beyond-the Sea (alternate symbol for God) at the time of creation. Edmund, she points out, is a traitor: he betrayed his siblings by joining the witch. The Deep Magic gives her the right to kill traitors. C. S. Lewis is saying, symbolically, that God has ordained that sinners will be consigned to the devil: they can't go to Heaven. The Deep Magic symbolizes Christian ideology, which includes the doctrine that sinners go to Hell.

Aslan's Sacrificial Death. Aslan makes a deal with the witch. He agrees to sacrifice his own life at the Stone Table in exchange for Edmund's. Leaving the children and his other followers, Aslan returns to the Stone Table. The witch orders her rabble to shave, muzzle, and bind Aslan. The ugly creatures then hit Aslan, kick him, spit on him, and jeer. They next place him on the Stone Table and bind him to the table with more cords. Then the witch, after first announcing that she intends to recapture and kill Edmund anyhow, stabs Aslan to death. Aslan has died for Edmund's sins, just as the Christ of Christian mythology died so that sinners could be saved from Hell. The event is witnessed from a hiding place by Lucy and Susan, who surreptitiously followed Aslan when he departed to turn himself in to the witch.

(Mythologically speaking, when a man dies his soul departs: he loses his soul. In the Gospel of Mark, when Jesus died he "yielded up his spirit [soul]."[11] In Pullman's trilogy, what character figuratively dies by losing his soul? That character, a symbol for Aslan, is someone who later figuratively comes back to life by regaining his soul. It is also someone who goes on to kill someone else who symbolizes the witch—just as, to anticipate, Aslan later kills the witch.)

Aslan's death obviously symbolizes Jesus's crucifixion. And Aslan's giving his own life to save that of a sinner symbolizes the Christian doctrine, "He died for our sins." Most people think Aslan's death and its corollary, "He died for our sins," is all there is to the death-of-Jesus symbolism. But there is really much more:

- Before being arrested, Jesus went to Gethsemane to pray, and "he began to be sorrowful and troubled."[12] Before being slain, Aslan "seemed [to Lucy and Susan] to be sad" and said, "I am sad and lonely."[13]
- Before being crucified, Jesus was hit, spat upon, and mocked. Before being killed, Aslan is hit, spat upon, and mocked by the witch's jeering mob—symbolization of what happened to Jesus.
- Before being crucified, Jesus had a crown of thorns placed upon his head. Before being killed, Aslan has a muzzle placed on his head. The muzzle symbolizes the crown of thorns (something uncomfortable worn on the head).
- Before being crucified, Jesus had his clothes stripped off (and divided among the Roman soldiers). Before being killed, Aslan has his "clothing," his fur, shaved off. The shaving symbolizes the stripping off of Jesus's clothes.
- Jesus was crucified on a cross. Aslan is executed on the Stone Table. Initially a symbol for Moses's stone tablets displaying the Ten Commandments, the Stone Table becomes a symbol for the cross when Aslan sacrifices his life to save Edmund.
- While being crucified, Jesus was nailed to the cross. While being killed, Aslan is bound with cords on the Stone Table. The cords that bind Aslan symbolize the nails that affixed Jesus to the cross.
- Jesus's cross was mounted on a hill outside Jerusalem, Calvary hill. Aslan's Stone Table, his "bed" of execution, rests on the top of a hill. The Stone Table's hill symbolizes Calvary.

- On the cross, Jesus had a spear thrust into his side by a Roman soldier. On the Stone Table, Aslan has a knife thrust into his body. The knife symbolizes the spear.

The Resurrection. Aslan, like the Christ he symbolizes, does not stay dead. While his body lies bound on the Stone Table, friendly mice come out and nibble away the cords. Then, as Susan and Lucy turn their backs in sorrow, the Stone Table breaks with a loud crack. The girls rush to the table, but Aslan is gone. Suddenly, he appears behind them: he stands resurrected. Aslan explains what happened. There is a Deeper Magic, unknown to the witch. The Deeper Magic's power determines that when a willing victim who is guiltless (the Christ) gives his life in exchange for a traitor's (a sinner's), the Stone Table will crack and death will reverse itself. Aslan's resurrection symbolizes the mythical resurrection of Jesus, and the Deeper Magic symbolizes the Christian belief that Jesus is immortal and was able to return to life.

Just as most people miss all the symbolic details of the death symbolism, so do they miss the details of the resurrection symbolism. The details are these:

- After Jesus died, Joseph of Arimathea was given permission to remove his body from the cross, which Joseph did by (we must assume) removing the nails. After Aslan dies, the mice cut the ropes—the symbolic nails—that attach Aslan to the Stone Table. The mice are Joseph.
- After being removed from the cross, Jesus was laid in a tomb hewn out of stone; its entrance was sealed with a stone. After dying, Aslan lay on a stone slab. The Stone Table where Aslan lies now symbolizes the stone tomb where Jesus lay. (The Stone Table is a triple symbol. It represents, first, Moses's Ten Commandments tables; second, in the crucifixion scene, the cross on which Jesus was crucified; and third, when Aslan returns to life, the stone tomb in which Jesus's body was laid to rest.)

- When Jesus returned to life, his stone tomb "broke" open: the stone rolled away. When Aslan returned to life, the Stone Table broke with a loud crack. Its breaking symbolizes the figurative "breaking open" of Jesus's tomb.
- After Jesus returned to life, Mary Magdalene and Mary the mother of James went to the tomb to anoint Jesus's body. They found the stone rolled back and the tomb empty. Then Jesus appeared to them and spoke to them: they witnessed the resurrected Jesus. After Aslan returned to life, Lucy and Susan heard the Stone Table crack, turned, and found the Stone Table empty. Then Aslan appeared to them and spoke to them: they witnessed the resurrected Aslan. Lucy and Susan now symbolize the two Marys. Aslan's speaking to them is Jesus's meeting and speaking to the two women.

The Harrowing of Hell. Back in action, Aslan carries Lucy and Susan on his back to the witch's castle (Lewis's Hell symbol). Leaping over the castle wall, he lands in the courtyard amid the stone statues, beings the White Witch turned to stone with her wand. Aslan uses his magical powers to restore the statues to life. When he breathes on them, they come back to life. Lucy and Susan help by searching for other statues in the castle's dungeons. Lucy finds Tumnus in one of the dungeons.

Aslan's breathing life back into the creatures symbolizes "the harrowing of Hell." The harrowing is some Christian mythology based on the Apostles' Creed and on the apocryphal Gospel of Nicodemus. This mythology was developed with variations by medieval theologians and by Dante in *The Divine Comedy*. After being crucified, Jesus supposedly "descended into Hell"—words from the Creed—and rescued the deserving among Hell's denizens. The deserving were, at the very least, the patriarchs and other stalwarts (e.g., Moses) and prophets from the Old Testament but, in some versions of the harrowing, every righteous person was rescued. The stone statues symbolize the prisoners of Satan who are rescued by Jesus.

The stone statues really serve two symbolic purposes in the castle scene. Twice in the Bible, Jesus restores dead persons to life. In Luke he restores a dead girl to life.[14] In John he restores to life Lazarus, who had been dead for four days.[15] The stone statues, in addition to symbolizing Satan's prisoners in Hell, symbolize the dead that Jesus restored to life. Aslan's restoring them to life symbolizes Jesus's restoring the dead to life.

After restoring the statues to life, Aslan and his crew ransack the witch's palace. One of the restored beings, Giant Rumblebuffin, uses his huge club to smash the castle's locked gates and demolish two towers flanking the gates. Rumblebuffin's prominent role in the harrowing sequence suggests that Lewis may be using the giant as a symbol, but this is doubtful. The only half-way relevant giant that comes to mind is Bunyan's giant Despair, from the Christian allegory *The Pilgrim's Progress*. Lewis could be using Rumblebuffin's coming back to life as a symbol for the overcoming of despair. But Rumblebuffin is a jolly chap who really doesn't fit the concept of despair.

The Witch's Death and Lucy's Saving Edmund's Life. With the palace out of commission, Aslan, the two girls, and the resurrected Narnians pour out of the castle and go charging off to fight the witch and her army of vile creatures. The girls ride on Aslan's back. Aslan and his reinforcements are almost too late. Peter and Edmund and the animals loyal to Aslan are struggling desperately against the witch and her superior force, but she is turning them one by one into stone with her magic wand. Edmund redeems himself by smashing the wand with his sword. In the process, however, he is gravely wounded by the witch's knife. Aslan leaps upon the witch and kills her. Lucy saves the dying Edmund with the cordial Father Christmas gave her: she pours a few drops of the cordial into his mouth. Father Christmas has again indirectly come to the rescue. More symbolism: God has forgiven the repentant sinner—Edmund has been "saved."

Once more, try to figure out on your own—in advance of chapter 4—what scene in *GC* symbolizes Lucy's reviving the dying Edmund by pouring her life-saving cordial into his mouth. Naturally, Lyra will be symbolizing Lucy in this scene. Lyra will put something in someone's mouth, thereby symbolizing Lucy's pouring cordial into Edmund's mouth. The *HDM* character receiving the symbolized cordial will, of course, have to bear an analogical resemblance to Edmund. He should symbolically be a sinner, perhaps someone who steals. And maybe he, like Edmund, has been seduced by a mean person who gives him a delicious drink (chocolatl?). When Lucy revives Edmund, she is in effect giving him back his departing soul. In *HDM* the humans (but not the armored bears, whose souls are their armor) have daemons for souls. So whatever Lucy puts in someone's mouth should be something that Pullman has designed to represent— to be a proxy for—the dying person's daemon.

The Four "Horsemen." In the denouement, the children grow up and become wise kings and queens of Narnia. They rule for many years, sitting on the four thrones at Cair Paravel, as foretold in the prophecy. Then one day the four go out on horseback to search for a White Stag. It has been sighted and is said to grant wishes. The four mounted siblings symbolize the Four Horsemen of the Apocalypse from the New Testament's book of Revelation. Each Horseman has "power over a fourth of the earth,"[16] power that is analogous to each sibling's having one-fourth of the power in Narnia. The arrival on the scene of the symbolized Four Horsemen symbolizes the beginning of Revelation's apocalypse.

Give yourself one more chance to anticipate some Pullman symbolism that will be revealed in this book's next chapter. Are there any characters in *HDM* who might symbolize four humans riding horses? First, look for a number analogy, *four* closely allied characters from Pullman's surface story who might represent *four* closely allied characters (the siblings) from his hidden story, which in this instance is *LWW*. Second, look for a mounted-on-a-creature analogy, persons who are riding some live creatures that might symbolize the horses *LWW*'s four siblings are riding.

The White Stag. The White Stag symbolizes Revelation's implicitly white "Lamb," the so-called Lamb of God, which in turn is a well-known symbol for Jesus. This means the stag is Aslan (Jesus), who has returned in another guise. But "returned" is the wrong word. Aslan's reappearance in Narnia is not just his return; it is his Second Coming. Lewis is symbolizing fundamentalist and conservative Christianity's Second Coming of Jesus. (Some moderates also believe the doctrine.) The Second Coming is a concomitant of the apocalypse, which Revelation says will precede the arrival on Earth of the Kingdom of God.

Jesus describes his near-future Second Coming in literal detail in the Gospels. When Jesus was arrested and brought before the priests and elders, the high priest asked him if he was the Christ. Jesus replied, "I am; and you will see the Son of man [Jesus] sitting at the right hand of Power [God], and coming with the clouds of heaven."[17] Jesus's description is amplified in Revelation, which describes the Second Coming in great detail—horrifying detail. Further confirmation of the White Stag's identity comes with the next symbol, the lamppost, which appropriately follows the Lamb of God symbolism in Lewis's story. We see that five parallels or analogies between the Lamb of God and the White Stag are present:

1. Both animals are associated with four horseback riders.
2. Both animals are white.
3. Both represent a Second Coming (that of Jesus and that of Aslan).
4. Both have the First Coming character (man or lion) assume a new form (lamb or stag).
5. Both are followed by a lamp (Revelation) or lamppost (*LWW*).

Together, the symbolized Four Horsemen and symbolized Lamb of God represent Revelation's tumultuous apocalypse, the devastating end-of-human-kingdoms upheaval that ushers in God's Kingdom on Earth, the Kingdom of God.

The Lamppost. The former children, now adults, see the stag. It leads them into a thicket. Soon they come to the lamppost, which they don't remember. At this point, C. S. Lewis is dipping his pen into the inkwell of Revelation in a big way. He has already symbolized the Four Horsemen of the Apocalypse, the Lamb of God, and the Second Coming of Jesus, all three of which are in Revelation. At the end of Revelation "the holy city, new Jerusalem," comes down from Heaven to Earth.[18] It will be the new dwelling of God and symbolizes the promised post-apocalyptic Kingdom of God on Earth that the early Christians, like some of today's, believed would follow the Second Coming of Jesus. "Behold, the dwelling of God is *with men*. He will dwell with them, and they shall be his people, and God himself will be with them" (italics added).[19] New Jerusalem will have a lamp, not a literal lamp but a figurative one: "And the city has no need of sun or moon to shine upon it, for the glory of God is its light, and its lamp is the Lamb."[20] The lamppost the children come to is the White Stag, magically transformed, when the stag (Aslan) later becomes a lamppost that symbolizes the lamp that lights new Jerusalem in the Kingdom of God. (In Revelation, the lamp is merely figurative— Jesus is a figurative lamp—but in *LWW* the lamppost is literal: it is a real lamppost.)

Back to the Professor's House. In a few more places the thicket's branches become coats; Lucy's original entering-Narnia experience has gone into reverse. The four siblings tumble out of the wardrobe and back into their own world: the stag has led them home, seemingly granting their subconscious wish. The four discover that they are children again and that no time has passed. C. S. Lewis is saying, metaphorically, that Revelation's apocalypse is over. The Four Horsemen of the Apocalypse and the Lamb of God have completed their work. This means that the Kingdom of God has arrived; the children are now with God in his Kingdom, New Jerusalem. God is the Professor, and the Kingdom of God is the Professor's house.

A final point: Edmund is among those admitted to the Kingdom of God. His return to the Professor's house is the culmination of his redemption, which began when he asked forgiveness and then battled the White Witch. Edmund has been "saved." Lewis has now finished symbolizing the redemption—salvation—of a sinner.

IS THIS ALLEGORY?

Religious symbolism and allegorical tendency have always been recognized in *LWW*, but nobody seems to regard the book as outright allegory. Yet it is allegory. The firm denials of C. S. Lewis and two of his admirers—Ford and Duriez—do not withstand scrutiny. Neither do the more subdued doubts of several more recent expositors—the authors of 2005 *Narnia* books timed to coincide with the 2005 film *The Chronicles of Narnia: The Lion, the Witch and the Wardrobe*. These 2005 writers represent the very latest thinking, insights, and knowledge about *LWW*. None of them considers *LWW* to be full-fledged allegory.

Why *LWW* Qualifies as Allegory. *LWW* easily qualifies as allegory. It overflows with symbols—symbols for (1–2) God, who has two symbols, (3) God's angels, (4) Heaven, (5) Earth, (6) Hell, (7) Jesus, (8) a Christian minister, (9) a Christian prophecy explained by the minister, (10) the minister's church, (11) a sinner, (12) Satan, (13–14) demons, who have two symbols, (15) Satan's power, (16) the weakening of Satan's power, (17) the impending end of Satan's reign, as prophesied in Revelation, (18) temptations placed before man by Satan, (19) sin, (20) Satan's role as a deceiver, someone who doesn't keep his promises, (21) a sinner's repentance, (22) forgiveness by good Christians, (23) redemption, or God's forgiveness of repentant sinners, (24) the Ten Commandments, (25) Christian ideology, including the doctrine that sinners go to Hell, (26) Jesus's crucifixion, (27) Jesus's resurrection, (28–39) twelve hitherto unrecognized details of Jesus's death and resurrection (e.g., the crown of thorns), (40) the Christian doctrine that "he [Jesus] died for our sins," (41) the Christian "Deeper Magic" belief that Jesus is immortal and could rise from the dead, (42) the "harrowing of Hell," (43) Satan's prisoners in Hell, from the "harrowing," (44) Jesus's restoring the dead to life, (45) victory over Satan, (46) Revelation's pre-apocalypse kingdoms (to be replaced by God's Kingdom), (47) Revelation's apocalypse, (48) the Four Horsemen of the Apocalypse, (49) the Lamb of God, (50) the

Second Coming of Jesus, (51) the lamp in new Jerusalem, and (52) the post-apocalyptic earthly Kingdom of God. The flow of symbols is continuous; they are not just occasional or isolated. And the symbols, all fifty-two of them, have the unifying theme that allegory demands. That theme is Christianity: Christian mythology, Christian doctrine, Christian history, Christian institutions.

Individually, some of these symbols might seem hard to recognize as symbols. Mr. Beaver's hiding hole as the symbol of a Christian church is an example. But part of the technique of recognizing allegorical symbols is looking for analogies that relate something in the surface story to the unifying theme that ties the various symbols together into an allegory. Lewis's theme, once again, is Christianity. In the hiding hole episode, Mr. and Mrs. Beaver and the children are being hunted by the White Witch, who is easily recognizable as the symbol for Satan. They use the hiding hole as a place of refuge, refuge from the symbolized devil and from the psychological stress imposed on them by being hunted. In Christianity, a church is, among other things, a place of refuge, not only from the devil but from whatever problems might be bothering someone who enters a church seeking solace. The hiding hole's role as a symbol becomes evident once you recognize three things: (1) *LWW* has a lot of allegorical symbols that can be found if you look for them, (2) there is an analogy between the hiding hole and a church, and (3) the hiding hole, interpreted as the symbol of a church, fits the allegory's unifying theme of Christianity.

The interpretation is reinforced by Mr. Beaver's earlier "preaching" to the children about a prophecy. Both Mr. Beaver and Christian ministers talk about prophecies: we have a coordinate analogy suggesting that Mr. Beaver symbolizes a minister. Mr. Beaver's role in guiding the children to Aslan, who is an obvious symbol for Jesus, is a supporting analogy: ministers lead people to Jesus. Notice how the minister and church symbols interlock. Mr. Beaver symbolizes a minister; the hiding hole is his church. Mr. Beaver is ministering to troubled souls in his hiding hole: a minister is ministering to troubled souls in his church.

LWW fits the various definitions of allegory presented in chapter 1. As specified by Bernstein's definition, "the surface story and characters are intended to be taken as symbols pointing to an underlying, more significant meaning." As specified by Friedman, the elements of the surface story "obviously and *continuously* refer to another simultaneous structure of events or ideas" (italics added). As specified by Fowler, we can read the tale and conclude "that under its surface meaning another is discernible as the true intent." And as should be the case with allegory, one story metaphorically tells another. *LWW* 's surface story tells the hidden story of a journey by humans (the four children) who are guided by a minister (Mr. Beaver) to Jesus (Aslan), becoming converts to Christianity in the process, and who then struggle through the quagmire of Christian mythology. The struggle includes battles with Satan, sin and redemption, a savior's death and resurrection, the harrowing of Hell, Revelation's apocalypse with its Four Horsemen, and finally salvation—life with God (the Professor) in the earthly Kingdom of God.

Lewis's Denial of Allegory. Despite the abundant evidence that *LWW* is allegory, we hear from time to time fervent denials that this is the case. Sometimes a denial reflects the protester's failure to recognize any symbolism beyond Jesus, his crucifixion, his resurrection, and maybe Satan and one or two details of the resurrection: three or six symbols don't make an allegory. But usually the denials rest on what C. S. Lewis wrote in a 1958 letter to a certain Mrs. Hook. There Lewis said his *Chronicles of Narnia* "is not allegory at all."[21] Paul Ford, a staunch defender of Lewis, interprets these and related words found in the Hook letter: "Lewis was adamant that he was not writing allegory when he wrote the *Chronicles*."[22] That being the case, shouldn't Lewis's word be the last word?

No. Lewis's denial that *LWW* is allegory in the face of overwhelming evidence to the contrary comes off as equivocation. Equivocation is seeming to say one thing, something that happens to be untrue and therefore misleading, while relying on ambiguity to establish another meaning that is technically true. Why Lewis would want to deceive is a matter for speculation, but a plausible reason is that he didn't want to undermine book sales, from which he was earning considerable income. Although Christian parents and other Christian book buyers would certainly approve of a Christian allegory, religiosity in Britain—Lewis was English—has long been much weaker than religiosity in the United States. Why risk discouraging British (and many American) buyers who would prefer not to buy religious literature for their children? Why not present the book in a light that appeals to *all* potential customers, the light of pure storytelling?

Another plausible reason for Lewis's refusal to concede that *LWW* is allegory is his possible wish to placate his good friend J. R. R. Tolkien, who disapproved of the allegorical elements in *LWW*. Colin Duriez writes that "Lewis's friend J. R. R. Tolkein was critical of the Chronicles [of Narnia] because he felt that they were too allegorical."[23] According to Duriez, "Lewis knew that his close friend, Tolkien, disapproved of his lay theologizing—he thought it should be left to the experts."[24] Lewis told another friend, Roger Green, "about how Tolkien had disliked the Narnia story intensely." Tolkien later told Green, referring to Lewis's *LWW* manuscript, "It really won't do, you know!" After Lewis died, Tolkien wrote, "It is sad that 'Narnia' and all that part of C. S. L.'s work should remain outside the range of my sympathy."[25]

How might Lewis have equivocated when denying that *LWW* is allegory? Two ways come to mind. First, Lewis never denied that *LWW* in particular is allegory; he denied that the seven-book *Narnia* series as a whole is allegorical. The other six books definitely contain Christian symbolism, but I have not analyzed them to see if the amount and continuity of the symbolism qualifies the overall series as allegory: such analysis would take us well beyond the scope of this study. The *Chronicles* in their entirety might not be allegory—they might simply display allegorical tendency—even though LWW, a particular book in the seven-book *Narnia* series, definitely is allegory.

The second approach to equivocation is found in the letter to Mrs. Hook. There Lewis uses a false definition of allegory. This definition, if applied to *LWW*, makes Lewis's denial of allegory—an untrue assertion—technically true. In substance, Lewis argues that allegory requires personification. "Personification" is derived from the word "person." Personification is using fictional persons to represent material things or abstract ideas (nonmaterial things such as despair, sin, love, courage, and wisdom).

Lewis's actual words are these: "By allegory I mean a composition . . . in which immaterial realities [abstract concepts] are represented as feigned [fictitious] physical objects [persons]."[26] His example is a giant (a physical object) from John Bunyan's *The Pilgrim's Progress*, possibly the best-known allegory ever written. The giant personifies—treats as a person—and thereby symbolizes the abstract concept of despair. In his letter, Lewis explains that "in Bunyan, a giant represents Despair."[27] This fact, according to Lewis, qualifies Bunyan's tale as allegory, whereas *LWW* does not use personification and therefore is not allegory. Paul Ford confirms what Lewis meant: "Lewis was not trying to take . . . abstract ideas and personify them; this would be to allegorize."[28]

In short, Lewis bases his denial that *LWW* is allegory on a ridiculous definition of allegory. That definition assumes personification is a *requirement* of allegory rather than what it really is—a characteristic of *some* of the allegorical symbols in *some* allegories.

The truth is, allegory does not necessarily use personification. The absence of personification in *LWW* has no bearing on whether *LWW* is an allegory. Some allegory does use personification. Bunyan uses it with the giant in *The Pilgrim's Progress*, and Pullman uses it with Xaphania, who personifies wisdom, in his *Paradise Lost* allegory. But personification has never been a requirement of allegory. No personification of abstract concepts like despair exists in Orwell's *Animal Farm* or in Pullman's *LWW* allegory.

The frailty of Lewis's personification argument becomes even more evident when we examine it further. In the Hook letter, Lewis proceeds by distinguishing between (*a*) the personification of abstract ideas—having a person symbolize an abstraction such as love or despair—and (*b*) the use of "supposals," which ask us to suppose that something or someone real existed in fictional ("supposed") form in a fictional world. Lewis speciously argues: "Allegory and . . . supposals differ because they mix the real and the unreal in different ways. Bunyan's picture of Giant Despair does not start from a supposal at all. It is not a supposition but a *fact* that despair can capture and imprison a human soul [i.e., that despair is real]. What is unreal (fictional) is the giant, the castle and the dungeon. The Incarnation of Christ in another world is mere supposal; but *granted* the supposition, He [Jesus] would really have been a physical object [real] in that world [Narnia] as He was in Palestine."[29]

Here Lewis is comparing two symbols: the giant and Aslan. Both symbolize real things: despair and Jesus. But Lewis is claiming that the giant (Bunyan's symbol) is "unreal," because nobody supposes that he is real; whereas Aslan (Lewis's symbol) is real, because Lewis has decided to *suppose* that Aslan is really Jesus, transported to another world. Lewis then implies that the "real" being, Aslan, cannot be an allegorical symbol because a real person—or even just a character an author "supposes" is real—cannot be a symbol.

This sort of verbal legerdemain will never do as a substitute for argument. Lewis's point seems to be that (*a*) an unreal being—Aslan, a fictional lion—becomes a real "physical object" if Lewis decides to "suppose" or imagine that he is a real historical being, in this case Jesus, and (*b*) a real being cannot be a symbol. Such nonsense! In the first place, a real being *can* be a symbol. Anything, including a real person, can be a symbol. In Dante's *The Divine Comedy*, Dante uses himself—a real person, like Jesus—to symbolize a sinner (or, some would say, sinners in general, which amounts to all humanity). And just as Lewis places his supposedly real Jesus in the supernatural world of Narnia, Dante places his actually real self in the supernatural world of Hell (and later in the supernatural worlds of Purgatory and Paradise). So by what logic is the supposedly real, morphed-into-a-lion Jesus not a symbol whereas the actually real, unmorphed Dante is a symbol?

Second, even if real beings couldn't be used as symbols, Aslan is not a real being. "Supposing" that Aslan is real—really Jesus—doesn't make him the real Jesus. The real Jesus was a human being; Aslan is a lion. What if Lewis's story had come right out and said Aslan is Jesus, magically transformed into an animal? That still wouldn't make him the real Jesus. In the story, Aslan is a lion. And he is in a fictional place, Narnia, where Jesus couldn't possibly go, because Narnia doesn't exist. Explicitly identifying Aslan as Jesus in disguise would still leave us with symbolism: a fictional lion in a fictional place representing the real Jesus.

Third, supposal is actually a requirement of allegory, not a destroyer of allegory. All allegory is fiction. If a narrative isn't fiction, it can't be allegory. Fiction is the use of imaginary but often realistic persons, places, things, and events in a narrative. Fiction is defined in *The American Heritage College Dictionary* as "a literary work whose content is produced by the *imagination* and is not necessarily based on fact" (italics added). *Supposal* is just another word for "imaginary"; the same dictionary says the intransitive verb *suppose* means "to imagine." Supposed persons and things are imaginary, hence fictional. Being fictional, they meet one of the basic requirements of allegory.

Fourth, Lewis's claim that Bunyan's giant's symbolizing despair is allegorical only because despair is "a fact" would, if the claim were true, validate many of Lewis's own symbols. Lewis symbolizes, among numerous other things, the mocking of Jesus, the crown of thorns placed on his head, and the hill where he was crucified. All of these things are facts, not supposals. Therefore, according to Lewis's own reasoning, the things that symbolize these facts in Lewis's story—the mocking of Aslan, the muzzle placed on his head, the hill where Aslan is crucified—qualify as allegorical symbols. I will add that Lewis is wrong when he says that, to be allegorical, a symbol must refer to something factual. In the next chapter I will show that Pullman allegorizes Lewis's story. Pullman symbolizes just about everything in *LWW*. Yet almost all of the things symbolized—the four children, the magical wardrobe, Tumnus, the witch's castle, and so on—are fiction, not fact.

Fifth, even if we were to concede that Aslan cannot be a symbol—a thoroughly unwarranted concession—we would still have fifty-one other allegorical symbols. Lewis can't argue that going from fifty-two symbols to fifty-one destroys the allegory. For that matter, many of the remaining death-and-resurrection symbols would still *symbolize*, rather than actually *be*, things that happened to Jesus two thousand years ago. Aslan's death and resurrection in Narnia are not the actual death and resurrection of the Christ on Calvary. Neither is the knife thrust into Aslan's body really the spear thrust into Jesus's body. And so on for many other death-and-resurrection symbols. Lewis's implicit idea that discrediting one symbol makes all the others vanish—turns allegory into nonallegory—is absurd.

The "supposal" argument gives the impression that Lewis regards *LWW* as a sort of alternate history novel. Alternate history is a literary form wherein a real historical person is placed in altered (fictional) historical circumstances. Lewis doesn't state this argument explicitly, but he seems to imply that *LWW* is alternate history and that alternate history can't be allegory. That may not be precisely his point, but it is what his point amounts to. Here Lewis is wrong on three counts: (1) Alternate history requires realism—the world remains real, historically plausible. You can't put Galileo in Oz and call it alternate history. By the same token, you can't put Jesus in Narnia and call it alternate history. Fantasy, whose definitive characteristic is supernaturalism, and alternate history are incompatible. (2) Alternate history requires that the historical person remain a human being. A historical man can't morph into a talking lion and still be a character in an alternate history novel. (3) Alternate history and allegory are not incompatible. There is no reason why an alternate history novel cannot be loaded with allegorical symbolism, with or without the author's using the real historical person as a symbol.

The rest of Lewis's argument gets even more muddled. Lewis writes that, whereas despair is real, Aslan "is an invention giving an imaginary answer to the question, 'What might Christ become like, if [we *supposed* that] there really were a world like Narnia and He chose to . . . die and rise again in *that* world as He actually has done in ours.'"[30] One problem here is that Lewis is comparing noncomparables. Despair, something real, is a thing that is *symbolized*, but Aslan is a *symbol*. Something symbolized and a symbol are not comparable things: we have an invalid comparison.

A valid comparison requires that both items being compared be a symbol's antecedent or referent—whatever is symbolized. Despair is the antecedent of Bunyan's symbolic giant. What is the antecedent of Lewis's symbolic lion? Answer: the real human Jesus who lived and died on this planet. Jesus is not a supposal; he is, like despair, a fact. We see that, when a valid comparison is made, Lewis can no longer claim that (*a*) Bunyan's story is an allegory because a certain symbol refers to something (despair) that is a fact whereas (*b*) Lewis's story is not allegory because a certain symbol refers to something (Jesus) that isn't a fact.

Now let's look at the other side of symbolism—the symbol itself rather than its antecedent. Lewis claims that a character (specifically, Aslan) based on a real person cannot be an allegorical symbol if that character is "an invention" and is given an "imaginary" setting such as "a world like Narnia." That idea is more foolishness. George Orwell's *Animal Farm* is widely recognized as allegory. Yet Orwell uses an imaginary pig—an "invention"—named Napoleon to symbolize a real human, Stalin, just as Lewis uses an imaginary lion named Aslan to symbolize a real human, Jesus. Furthermore, Orwell places his pig in what Lewis would call a "supposal" world: a supernatural farm populated by intelligent, talking animals who behave like humans, just as lions, fauns, beavers, and wolves talk and behave like humans in *LWW*. Orwell's technique does not cause *Animal Farm* to be something other than allegory.

Lewis's semantic gamesmanship relies on the idea that Lewis is imagining, or "supposing," that Jesus actually went to a place like Narnia and assumed the form of a lion. (In *LLW* Aslan really assumes three forms—lion, stag, and lamppost—and in *The Voyage of the "Dawn Treader"* he goes on to become a lamb.) Lewis would presumably argue that, in contrast, Orwell was not "supposing" that Stalin actually went to a supernatural farm in a supernatural world very similar to Earth and assumed the form of a pig. Lewis is arguing that allegory depends on what and whether an author is pretending or supposing.

But that isn't true. The concept of allegory is unrelated to what Lewis calls "supposing." Rather, the concept of allegory is based on symbols. One thing symbolizes—represents—*something else*. In *LWW*, a lion represents Jesus—*something else*—and is thus a symbol, whether or not Lewis wants to pretend that Aslan really is Jesus beneath the fur. Aslan is not representing Aslan; a lion is not representing a lion. A fictional lion is representing a real human, and that is symbolism.

LWW not only has its Christ symbol, it also has fifty-one other symbols and displays the continuity of symbolism that allegory requires. Likewise, the symbols have a unifying theme, Christianity—in some respects the same theme Bunyan's allegory has. *LWW* is definitely allegory.

Ford's and Duriez's Denials of Allegory. Two authors of books about *The Chronicles of Narnia* are particularly forceful in denying that *LWW* is allegory. These two authors present arguments purporting to show that *LWW* is not allegory.

In *Companion to Narnia*, Paul Ford tries to salvage Lewis's confused rhetoric by offering two interpretations. He begins by saying, "In the *Chronicles* Lewis is beginning with the supposition that there *is* a world like Narnia, . . . that this world needs redemption, and that [Aslan] is to carry out the [role of the Christ]."[31] Ford is implying that a "real" setting, either actually real or supposedly real, is incompatible with allegory. But Ford is just engaging in word play. Supposing that something fictitious is real does not make it real, especially when the supposed setting is as far from reality as Narnia is. Even if Narnia were a realistic place, or even a real region actually located somewhere here on Earth, that would not be incompatible with allegory. No rule of allegory says the story cannot be set in a real place. John Bunyan's *The Pilgrim's Progress* is a widely cited example of allegory. Bunyan's setting is a real place, England.

Ford next says that "for Bunyan the giant is unreal but the despair [symbolized by the giant] is real; for Lewis in the *Chronicles* giants and talking beasts and the like *are* real."[32] That too is just world play. Ford is claiming that to pretend imaginary things like talking beasts are real makes them real ("*are* real"). But pretending, or supposing, doesn't change imaginary beings into real beings. Aslan, a supernatural lion living in a supernatural world, is just as unreal as Bunyan's giant. Indeed, Aslan is more unreal: whereas humans (including giants) can talk, lions can't; and whereas Bunyan's giant lives on Earth, our own real world, Aslan lives in a magical world that couldn't possibly exist. Lewis and Ford can imagine and suppose all they want, but *LWW* will continue to be allegory.

Colin Duriez, in *A Field Guide to Narnia*, devotes slightly more than two pages to the topic "Are the Chronicles Allegory?" He observes that Tolkien criticized the Chronicles for having "too many allegorical elements." Duriez acknowledges the presence of these "allegorical elements" but denies that they constitute allegory.

His first argument is that, "as a genre, however, the Chronicles are not allegory but rather fairy tale, a branch of fantasy."[33] This argument collapses under the weight of Duriez's misunderstanding of the meaning of "genre." A literary genre is a subject matter category used in classifying works by *type*. Examples (these sometimes overlap) are romance, western, sports, maritime, war, foreign intrigue, exotic locale adventure (jungle, desert, island, etc.), historical, mystery, humor, science fiction, fantasy, and children's story. Allegory, on the other hand, is a literary device or *technique*, analogous to satire. Allegory can be used with any genre, including fantasy. Fantasy and allegory are not mutually exclusive categories; they don't belong to the same typology. Being fantasy or fairy tale does not deny *LWW* the chance to be an allegory.

In developing his argument that *LWW* has allegorical elements but is not fully allegorical, Duriez accurately defines allegory as "a figurative [metaphorical, analogical] narrative [a hidden story] . . . sustained throughout a [surface] story, one that conveys a particular and well sign-posted pattern of meaning [a unifying theme and continuity]."[34] The "well sign-posted" aspect of this definition leads to Duriez's second argument. Although Duriez doesn't say it in so many words, he implies that *LWW* is not sufficiently "well sign-posted" to constitute allegory. It has those occasional "allegorical elements" but not enough of them—not enough continuity of symbolism—to be considered allegory.

This argument is easily refuted. The answer is, Duriez has failed to recognize most of those "allegorical elements," better described as symbols. Where *LWW* is concerned, he recognizes symbols for (1) Jesus, (2) the crucifixion, (3) the resurrection, (4) Jesus's sadness before being crucified, and (5) Jesus's conversation with two women after his resurrection. That's all. Duriez finds five symbols where this analysis finds fifty-two. All five of his symbols relate to Jesus. He hasn't spotted a single one of the many other symbols referring to other facets of Christianity. No wonder he refuses to acknowledge that *LWW* is allegory.

Tolkien, though he may not have recognized the full extent of Lewis's allegorizing, was nevertheless basically correct. *LWW* is allegory. There is no doubt about it. The arguments denying that *LWW* is allegory wither under analysis.

The 2005 Books: The First Four. The year 2005 saw the publication of eight books (not counting some that are essentially for children) intended to explain either *LWW* alone or the entire *Narnia* series. Seven of these books either defer to Lewis's claim that *LWW* is not allegory or recognize just a small part of Lewis's story as allegorical. The first four books are especially weak in their treatment of the allegory issue. What unites these four books is their authors' (1) deferential, uncritical acceptance of Lewis's preposterous arguments about personification and "supposals" and (2) their apparent lack of understanding of what constitutes allegory. Bruce Edwards has the least to say. He simply bows to Lewis's characterization of *LWW*: "It's not an allegory, he would chide us."[35] Edwards identifies no symbols and offers not even a hint of disagreement with Lewis.

Richard Wagner has more to say about allegory but gets allegory and personification mixed up. Apparently seduced by Lewis's false assertion that allegory requires personification, Wagner confuses the definition of allegory with the definition of personification. He defines allegory as "a literary device in which an author uses the form of a person, place [*sic*], or animal to represent an abstract idea."[36] That's really a definition of personification (though not a good one). Wagner's implication that allegory must include—or be limited to?—symbols that personify is absolutely false. But Wagner thinks allegory requires personification and, consequently, denies that *LWW* is allegory.

Wagner goes on to say that the *Narnia* series "bears no parallels to allegorical works like . . . *Animal Farm*."[37] Oh? Don't both use surface story symbols with a unifying theme to convey a deeper meaning? That, after all, is the very essence of allegory. And beyond this general parallel are thirteen specific ones, enough to make you wonder if Lewis didn't use *Animal Farm* as a source of ideas. The specific parallels:

1. Both works use intelligent, talking animals to symbolize real historical persons: (*a*) Aslan symbolizing Jesus, (*b*) Napoleon and Snowball (pig leaders from *Animal Farm*) symbolizing Stalin and Trotsky.

2. Both works use human beings to symbolize authority figures: (*a*) the Professor symbolizing God, (*b*) Farmer Jones symbolizing Russia's czar.

3. Both works use canines to represent secret police: (*a*) the White Witch's wolves as her secret police, who are agents of the witch and thus additional symbols of demons, agents of Satan, (*b*) Napoleon's enforcer dogs as Stalin's secret police.

4. Both works use surface story places to symbolize hidden story places: (*a*) the White Witch's castle as Hell, (*b*) Farmer Jones's Manor Farm as Russia.

5. Both works use inanimate objects to symbolize other objects of the same type: (*a*) the Stone Table's hill as Calvary hill, (*b*) the animals' flag as the Soviet flag.

6. Both works use number analogies: (*a*) the four horseback-riding siblings as the Four Horsemen of the Apocalypse, (*b*) the two "tool" symbols (hoof and horn) on the *Animal Farm* flag as the two tool symbols (hammer and sickle) on the Soviet flag.

7. Both works use color analogies: (*a*) the white color of Lewis's White Stag as the white color of the Lamb of God, (*b*) both the white color of a snowball (white as a sign of goodness) as a sign of Trotsky's goodness and the green background color of the *Animal Farm* flag as the red background color of the Soviet flag.

8. Both works use writing analogies: (*a*) the symbols inscribed on the Stone Table as the Ten Commandments, (*b*) the animals' Seven Commandments as the Communist Manifesto.

9. Both works use horrifying events to symbolize a good person's persecution: (*a*) Aslan's slaying as the slaying of Jesus, (*b*) Snowball's being chased away and almost killed by Napoleon's dogs as the exile of Trotsky (who was later assassinated).

10. Both works use betrayals as symbols: (*a*) Edmund's betrayal of his siblings as a symbol of sin, (*b*) Napoleon's betrayal of the animal revolution's aims (e.g., replacing "all animals are equal" with "some are more equal than others") as a symbol of Stalin's betrayal of the Bolshevik Revolution's aims.

11. Both works use fictional ideologies in their surface stories to symbolize real ideologies found in our society: (*a*) Narnia's Deep Magic laws as the religious ideology of Christianity, (*b*) the revolution-inciting philosophy of Old Major, Farmer Jones's prize Middle White boar, as Marxist ideology.

12. Both works have symbolic characters who promulgate the surface story ideologies: (*a*) the Emperor-beyond-the-Sea

(alternate symbol for God) as the author of the Deep Magic, (*b*) Old Major (who symbolizes Karl Marx and, like Marx, dies before the revolution) as the author of the revolutionary ideology of Farmer Jones's animals.

13. Both works use surface story prophecies to symbolize prophecies from our human society: (*a*) the Narnia prophecy that the White Witch will meet her demise when four humans sit on the four thrones at Cair Paravel as biblical prophecies in general and, particularly, Revelation's prophecy that Satan will meet his demise, (*b*) the dream of Old Major (Marx) that Man (capitalists) will vanish as Marx's prophecy that capitalists and capitalism will vanish.

The parallels are there, but Wagner doesn't see them. Consequently, he denies that *Narnia* is allegory.

Devin Brown is another confused analyst, confused about the difference between an allegory and a symbol. He writes that "Lewis did not intend for Aslan be an allegory for Jesus."[38] But persons and animals can't be allegories. Symbols aren't allegories. Allegories are *stories*. Aslan is a *symbol*, not someone rightly or wrongly said to be an allegory. Brown does recognize Aslan as a "Christ-figure"—that makes Aslan a symbol—but also says *LWW* "is not an allegory."[39]

David C. Downing writes that "it does a great disservice to the chronicles to read them as allegories, as if all the major characters and incidents are merely disguised Bible stories."[40] He is badly confused. Allegory does not require that *all* major characters and incidents be symbolic, and a Christian allegory's symbols need not all take their antecedents from the Bible. *The Pilgrim's Progress* is a Christian allegory. Does Bunyan's Giant Despair symbolize something in the Bible? But even if Downing recognized these facts he would still conclude, falsely, that Lewis "was not trying to write a Christian allegory": the only symbolic character—indeed, the only symbol—Downing acknowledges is Aslan.[41]

The 2005 Books: The Next Three. Three more books published in 2005 are slightly, but only slightly, more open to the possibility that *LWW* is an allegory. Coauthors Leland Ryken and Marjorie Lamp Mead concede that "Aslan was . . . conceived by Lewis as corresponding in the world of Narnia to Christ in the world of Palestine."[42] But they implicitly deny the presence of allegory by citing Lewis's claim that *LWW* is not allegorical.[43] Still, the authors later undercut their own authority, Lewis, by quoting additional statements where "Lewis as a literary critic . . . makes it clear that the author does not always know best about the meaning of his own story."[44]

Ryken and Mead further weaken their tentative denial that *LWW* is an allegory by making it apparent that this denial rests, in part, on their own failure to recognize the presence of dozens of allegorical symbols. They even express uncertainty about one of the clearest symbols of all—the White Witch as Satan. Specifically, they say that, although the White Witch is a "figure of evil," interpreting her as Satan "is extending the image too far."[45] In any case, Aslan, Aslan's death, his resurrection, his being sad and lonely as he goes to his place of doom, and the jeering crowd at his execution are about the only symbols recognized.[46] Five symbols don't make an allegory. But fifty-two can do the job.

Peter J. Schakel's position on allegory in *LWW* is this: "Today many readers come to the Chronicles aware that they have Christian overtones, and they are tempted to look for one-to-one parallels between characters, objects, and events in Narnia and corresponding ones in the Bible. However, that is not the way Lewis wanted the Chronicles to be read."[47] Schakel goes on to quote from the usual Lewis denials that *LWW* is allegory. He later adds that "the account of Aslan's death is the only section of *The Lion, the Witch and the Wardrobe* that can justifiably be said to invite an allegorical reading."[48]

Quite apart from the fact that not all of *LWW*'s Christian symbols relate to the Bible, Schakel's refusal to acknowledge *LWW*'s pervasive allegorical structure is based on the usual two flawed considerations: (1) unwarranted deference to Lewis's false definition of allegory and foolish "supposals" argument and (2) failure to recognize more than a tiny number of *LWW*'s allegorical symbols (those symbolizing Jesus's death, his resurrection, and supposedly the tearing of the temple curtain when Jesus died). Not even the Satan symbol (the White Witch) or the Hell symbol (the witch's castle) is recognized. Schakel even expresses strong doubts that the White Witch represents Satan.[49]

I should add that "the way Lewis *wanted* the Chronicles to be read" is irrelevant. Even if Lewis wanted *LWW* to be read as a children's story—even if he wanted his allegorizing to go unrecognized—his wants and *LWW*'s allegorical structure are two different things. The children's story is certainly there (all allegories have a surface story), but the allegory is there too.

Gene Veith, to his credit, does not invoke Lewis's slippery denials that *LWW* is allegory.[50] On the contrary, Veith actually regards *LWW* as allegory: "With Aslan, the fantasy becomes an allegory."[51] And he explicitly recognizes allegorical symbolism: "Aslan, of course, is Lewis's symbol for Jesus Christ."[52]

So far, so good. The trouble is, Veith substantively agrees with Schakel, who says that only the scenes describing Aslan's death and resurrection constitute allegory. Those scenes take up only three of *LWW*'s seventeen chapters, specifically, chapters 13–15. Veith does not consider the book as a whole to be allegory. He makes this clear in earlier remarks: "*The Chronicles of Narnia* are not full-fledged, point-by-point allegories as such. Still, Lewis follows Spenser [Edmund Spenser, in *The Faerie Queen*] in giving each novel [of the seven] an 'allegorical core.'"[53] The upshot is that Veith denies that *LWW* in its entirety is allegorical. He sees almost no allegorical symbolism beyond that relating to Aslan's giving his life for the sins of Edmund. That symbolism occupies only about one-sixth of the book.

Veith does refer to "the breath of Aslan" as God's Holy Spirit. Here he implies that Aslan's breath is an additional symbol, beyond the death and resurrection symbols. The New Testament, where Christianity's Holy Spirit comes into view, was written in Greek. The Greek word for spirit is *pneuma*. *Pneuma* has three related meanings—soul, spirit, and breath. Veith chooses to construe the Holy Spirit, God's *pneuma*, as the "Breath of God."[54] Since the Jesus of John 1:14 is God incarnate—God in the flesh—Veith can suggest that Aslan's (Jesus's) breath is God's breath, which in turn is the Holy Spirit.

Veith could be right, but I strongly doubt that Lewis intended Aslan's breath as a symbol, except possibly as a symbol of Jesus's ability to perform miracles. One problem is that the Jesus Aslan symbolizes is not the God-incarnate Jesus of the Gospel of John. Aslan is, rather, the Son-of-God Jesus of the three so-called synoptic Gospels—Matthew, Mark, and Luke. Aslan is the son of the Emperor-beyond-the-Sea (God). So Aslan's breath is Jesus's breath, not God's.

Another problem is that, though "breath" is one possible translation of *pneuma*, that translation does not fit the concept of the Holy Spirit. Early Christians, like many of today's, viewed God as an anthropomorphic being—a manlike being with a head, arms, and legs who sat on a throne in Heaven, a place in the sky, with Jesus (a separate being) seated at his right hand. Genesis 1:27's words "God created man in his own image" express the belief of the ancients that God and man have essentially the same physique. Man was believed—and is still believed by most of today's Christians—to have an invisible, nonmaterial inner self called the soul or spirit. This spirit departed at death and possibly also in dreams. When Jesus died, his spirit departed: he "cried again with a loud voice and yielded up his spirit."[55] Similarly, when Jesus restored a dead girl to life, "her spirit returned."[56]

Because God was essentially a man, God had a man's inner self—God's soul or spirit—called the Holy Spirit. The Holy Spirit was essentially an agent of God, used by God to perform errands. These errands involved the ancient superstition of spirit possession: humans became possessed by an alien spirit, God's Holy Spirit. The Holy Spirit entered Mary's womb to make her pregnant,[57] gave the disciples the power to work miracles,[58] caused Christian converts to speak in tongues,[59] and gave men the gift of prophecy.[60]

Nowadays, most educated, intellectually sophisticated Christians think of God himself as a spirit—invisible, nonmaterial, shapeless (no

arms or legs), and maybe everywhere at once, not even spatially local-
ized like a man. If it once made sense for a manlike God to have a
man's spirit, it makes no sense today for a spirit God to have its own
spirit. The idea of a Holy Spirit has become an anachronism, not com-
prehended by modern Christians but retained as an enigma because
the Holy Spirit is part of the Trinity. My point is, though, that Christianity's Holy Spirit is not God's breath but a supernatural spirit used
to achieve spirit possession. Hence Aslan's breath is just that, breath,
not spirit—not the Holy Spirit.

The 2005 Books: Hinten. Easily the best of the eight film-
inspired *Narnia* books published in 2005 is Marvin D. Hinten's *The
Keys to the Chronicles: Unlocking the Symbols of C. S. Lewis's
Narnia*. Rather than downplaying the role of allegory in *LWW* (and in
the other six *Chronicles* books), Hinten does what his book's subtitle
suggests: he searches for—and finds—symbols and allusions that are
hidden in Lewis's text. In doing so, he challenges rather than accepts
Lewis's denials of allegory.

Hinten's most telling points are the ones challenging Lewis's
denials. I have shown that Lewis relies on a false definition of allegory:
he says allegory requires personification, which simply isn't true.
Lewis also says, again falsely (doubly so), that his "supposing" that fictional characters (specifically, Aslan) are real makes them real and that
such supposed-to-be-real things cannot be symbols. But "supposing"
can't make fictional things real. And even if it could, the "real" symbol
(Aslan, a lion) and what the symbol represents (Jesus, a human being)
are two different things, which is all that symbolism requires.

Hinten presents the gist of my points abstractly when he writes:
"*Allegory* is a slippery term, and our answer to the question of whether
the Chronicles are allegories may well depend on how the term is
defined. . . . This explains why J. R. R. Tolkien could condemn *Lion*
[*LWW*] as allegory while Lewis denied it even fit the category."[61]
Hinten also attacks the "common and erroneous view that allegory
means every incident and character from the created world must have
a corresponding incident or character from our world."[62] (Downing,

please note.) That view means, for example, that *LWW* is not disqualified as allegory simply because Tumnus, Giant Rumblebuffin, and the meal the siblings enjoy at Mr. Beaver's house are not symbols.

More to the point, Hinten's statement also means that Ryken and Mead are wrong and Schakel is wrong when they demand detailed parallels between the symbol and whatever is symbolized. Ryken and Mead think that "to allegorize . . . [would be] to make virtually all details correspond to something in the life of Christ."[63] Schakel says that "Aslan's death does not parallel Christ's death . . . as closely as 'allegory' would require."[64] Here Schakel naively argues that (*a*) Aslan dies to save one person rather than all Narnians, (*b*) Aslan is stabbed to death rather than crucified, and (*c*) Aslan arises the next morning, not on the third day as Jesus did. What Schakel doesn't realize is that, as I said earlier, one good analogy is all it takes to make a valid symbol. Symbolism relies on analogy. In *The American Heritage College Dictionary* we learn that analogy means "similarity *in some respects* between things that are *otherwise dissimilar*" (my italics).

Unfortunately, Hinten's laudable willingness to ignore Lewis's warped concept of allegory fails to lead Hinten much beyond the conclusion reached by Schakel and Veith: that only a small part of *LWW*—what Veith calls an "allegorical core"—is allegorical. Hinten's main concern is to demonstrate the presence in the *Chronicles* of symbols and allusions. The emphasis is on allusions. An allusion is an indirect reference to something, whereas a symbol is an analogical representation of something; allusions don't represent. Since allusions are not symbols, they are not evidence of allegory.

Hinten shows, as one example of allusion, that the faun's name, Tumnus, alludes to the last two syllables of the name of the Roman god Vertumnus.[65] Hinten's allusions include quite a few pointing to Norse mythology. Norse mythology is not Christian mythology. So even if the allusions were symbols, the Norse allusions would not be evidence of an allegory whose unifying theme was Christianity. Though interesting, the allusions provide no support for the idea that *LWW* is allegory (and Hinten doesn't claim that they do).

When it comes to Christian *symbols* (these exclude allusions to phrases from the Bible), Hinten comes up with only five that the previous authors have usually overlooked, and I am skeptical about two of these. Hinten's five additional symbols are (1) Peter, Susan, and Lucy as Jesus's "inner circle" of disciples, namely, Peter, James, and John, (2) the hill where the Stone Table sits as Calvary, (3) the Stone Table as Moses's stone tables (tablets) on which the Ten Commandments were written, (4) the breaking in two of the Stone Table as the tearing in two of the temple's curtain when Jesus died—Hinten qualifies this symbol with "perhaps"—and (5) the harrowing of Hell. Strangely, despite recognizing the harrowing of Hell symbolism, Hinten fails to mention three corollary symbols: (6) the White Witch as Satan, (7) the witch's castle as Hell, and (8) the stone statues as the righteous inmates of Hell who Jesus rescues.

Item 2 is validated by a clear analogy between the Stone Table's hill as Aslan's place of execution and Calvary hill as Jesus's place of execution. Item 3 is validated by its coming from the previously mentioned letter Lewis wrote. Item 5 is validated by strong analogies, discussed earlier. These include the White Witch's (Satan's) castle as the symbol of Hell and the rescue of the castle's prisoners as the rescuing of Satan's prisoners in Hell.

But in item 1, I don't think the three siblings, who have just met Aslan and hardly know him, qualify as disciples. If the children symbolize anything before they climb on their four horses, it is simply Christians or, more particularly, converts to Christianity. Aslan's loyal followers—the dryads, centaurs, leopards, and others in attendance when the children arrive at the Stone Table—more closely resemble disciples. One of the two leopards, for example, carries Aslan's crown, and the other carries his banner. Likewise, I am not persuaded that Peter's name makes him a symbol for the disciple Peter: that's a bit too literal for a Lewis symbol. It's more like something from Bunyan, the literalist who in *The Pilgrim's Progress* gives the name "Despair" to the giant who symbolizes despair.

As for item 4, the Jewish temple's curtain tore when Jesus died, whereas the Stone Table breaks when Aslan comes back to life. The Stone Table's association with Aslan's return to life points to the real symbolic analogy, the analogy between the breaking of the Stone Table and the breaking open of Jesus's stone tomb (the rolling away of the stone blocking the entrance) when the Jesus of mythology arose from the dead.

So, despite his much better understanding of allegory and his consequent willingness to look for the presence of allegory in *LWW*, Hinten reaches essentially the same conclusion that Schakel and Veith reach: *LWW* has a limited allegorical core—the death and resurrection of Christianity's Christ—but is far from being a full-fledged allegory.

All three authors—Schakel, Veith, and Hinten—fail to recognize that *LWW*'s allegorical content goes way beyond what Schakel calls "the account of Aslan's death." Before symbolizing the crucifixion, Lewis symbolizes God, angels, Heaven, Earth, Hell, Satan, demons, Satan's power, the weakening of Satan's power, temptation, sin, a Christian prophecy, a minister, the minister's leading his flock to Jesus, a church, the Ten Commandments (recognized by Hinten), Christian ideology, and Satan's being a deceiver. After symbolizing the resurrection, Lewis symbolizes the harrowing of Hell (recognized by Hinten), Jesus's restoring dead persons to life, Jesus's defeat of Satan, repentance, forgiveness, redemption, Earth's human kings and their doomed kingdoms, the apocalypse, the Four Horsemen of the Apocalypse, the apocalypse's Lamb of God, the disappearance of earthly kingdoms, the Second Coming of Jesus, the lamp in new Jerusalem, and the arrival of the Kingdom of God. *LWW* has symbols from its beginning to its end, not just in one short stretch. *LWW* definitely is allegory.

CHAPTER 4

THE LION, THE WITCH AND THE WARDROBE RETOLD

Pullman's Allegory

Although Pullman could allegorize *LWW* without symbolizing every significant character, action, and object, it happens that he does an amazingly thorough job of symbolically retelling the C. S. Lewis story. Pullman uses forty-one characters (sometimes groups, such as witches or dragonflies) from his surface story to symbolize thirty-seven characters (or groups, or in one case the lamppost) from *LWW*. Each of the four siblings is symbolized, in separate scenes, by two or three Pullman characters; Lyra, in separate scenes, symbolizes both Lucy and Susan. Four of the symbolized characters, major figures from World War II, are not actually mentioned in *LWW*, but their presence in the story's wartime background is implied. In addition to creating forty-one character symbols, Pullman symbolizes sixty-two places, things, and events from Narnia. Were Pullman to selectively symbolize just half or even a third of the referents of his symbols, he would have a fine allegory. As it happens, though, he somehow conjures up 104 symbols that symbolize almost everything in Lewis's story. This is an astonishing achievement. Let's see how he pulls it off.

THE *LWW* ALLEGORY'S SETTING

The surface story symbols Pullman uses to depict the many details of *LWW* include ones describing both the historical setting and the spatial setting of the hidden C. S. Lewis story.

The Historical Setting: Ruta Skadi's Witches. Late in *The Amber Spyglass* (*AS*), the long-awaited clash between the Authority's forces and Asriel's rebels begins. Ruta Skadi's witch clan, accompanied by seven other clans, participates in a big way and slyly delivers to us a message about the setting. In the action about to be described, see if you can recognize what is being symbolized. Metatron's "Chariot," the Clouded Mountain, is moving in on Asriel's fortress: the great battle is on. A large group of witches from Ruta Skadi's clan and the other clans, flying on their cloud-pine branches, rises to meet the attack. Each witch carries a flaming torch. From the Clouded Mountain comes an opposing flight of angels armed with spears and swords. The angels move in fast, but the witches have their own tactics. They soar high, then dive on the angels from above, "lashing to left and right with their flaring torches" as "angel after angel, outlined in fire, . . . wings ablaze, tumble[s] screaming from the air."[1]

What's going on here? What's going on is the Battle of Britain. The action is over London. British Spitfires and Hurricanes, machine guns flaring, are diving on incoming German Heinkel He 111 bombers and sending them down in flames, screaming as crippled planes do when plummeting to earth.[2] The witches are the RAF! Or, more precisely, the witches are the RAF pilots, and the cloud-pine branches are the Spitfires and Hurricanes. The several clans of witches are squadrons. And Metatron's angels? Collectively, they are Hermann Goering's Luftwaffe; their wings are the wings of the German bombers, aflame because their engines are on fire. The angels' spears and swords are the German bombs. Pullman's father and stepfather, by the way, were both RAF pilots, so we shouldn't be surprised that the RAF gets into the act.[3]

Four characters from Pullman's surface story probably symbolize background participants in the Battle of Britain, Hitler's abortive effort to bomb the British into submission and prepare the way for a German invasion. It's hard to be sure of Pullman's intent regarding this symbolism, since the four symbolized persons are offstage in *LWW*; their roles in directing the aerial warfare over London are merely implied. But Pullman seemingly intends, and certainly should intend, that Ruta Skadi symbolizes the head of the Royal Air Force Fighter Command, Air Chief Marshall Hugh Dowding. Skadi's superior, the leader of the rebel defenders, is Lord Asriel, who becomes the symbol for British Prime Minister Winston Churchill. On the other side, Metatron symbolizes Dowding's immediate adversary, Reichsmarshall Hermann Goering, chief of the German air force, the Luftwaffe. Metatron's boss, the leader who made him Regent, is the Authority. He symbolizes Goering's boss, der Fuehrer, Adolf Hitler. These symbols apply only to this allegory. In the *PL* allegory Asriel, Metatron, and the Authority play different and considerably more important—and visible—roles. (Ruta Skadi does not have a role in the *PL* allegory.)

You may, with good reason, be reluctant to believe that the Authority could symbolize anyone but God. And he certainly does symbolize God in the *PL* allegory. But according to Chris Weitz, hired to direct the planned *HDM* movies, Pullman does not narrowly interpret the Authority as describing God alone: "I have visited with Pullman and spoken with him about this subject at great length. His feeling, and I say this with absolute certainty that I am not unfairly paraphrasing him, is that the 'Authority' . . . could represent any arbitrary establishment that curtails the freedom of the individual, whether it be religious, political, totalitarian, fundamentalist, communist, what have you."[4] Why would Pullman say this? The Authority is plainly designed to represent God, so Pullman must have a reason for insisting that someone else can also be represented. The apparent reason is that Pullman has a secondary role in mind for the Authority, in addition to the primary role, God. Pullman wants an Authority who can, in different contexts (different allegories), represent both Hitler—a "totalitarian" despot—and God.

Pullman's disgression into World War II symbolism provides the hidden story's historical setting. The four children, you may recall, have been sent to the Professor's house in the country for their safety. They have been removed from the threat of the German bombs raining down on London during the Battle of Britain. Pullman is portraying the second sentence of *LWW*: "This story is about something that happened to them [the children] when they were sent away from London during the war because of the air-raids."[5] Although Pullman's air war symbols come near the end of the trilogy, they are not out of place. The Battle of Britain is going on during the entire *LWW* story.

Two witches—Serafina Pekkala and Ruta Skadi—have featured roles in *HDM*. Serafina is off somewhere helping the gyptians, who are trying to help Lyra, when the aerial combat takes place: the combat scene belongs to Ruta Skadi. The origin of her name is a matter of speculation. It might be nothing more than a representative Scandinavian name, signifying that the witches are from Lapland, the northern part of Scandinavia. (Serafina Pekkala also has a Scandinavian name.) "Ruta" is a real Finnish first name—it means beautiful—and "Skadi" could be either a genuine Finnish surname or, more likely, a drop-the-*n* derivative of the first two syllables of "Scandinavia." Yet "Ruta Skadi" also happens to be an anagram for "A Dark Suit." And Pullman's witches do wear dark suits of a sort. When Serafina Pekkala first shows up, she is "clad like *all* the witches in strips of black silk."[6] A coincidence? Probably. "A black uniform" (Franci Kolbaum) or "a black silk flier" (Karla Flickbleis) would certainly be a more precise description of a witch or her outfit. But "a dark suit" provides a Scandinavian name (unlike Kolbaum or Flickbleis) and just might be an intentional anagram.

The Spatial Setting: Places. The *HDM* symbols that describe the spatial setting—the places where the hidden story unfolds—are on two levels. The first-level symbols are found in *The Golden Compass* (*GC*) and use a micro scale. These symbols depict four places in Lewis's story: (1) the Professor's house, (2) the room with the wardrobe, (3) the wardrobe itself, a passage between worlds, and (4) Narnia. In Pullman's story, Lyra lives at Jordan College, part of her world's Oxford University. Her Oxford is different from but similar to the real Oxford in England, which is also in Pullman's surface story. Jordan College symbolizes the Professor's house. The Retiring Room at Jordan College symbolizes the room where the children find the wardrobe. The wardrobe in the Retiring Room symbolizes the wardrobe the children find. And that part of Lyra's world that lies outside of Jordan College symbolizes Narnia. Like Narnia, Lyra's outside world is full of supernatural creatures, including witches, armored bears, and cliff-ghasts, not to mention a human shaman with supernatural powers.

In *The Subtle Knife* (*SK*), Pullman introduces a second symbol for the wardrobe, and in *The Amber Spyglass* (*AS*) he uses this additional symbol to depict the four siblings' return through the wardrobe at the end of *LWW*. This symbol uses the macro scale: the symbolic place is huge instead of relatively small. The macro symbol is the world of Cittàgazze (City of Magpies), where the Specters live. Cittàgazze's world is modeled after the wardrobe from *LWW*. Just as the wardrobe must be passed through to get from Earth to Narnia and back, Cittàgazze's world must be passed through to get from Lyra's world to Will's and back: it is an intermediate place that serves as a gateway between two other places.

PULLMAN'S *NARNIA* ALLEGORY'S SYMBOLIC CHARACTERS

A multitude of characters from the *HDM* surface story symbolize persons from *LWW*—or in some cases animals and other creatures and in one case the lamppost. Ruta Skadi and the other witches from the eight clans in Asriel's Air Defense Command have already been cited; so have Asriel, Metatron, and the Authority. The other surface story characters Pullman uses as symbols in the *LWW* allegory are the Master of Jordan, his housekeeper and three servants, Lyra (as Lucy), Lord

Boreal (a.k.a. Sir Charles Latrom), Roger (Lyra's Jordan College friend), Tony Makarios (a kidnaped boy), Mrs. Coulter and her golden monkey daemon, Serafina Pekkala (a witch), John Faa and Ma Costa (Lyra's gyptian protectors), Lee Scoresby (the balloonist), the other witches of Serafina's clan (counted as one symbol), Lyra again (as Susan), Father Gomez, the *tualapi* (great white sailing birds), Balthamos (an angel), the spy-fly, Iorek (the good armored bear), Iofur (the bad armored bear), Will, the intercised children, the cliff-ghasts, the four principal Gallivespians (Roke, Oxentiel, Tialys, and Salmakia), Mary Malone, and Xaphania (the leader of the rebel angels).

The Master of Jordan and His Staff. Recall that, in C. S. Lewis's story, a kindly old Professor owns the house the four siblings are living in to escape the air raids. The house has the room with the wardrobe. In examining the allegory's spatial setting, we saw how Pullman has symbolized these things. Jordan College, where Lyra has lived for most of her life and which the Master is administrator of, is the Professor's house. The college's Retiring Room, where the story begins, contains a wardrobe in which Lyra hides, so the Retiring Room symbolizes the room with the wardrobe in the Professor's house. And the wardrobe symbolizes the wardrobe. Against this background, the Master of Jordan has to represent the Professor.

If you're not convinced, consider some additional evidence. *LWW*'s Professor has a housekeeper and three servants. The Master of Jordan likewise has a housekeeper and three servants: Mrs. Lonsdale, the housekeeper; Mr. Cawson, the steward; Mr. Wren, the butler; and Mr. Shuter, the porter. Mrs. Lonsdale symbolizes *LWW*'s Mrs. Macready. Cawson, Wren, and Shuter collectively symbolize Ivy, Margaret, and Betty.

Lyra. As a particularly versatile actress, Lyra has been given several parts in the Pullman drama. In the present allegory she has two roles, and in the next she has a third role. Her *LWW* allegory roles are those of Lucy and Susan, the two girls among the four siblings of the C. S. Lewis story.

When Lyra hides in the Retiring Room's wardrobe at the beginning of *GC*, she symbolizes Lucy (the youngest sibling), who hides in the wardrobe in the Professor's house during a game of hide-and-seek (the second time she enters the wardrobe). Later, when Lyra goes from her world to the intermediate world of Cittàgazze and from there to Will's world, Cittàgazze becomes a macro symbol for the wardrobe; Lyra's passing through the intermediate world symbolizes Lucy's going from her world through the wardrobe to Narnia. To anticipate some still later symbolism, when Lyra converses with Lord Boreal she again symbolizes Lucy, who is having a conversation with Tumnus. To further anticipate, when Lyra puts the "Ratter" coin, which symbolizes Tony Makarios's daemon (his soul), in the dying Tony's mouth, her action symbolizes Lucy's act of pouring her life-saving cordial in the dying Edmund's mouth: Lucy is restoring Edmund's departing soul.

But when Lyra is hunted by Father Gomez, she represents Susan (second oldest), who is being attacked by the wolf Maugrim. In related symbolism, when Lyra goes up in the balloon with Lee Scoresby, she again symbolizes Susan, who is trying to get away from Maugrim by going up in a tree with the gift horn given to her by Father Christmas. (Guess which Pullman character—someone who travels through the air—symbolizes Father Christmas, a.k.a. Santa Claus, who helps Susan by giving her the gift.) The analogical bases for these two identities—Lucy and Susan—are clarified under the "Lord Boreal," "Lee Scoresby," and "Father Gomez" subheadings.

Let's go back to that gift horn. Does Lyra take anything that might symbolize a gift horn with her when she goes up in Lee Scoresby's balloon (i.e., when Susan goes up in the tree)? Yes, she takes the alethiometer with her. The alethiometer is the gift horn given to Susan by Father Christmas. To ensure that we don't overlook the alethiometer's presence in the up-in-the-balloon action, Pullman has Serafina Pekkala fly alongside the balloon and ask Lyra, "Have you got the symbol reader?" Lyra replies, "Yes, I got it in my pocket, safe."[7]

Lyra's name (*a*) has four letters, (*b*) begins with *L*, and (*c*) has *y* as one of its three lowercase letters. Lucy's name has the same three attributes. This is unlikely to be a coincidence. The statistical odds that both of two four-letter names would begin with L and have one more letter (of three) in common, but not necessarily in the same position, are $1/26 \times (3/26 + 3/25 + 3/24) = 1/26 \times 5,622/15,600 = 5,622/405,000 = 1/72$, or 1 chance in 72.[8] Now assume that the chance that two girls' names will both have four letters is one in seven. (Most girls' names have three to nine letters, giving us seven options. For present purposes, the rare two-letter names can go with the three-letter names, and the scarce ten-letter and eleven-letter names can go with the nine-letter names.)[9] The odds that both of two names will have all three attributes—an initial L, a second letter in common (not necessarily y), and a total of four letters—are $1/7 \times 1/72 = 1/504$, or less than 1 chance in 500.

Lord Boreal, a.k.a. Sir Charles Latrom. Truly inspired symbolism radiates from the sinister character known as Lord Boreal (from "aurora borealis") in Lyra's world, his home world (he has a daemon), but known as Sir Charles Latrom ("mortal" spelled backward) in Will's world. We know he is sinister because, among other reasons, his daemon is a serpent. Boreal-Latrom seems important enough to be a symbol, but who or what might he symbolize? The essential clue is his resemblance to a character in *LWW*. The first person Lucy meets in Narnia is the faun, Mr. Tumnus. A faun is part human, part goat. The White Witch has assigned Tumnus the task of inviting humans to his home (a well-furnished cave), pretending to be friendly, and then handing the victims over to the witch. But Tumnus lets Lucy go.

Like Tumnus, Charles Latrom is the first person (well, the first of any consequence) Lyra meets after entering Will's world. (Lyra is now playing the part of Lucy.) Also like Tumnus, Latrom more or less invites her to his home: he gives her his card with his home address and invites her to get in touch, which she later does. And again like Tumnus, he has evil doings in mind. He steals her alethiometer and then tries to deceive her into stealing the subtle knife and giving it to him in exchange for the return of the alethiometer, which he does not really intend to return. Finally, when she does go to his house and confronts him, he lets her go. These analogies by themselves imply that (*a*) Boreal-Latrom symbolizes Tumnus and (*b*) his house symbolizes Tumnus's cave. Granted, Boreal-Latrom exudes wickedness, whereas Tumnus is nice; but that character reversal agrees with other bad-becomes-good and good-becomes-bad role reversals (e.g., Satan's being on the side of good in Pullman's story).

The interpretation does seem to have a problem. Lucy meets Tumnus in Narnia, the world of supernatural beings. In Pullman's trilogy, that world's counterpart is Lyra's world, the world of daemons, witches, armored bears, and cliff-ghasts. Lyra's world of supernatural creatures is where Lyra should meet Boreal-Latrom, if he symbolizes Tumnus. But the answer is that she *does* first meet him in her world—at Mrs. Coulter's cocktail party in London, where his identity is Lord Boreal. This meeting, to be sure, does not at first seem to take place (as it should) right after Lyra enters a new world. But closer inspection reveals that the world *is* new. Lyra has just left her "world" at Jordan College and has just arrived at a new "world," London. Under the "Spatial Setting" heading, we saw that the part of Lyra's world that lies outside of Jordan College symbolizes Narnia: London is in Narnia.

But the meetings are just the cake. The icing—the really convincing, and superbly clever, analogy—is Boreal-Latrom's double identity. Tumnus, being a faun, has two identities. He is part man, part goat. Similarly, Pullman's faun symbol is part Boreal, part Latrom.

Tony Makarios. Tony Makarios is a boy of about nine, the son of an alcoholic mother. He steals to eat, so he is a sinner—like Edmund, the liar and traitor among the Lewis story's four siblings. Tony is one of the first children to be kidnaped by the Gobblers. What happens is that Mrs. Coulter uses her golden monkey daemon to beguile Tony's sparrow daemon (its form at the moment) and gain Tony's confidence. Then she lures Tony into a warehouse by promising him a delicious drink of chocolatl. (In Lyra's world, chocolate is called chocolatl.) The chocolatl is obviously a combination of the hot drink and the delicious Turkish Delight candy the White Witch uses to lure Edmund into her clutches. So Tony, the sinner seduced with chocolatl, must be Edmund (the second youngest sibling), the *LWW* sinner who is seduced with sweets.

The above evidence is all we need to establish beyond doubt that Tony is Edmund, but there is still more evidence. When Lucy and Susan ride on Aslan's back from the witch's ransacked palace to where Peter's army is battling the witch's army, they arrive just as Edmund gets gravely wounded by the witch. He is dying. But Lucy saves Edmund by pouring into Edmund's mouth a few drops of the magical cordial Father Christmas gave her. Pullman reenacts this action. Lyra (symbolizing both Lucy and Susan here) rides on Iorek's (Aslan's) back to a village where Tony Makarios (Edmund) has been sighted. Tony is near death, because Mrs. Coulter (the witch) has cut away his daemon (his soul) with her silver guillotine. "Ratter" (his daemon's name), moans the dying Tony. "Where's Ratter?"[10] Lucy and Iorek bring Tony to the gyptians, but they can't save him. He dies.

Lyra takes a gold coin, scratches the word "Ratter" into it with a borrowed knife, and places the coin in Tony's mouth. Lyra intends that the coin represent Tony's daemon, "Ratter," who is his soul. Way back near the beginning of *GC*, Lyra and Roger went down to the crypt below the Jordan College oratory. This was where previous Jordan College Masters had been buried. There, on shelves, the children found the skulls of dead Masters. Turning a skull over, Lyra found a coinlike bronze disc with the image of that dead Master's daemon scratched on it. "Each of the other skulls, they found, had its own daemon-coin, showing its owner's lifetime companion still close to him in death."[11] By placing the "Ratter" coin in Tony's mouth—inside his skull—Lyra is making a token gesture: returning Tony's daemon-soul to him. Tony is then cremated.

In the allegory, the "Ratter" coin symbolizes the magical cure-all cordial Father Christmas gave to Lucy. When Lyra (now playing Lucy) puts the coin in Tony's (Edmund's) mouth, Lucy is restoring

Edmund's health by pouring cordial into his mouth. Figuratively speaking, Lucy is returning to Edmund his departing soul, which the coin also represents. The coin can therefore be viewed as a double-duty symbol. It represents the cordial Lucy administers to Edmund, and it also represents Edmund's soul, which is being returned to him.

The symbolism is flawed, because Tony shouldn't die: Edmund didn't die. Yet there is absolutely no doubt about what Pullman is trying to do here. He is symbolizing Lucy's (*a*) riding to the battlefield on Aslan's back, (*b*) seeing Edmund near death, his soul in the process of departing, (*c*) pouring cordial into his mouth, and (*d*) causing Edmund to return to health by putting his departing soul back inside him. Tony does not actually return to life, at least not in a literal sense, but he does *symbolically* return to life when his soul—in token form—is returned to him.

The Jordan College episode in which Lyra and Roger visit the vaults and find the skulls and daemon-coins has an amusing sidelight, a subtle pun thrown in by Pullman. On a follow-up trip to the vaults, they are spotted by a Jordan College priest, Father Heyst. Father Heyst is hanging around the vaults. Get it? If not, try respelling his name without changing the pronunciation: Heist. What better place to pull off a heist than at some vaults? (The man is confused: he can't tell a bank vault from a burial vault.)

The deduction that Tony is Edmund is stronger still because, without an Edmund symbol, the symbolization of the four *Narnia* children would be incomplete. To recapitulate, Lyra represents both Lucy (who meets Tumnus and who later administers cordial to Edmund) and Susan (who the wolf tries to kill and who goes up in a tree). Balthamos, as we shall see in a moment, is Peter (who slays the wolf), and Tony is Edmund (the sinful sibling who is seduced with Turkish Delight candy). And if that weren't enough, we could observe that the woman who lures Tony into her clutches with chocolatl is the woman who symbolizes the White Witch, who will be discussed next.

Makarios is a Greek name meaning blissful or happy. Tony is blissful when Mrs. Coulter gives him the chocolatl, thereby entrapping him.

Mrs. Coulter and her Golden Monkey Daemon. Two of Pullman's thespians share the role of the White Witch. In the scene where Mrs. Coulter lures Tony Makarios (Edmund) into the warehouse, the witch is Mrs. Coulter. Further evidence that Mrs. Coulter symbolizes the witch (most of the time) comes to light when Coulter poisons Boreal-Latrom. Boreal-Latrom, remember, symbolizes Tumnus, the faun. Mrs. Coulter, in administering the poison, is again playing the White Witch, who is using her wand (the poison) to turn Tumnus into stone. When Mrs. Coulter intercises the children with her silver guillotine at her Experimental Station, figuratively killing them (separating them from their souls), she is the witch stopping her sledge to turn the tea-partying little forest creatures into stone statues. The silver guillotine is the witch's magic wand. Once more, when Mrs. Coulter pursues and temporarily recaptures Lyra after Lyra leads the escape from Bolvangar, Mrs. Coulter travels on a sledge (sleigh), just as the witch does. Mrs. Coulter's sledge is the witch's sledge.

Mrs. Coulter's daemon, the golden monkey, is the witch's servant, the dwarf. Like the dwarf, the golden monkey is smaller than his master and is a servant of sorts. For example, at the London cocktail party, the monkey daemon searches Lyra's room while Lyra is mingling with the guests. When Mrs. Coulter is holding Lyra prisoner in the cave, the monkey serves Mrs. Coulter by capturing Lady Salmakia, one of the two Gallivespians sent by Lord Asriel to help rescue Lyra. The monkey daemon also displays the dwarf's nasty personality. Shortly before the cocktail party, Lyra balks at removing her handbag; Pantalaimon turns into a polecat, arching his back. The consequence: "Mrs. Coulter's daemon sprang off the sofa in a blur of golden fur and pinned Pantalaimon to the carpet before he could move . . . [and then] took one of Pantalaimon's ears in his . . . paw and pulled as if he intended to tear it off."[12]

Mrs. Coulter's name comes from a surprising source, a plow. A coulter is a vertical blade—sometimes a sharp wheel—attached to the front of a plow and used to make a vertical cut in the soil in advance of the plowshare. It can be likened to a pilot engine, a locomotive that proceeds ahead of a train to ensure that no hazards lie ahead. The Indo-European root word from which "coulter" is derived means "to cut." That meaning, and the function of a plow's coulter, point to Mrs. Coulter's favorite pastime: intercision. Intercision is cutting children apart from their daemons with the blade of her silver guillotine. "The blade is made of manganese and titanium alloy, and the child is placed in a compartment—like a small cabin—of alloy mesh, with the daemon in a similar compartment connecting with it. . . . Then the blade is brought down between them, severing the link [between the child and its daemon] at once."[13]

The golden monkey, Mrs. Coulter's daemon, has no name. Pullman has explained why. "Every time I tried to think of one, he snarled and frightened me. What's more, he hardly speaks either."[14]

Serafina Pekkala. The good witch Serafina Pekkala helps Lyra on several occasions. One of the things Serafina does is guide Lyra to where she needs to go. First, Serafina sends her goose daemon, Kaisa, to tell the gyptians how to get to the Experimental Station at Bolvangar, where the kidnaped children are being held. Lyra is with the gyptians. Later, after Lyra has helped the children escape, Serafina and her witch companions, flying on their cloud-pine branches, tow Lee Scoresby's balloon as it proceeds toward Svalbard. Lyra is a passenger. She thinks she needs to get to Svalbard to deliver the alethiometer to Lord Asriel, who really doesn't want it.

Serafina is an important character, so we can be sure she symbolizes someone. Who does she symbolize? Her service as a guide is the vital clue, and her ability to fly on broomlike cloud-pine branches is a second clue. Early in *LWW*, the four children are *guided* to Mr. Beaver by a robin. The robin flies from tree to tree, leading the children to Mr. Beaver. There really isn't much room for doubt: Serafina, a flying guide, is the robin.

The name Serafina Pekkala provides food for speculation. "Serafina" is apparently based on the name of a high order of angels, the Seraphim, sometimes associated with a lower order, the Cherubim (whence "cherub"). Like witches, angels (i.e., the Seraphim) fly.

Choosing a flier's name seems to be a way of emphasizing Serafina's most important characteristic, the ability to fly. The name also alludes to religion.

Pullman has said in several interviews that he got the witch's name from the Helsinki telephone directory.[15] Pullman's witches make their home in Lapland, which includes northern Finland, and Pekkala is an obviously Finnish name; so the choice is geographically excellent. But Pullman surely chose the first name, Serafina, after searching diligently in the phone book for a name with useful connotations, preferably religious. Serafina is definitely a name that might be found in the Helsinki phone book, although the name is actually Swedish. The Finnish variant, *Serafiina*, is spelled with a double *i*.

John Faa and Ma Costa. When Lyra runs away from Mrs. Coulter in London, gyptians (gypsies) rescue her from kidnappers and bring her onto Ma Costa's "narrowboat," a houseboat. The gyptians are boat people who live in Lyra's world and travel on canals. John Faa, Lord of the western gyptians, and Ma Costa, Lyra's nanny from early childhood, are Lyra's gyptian guardians. These two play important roles in Pullman's story. They and their gyptian companions take Lyra north to Iorek Brynison, the armored bear. To anticipate, he symbolizes Aslan, the lion.

In the *Narnia* story, Mr. and Mrs. Beaver take the children to Aslan. Just as the gyptians are water people, beavers are water animals. The Beavers' house is in the middle of a pond. Also, just as gyptians live in the world that has supernatural beings—armored bears, witches, and the like—the Beavers live in Narnia, a world full of supernatural creatures. This gives us three analogies relating the gyptians to the Beavers: (1) both are at home on or in water, (2) both take a child or children to the Aslan character or to Aslan himself, and (3) both belong to worlds where supernatural beings live. John Faa and Ma Costa unmistakably symbolize Mr. and Mrs. Beaver.

Pullman's story has other Beaver-related symbols besides John Faa and Ma Costa. Ma Costa's narrowboat, which the men who rescue Lyra take her to, is the Beaver house in the pond. After rescuing Lyra, Ma

Costa, John Faa, and the other gyptians take Lyra north on the Grand Junction Canal, then across the sea to where they meet Iorek (Aslan). The Grand Junction Canal symbolizes the path by the river that Mr. and Mrs. Beaver take Lucy, Susan, and Peter along as they head for the Stone Table and Aslan. On the way north, police search the narrow-boat, looking for Lyra, but she is safely hidden in a secret compartment under Ma Costa's bunk. The hidden compartment symbolizes the river bank hiding hole where Mr. Beaver hides the three siblings while the witch searches for them. The trip Lyra and the gyptians take from London, where the houseboat was tied up, to Trollesund, the Lapland port where they meet Iorek, symbolizes the trip the three siblings (sans Edmund) take from the Beaver house to the Stone Table, where they meet Aslan. In this chapter's next section ("Other Symbols Referring to the Lewis Story"), some more Beaver-related symbols will emerge under the subheading "The Visit to the Wine Cellars."

John Faa's name comes from an old ballad, probably of Scottish origin, that has many variations in both tune and title. The titles include "Johnny Faa," "The Gypsy Laddie," "Davy Faw," and "Gypsy Davy." John Faa, also spelled John Faw, was a common gypsy name in the 1500s, and more than one John Faa was hanged in Scotland after the gypsies were banned from Scotland in 1541.

The derivation of Ma Costa's name is unknown. One possibility is that it comes from Costa del Sol ("Sun Coast"), a resort region in southern Spain that includes the city of Granada. Sacromonte Hill, just outside Granada, has famous caves that once housed a large gypsy community. Another possibility is that Pullman is giving a friendly salute to Maddy Costa, whose first name's first two letters spell "Ma." Costa is the author of a Pullman-interview article titled "Kid's Stuff" in the August 22, 2001, *Guardian*, a leading English newspaper. Was Maddy Costa a friend or acquaintance of Pullman before the first *HDM* book was written?

Trollesund's name has a charming derivation, one that displays Pullman's keen sense of humor. A port city, Trollesund is in Norroway, which undoubtedly is famous for its trolls, as is our own Norway. That takes care of the first syllable. *Sund*, for its part, is the Old Norse word for strait or sound, a long wide ocean inlet; the word could be applied to a Norwegian fjord. Trollesund, we can see, is a city on a sound or fjord where trolls hang out.[16]

Lee Scoresby. Lee Scoresby, the balloonist, is one of the more important secondary characters: he appears in all three *HDM* books. He definitely symbolizes someone. Whoever it is, it should be someone who flies through the air. And it doesn't seem to be anyone from Pullman's *Paradise Lost* (*PL*) allegory. The only people besides Jesus and Mary who travel through the air in Christian theology (plus Catholic "Assumption" dogma) are angels and the prophet Elijah, who ascended to Heaven in a chariot of fire. We can eliminate those candidates, because (*a*) in Pullman's story the angels represent themselves and (*b*) Elijah, according to Jewish mythology, became the angel Metatron. Most likely, then, Scoresby symbolizes someone from *LWW*. Once we eliminate Maugrim, Susan, and Peter, whose symbols will be discussed next, the only important character from *LWW* who has not yet been accounted for is Father Christmas. "Father Christmas" is British terminology (C. S. Lewis was English); Americans know the gentleman as Santa Claus. And what do you know: Santa travels through the sky (on a sleigh pulled by reindeer), just as Lee Scoresby does. (In *LWW* Father Christmas travels on the ground, but the traditional bringer of Christmas presents prefers the sky.)

There is a problem, though. Whereas Scoresby helps Lyra and others on several occasions, Father Christmas does not do anything comparable. All he does is give gifts to three of the children—Edmund is off with the witch—and to Mr. and Mrs. Beaver, who are taking the children to Aslan. But problems often have solutions. In this instance, the gifts become proxies for Father Christmas. Although he doesn't personally come to anyone's aid on several occasions the way Scoresby does, he does return and provide aid indirectly, through his gifts. When Susan is chased up a tree by the wolf, the ivory horn "Santa" gave her summons help, and the sword "Santa" gave Peter slays the wolf. Later, when Edmund is dying after having heroically broken the witch's magic wand in combat, the bottled cordial that was Santa's gift to Lucy restores Edmund to good health. So Father Christmas, represented by proxies, does help not only Susan but Peter and Edmund on later occasions.

Two other events strengthen the connection between Lee Scoresby and Father Christmas. When Lyra goes up in the balloon with Scoresby, Susan is climbing the tree—going up in the air—with her ivory horn (the alethiometer), her Santa proxy. Later, some witches tow Scoresby's balloon across the sky. The Santa Claus symbolism in that action will be explained when we get to the next subheading—in case you don't see it already.

Pullman coined the name Lee Scoresby by combining the names of movie actor Lee Van Cleef and arctic explorer William Scoresby. He took the Lee from Van Cleef's name "because I thought my Lee would look like him."[17] Van Cleef, who appeared in spaghetti westerns with Clint Eastwood, is thin and has a rough-hewn face, not what you'd call handsome. Pullman used the last name Scoresby because William Scoresby (1789–1857), like Lee Scoresby, spent considerable time in the arctic. The arctic is where Lee Scoresby meets Will's father, who goes by the name Stanislaus Grumman in the world where Lyra and Scoresby live.

Serafina Pekkala's Witches. Serafina Pekkala, the robin symbol, is the queen of the Lake Enera clan of witches. She has a featured role, but she isn't the only clan member in the cast. Some of the other witches of her clan, the anonymous ones, have bit parts; they are like movie extras. When Lyra is being transported in Lee Scoresby's balloon from Bolvangar toward Svalbard, the island home of the armored bears, the witches decide to give Lee a hand by towing the balloon. Lee attaches "a coil of stout rope to the leather-covered iron ring that gather[s] the ropes running over the gas bag," tosses the free end of the rope to the airborne witches, and off they go.[18] Why should Pullman have the witches do that? On other flights Lee has never needed a helping hand. The tow he gets from the witches has all the earmarks of something contrived for symbolic purposes.

The symbolism isn't hard to find. Lee Scoresby, remember, symbolizes Father Christmas—Santa Claus from the American perspective. Father Christmas travels in a sledge pulled by reindeer. And Lee travels in a balloon. The balloon represents Father Christmas's sledge (British terminology), or Santa's sleigh (American terminology) if you prefer. But where are the reindeer that should be pulling Santa's sleigh across the sky? The reindeer are the witches towing the balloon across the sky. Pullman does have a glitch in his symbolism. He has *six* witches towing the balloon. There should be eight, starting with Dasher and ending with Blitzen—or maybe nine, with the lead witch wearing a red hat instead of the usual black one. But Pullman is an Englishman and can't be expected to be familiar with Clement Moore's American poem "The Night before Christmas" or with our beloved Rudolph. (Perhaps future editions of *GC* will have a correction.)

Father Gomez. Father Gomez, the priest sent to assassinate Lyra, is another symbolic character. He participates in a nonessential subplot whose nonsymbolic purpose is to pump additional suspense and excitement—plus a bit of humor—into the main plot. Gomez is "blazing eyed" and "trembling with zealotry."[19] So zealous is he that he has done "preemptive penance," penance for a sin not yet committed, every day of his adult life. And the mission he volunteers for is to destroy Sin, symbolized by Lyra. (The Sin symbolism will be explained when we get to the next allegory.) He must kill her. He must kill Sin.

When we search Christian theology, *Paradise Lost* (*PL*), and *LWW* for assassins Gomez might symbolize, an excellent fit appears in the third source. Think back to what happens shortly after Lucy, Susan, and Peter meet Aslan, the lion who symbolizes the Christ. A monstrous wolf, Maugrim, attacks Susan. Susan blows on the ivory call-for-help horn Father Christmas has given her, and Peter rushes to save her. He slays Maugrim with the sword given to him by Father Christmas. Gomez dies at the hands of Balthamos, a protector of Lucy, who is Gomez's intended victim. Gomez's death mirrors Maugrim's death at the hands of a protector of his intended victim. These two analogies—assassin and assassin's death at the hands of a protector—offer reasonable certainty that Father Gomez symbolizes Maugrim. Gomez's target, Lyra, serves as additional evidence that Gomez is Maugrim. Lyra symbolizes Susan, Maugrim's target.

The analogical evidence is all the stronger because eliminating the Gomez subplot would not weaken the main plot. The real purpose of the subplot is to symbolize Susan, Maugrim, Maugrim's attack, and his death. Pullman is determined to symbolize every significant person and event from *LWW*.

The name Gomez does not seem to have any special significance. It is a Spanish name, and Spain is a Catholic country. Gomez seems to be nothing more than a stereotypical Catholic name. As such, it has little meaning other than, maybe, a token effort at humor. Actually, Pullman has more skillfully crafted the names of two of the other neo-Catholic clergymen who share with Gomez the scene where Gomez gets his assignment. The name of Father MacPhail, president of the Church's Consistorial Court of Discipline, is a variant of Make-Fail: he is going to fail—and lose his life—in his effort to kill Lyra with the hair bomb. The oldest member of the court, Father Makepwe, seems to have changed his name from Makepew (= "make pew") as an act of humility. Possibly he made pews for a local church back in his seminary days, donating his services. Pullman apparently got the idea for the two "make" names from C. S. Lewis. In *LWW* the Professor's housekeeper is Mrs. Macready, who must "make ready" the Professor's house.

The *Tualapi*. Well before Father Gomez dies, he finds and goes through the window Mary took to get from the world of Cittàgazze to the world of the *mulefa*. In this new world he encounters the *tualapi*. At first they try to attack him but, when Gomez uses his rifle to blow the head off the nearest bird, the two sides quickly reach an understanding. Gomez realizes that "once they had truly learned to fear him, they would do exactly as he said."[20] Gomez has become the chief of the *tualapi*.

What is the point of this scene? The scene where the *tualapi* attack the *mulefa* village has already been performed, well before the arrival of Gomez in the *mulefa* world. And in no scene subsequent to Gomez's becoming the birds' chief does Gomez actually use his power over the birds. So why did Pullman bother to insert the encounter between Gomez and the *tualapi*? Why did Pullman digress to make Gomez the chief of the *tualapi*? There must be a reason. And once we recognize that Gomez symbolizes Maugrim, that reason is plain to see. The birds work for Maugrim (Gomez), Captain of the White Witch's Secret Police; they are Maugrim's Secret Police.

Balthamos and Lyra (Again). The protector who slays Father Gomez is the angel Balthamos. He is one of a pair of angels, Balthamos and Baruch, sent by Lord Asriel to guide Will to Asriel. Baruch has returned to Asriel with important information, but Balthamos has remained with Will. After helping Will find Lyra, Balthamos watches over the two as a sort of guardian angel. And when Father Gomez finds Lyra and prepares to shoot her, Balthamos does what any good guardian would do: he kills the assassin. If the deduction that Gomez symbolizes the assassin wolf, Maugrim, is correct, Balthamos must symbolize Peter (the oldest sibling), who kills Maugrim. (In another scene, discussed later in this chapter, Roger is a second symbol for Peter.) Lyra, who previously symbolized Lucy vis-à-vis Tumnus, the faun, now symbolizes Susan, who Maugrim was attacking.

The name *Balthamos* could be derived, at least in part, from biblical names. The first syllable, Bal, suggests Yahweh's rival Baal, who the Bible treats as an enemy of Yahweh. (Yahweh is God's Hebrew name.) Balthamos is an enemy of the Authority, who symbolizes Yahweh. In addition to the Baal resemblance, the first five letters of *Balth*amos look like an *l*-for-*r* respelling of the first five letters of Bartholomew, the name of one of Jesus's twelve disciples. Bartholomew could likewise be the source of the letters *o*, *l*, and *m*. Just as Bartholomew is a disciple of Jesus, Balthamos is a disciple of Xaphania, although Xaphania doesn't symbolize Jesus. Be that as it may, the last part of Balthamos's name, thamos, looks like a cryptic variation of Thanatos, who in Greek mythology was Death. Because Balthamos brings death to Father Gomez, this derivation has a sound analogical basis, although the severely corrupted spelling invites considerable skepticism.

The Spy-fly. Just before Lyra and the gyptians sail for Norroway (her world's Norway) on a chartered ship, she is attacked by two spy-flies. Resembling flying beetles and about the length of Lyra's thumb, these are best described as crosses between robots and spirits. Inside each one is a spring-driven clockwork mechanism: this much is robot. But attached to the spring is "a bad spirit with a spell through its heart."[21] The cormorant daemon of one of the gyptians knocks one down. That one is captured. Unfortunately, the other spy-fly escapes. The spy-flies were sent by Mrs. Coulter. And the one that escaped reports back to her, telling Mrs. Coulter of Lyra's whereabouts.

This incident symbolizes what happens next after Peter kills Maugrim. Aslan notices a second wolf hiding in the thickets. He is a spy for the witch. The spy-wolf escapes and reports back to the witch. In Pullman's allegory, Mrs. Coulter is the witch. The spy-fly who reports back to her has to be the spy-wolf.

Iorek—The Good Armored Bear. The two principal armored bears—Iorek Brynison and his adversary, Iofur Raknison—are coordinate symbols. Iorek is the more important of the two: he symbolizes the lion Aslan, who is C. S. Lewis's Christ symbol. The first analogy between Iorek and Aslan is that Iorek lives in that part of Lyra's world that is outside of Oxford—the territory that symbolizes Narnia. Narnia is where Aslan lives. The second analogy is that both Iorek and Aslan are intelligent, talking animals. The third analogy is that both befriend, help, and ultimately save the lives of children. The fourth analogy is that, just as Aslan is particularly close to Lucy and Susan, who witness his death and resurrection and who twice ride on his back, Iorek is a close friend and protector of Lyra, who symbolizes both Lucy and Susan, witnesses Iorek's resurrection (but not his death), and rides on his back.

These analogies are just the starters. The really powerful analogies—the fifth and sixth—are the death and resurrection of Iorek, which symbolize the death and resurrection of Aslan. Your skeptical eyebrow might well have lifted at that assertion, for Iorek does not literally die. But he does die figuratively. He is separated from his soul, which Christians believe is what happens when a person dies. Iorek's soul, and every armored bear's soul, is his armor. To ensure that we don't miss this vital point, Pullman states it in five places.[22] Iofur, the bad armored bear, drugged another bear, causing him to challenge Iorek. When Iorek killed the other bear, violating a bear taboo, he became an outcast. His depressed state allowed conniving humans to get him drunk and steal his armor when he passed out. This has reduced him to the status of a slave, working strictly for food and drink. For Iorek, this predicament—armorless and enslaved—is a state of Hell. After dying on the cross, the Christ descended into Hell, according to the Apostles' Creed. Then he arose from the dead. So it is with Iorek. He first metaphorically dies—he loses his armor (soul)—and descends into a metaphorical Hell. Then, with Lyra's help, Iorek regains his armor—regains his soul. He arises from the dead.[23]

Iorek's loss of his armor includes an extra detail that gives a double meaning to the loss-of-armor symbolism. Recall that Aslan was shaved before being killed; the shaving was C. S. Lewis's way of symbolizing what the Roman soldiers did when they stripped Jesus of his clothes and then divided the clothes among themselves. Having the men of Trollesund take Iorek's armor while he is sleeping is a seventh analogy: Pullman is symbolizing what the witch's rabble did when they shaved off Aslan's fur.

While Iorek is "dead"—separated from his armor—the armor lies hidden in the cellar of the Trollesund priest's house. Lyra uses her alethiometer to find out where it is. She then tells Iorek. He tears open the door of the priest's house, rips up the house, descends to the cellar, dons his armor, and then climbs out of the cellar through a window. Lyra sees Iorek climb out of the priest's cellar, reunited with his soul. This is more symbolism, an eighth analogy: Lucy and Susan, once more symbolized by Lyra, are witnessing Aslan's resurrection.

The significance of the armor's being hidden in the cellar is worth noting. This adds an extra touch of color to the resurrection symbolism by requiring Iorek to climb out of the cellar, an act analogous to a dead man's returning to life and climbing out of his grave. At the same time, the act provides a ninth analogy and an additional symbol of Aslan's resurrection. When Iorek arises from the cellar, Aslan is arising from the Stone Table (and C. S. Lewis's symbolized Christ is arising from his stone tomb).[24]

A tenth analogy reinforces the already unbreakable symbolic link between Iorek and Aslan. Aslan, we have seen, uses his magical powers to restore other dead creatures to life. Correspondingly, Iorek, after his "resurrection," helps Lyra restore to life psychologically dead children at the Experimental Station. (This restoration indirectly symbolizes theology's "harrowing of Hell," wherein Jesus descends into Hell for three days and rescues those who deserve to be rescued; the harrowing is directly symbolized by Aslan's restoring the dead creatures to life.) This point will be developed more fully in a moment.

There is even an eleventh analogy between Iorek and Aslan. This analogy is almost as powerful as the fifth and sixth (death and resurrection). Aslan kills the witch, and Iorek kills Iofur, who shares with Mrs. Coulter the role of the White Witch. The eleven analogies establish beyond all doubt that Iorek symbolizes Aslan.

Opinions differ on whether Pullman himself is saying Yo-rek or Yor-ik (it really comes out slurred: Yo-rk) when he pronounces Iorek's name out loud on the audio books and on a recorded BBC program. But in view of the *e* in the name's spelling, common sense tells us that the *rek* sound is right. Pullman's surprising pronunciation of the second bear's name, Iofur, is Yoo-fur: the pronunciation of Io has changed. Yoo-fur puts Iofur's first consonant, *f*, into the second syllable, not the first. That certainly justifies treating the first consonant of Iorek's name, *r*, as part of the second syllable, which gives us Yo-rek. Now, what does Yo-rek suggest? A short *I* combined with a long *o* produces an ee-oh sound that becomes Yo (as in "Yo ho ho") when spoken rapidly. Yo is Spanish for "I." The straightforward "rek" pronunciation of the *rek* syllable is phonetically identical to "wreck." Io-rek becomes Yo-rek, which becomes "I wreck," a colorfully accurate description of Iorek's personality. Iorek is indeed a wrecker. Recall the scene where Iorek recovers his armor: "Three steps led up to the front door, which was now hanging in matchwood splinters, and from inside the house came screams and the crashing and tearing of more wood."[25]

Iofur—The Bad Armored Bear. The other prominent armored bear, Iofur Raknison, has gained Iorek's rightful position as king of the armored bears. Iorek challenges Iofur to a fight to the death for the kingship. Iorek wins. Iofur dies. Given that Iorek symbolizes Aslan, this battle has to represent the fight in which Aslan slays the White Witch. So Iofur must symbolize the White Witch.

Iofur thus shares the White Witch role with Mrs. Coulter. Mrs. Coulter is the witch in several scenes: (1) where the witch lures Edmund (played by Tony Makarios) into her clutches with chocolatl, (2) where the witch "kills" Tumnus, the faun (played by Boreal-Latrom), by turning him into stone, (3) where the witch "kills" the tea-partying forest creatures (played by the intercised children) by turning them into stone, and (4) where the witch travels on her sledge. But in the climactic battle in which Aslan slays the witch, Iofur takes over the role of the witch. Having two symbols (Mrs. Coulter and Iofur in this allegory) for one thing is not without precedent in allegory. Stanley Kubrick, in his allegorical film *2001: A Space Odyssey*, symbolically depicts Nietzsche's magnum opus, *Thus Spake Zarathustra*. Kubrick has two symbols for Nietzsche's lower man, two for higher man, two for God, and two for the death of God. For example, both Hal-*Discovery*—the computer brain and its spaceship body—and the wine glass symbolize God, and both meet their demise, symbolizing Nietzsche's famous phrase "God is dead."[26]

Besides being slain by Iorek, Iofur has something else in common with the White Witch: both pretend to be human although they are not. The witch isn't human, explains Mr. Beaver to the children, but "she'd like us to believe it."[27] Why? Because "she bases her claim to be

Queen" on her claim to be human.[28] So, we have a witch who *pretends* to be human.

And that is what Iofur also does. Early in the story, while hiding in the wardrobe in the Jordan College Retiring Room, Lyra overhears the Palmerian Professor say about Iofur: "He wants a daemon. Find a way to give him a daemon, and he'd do anything for you."[29] Much later, at Iofur's palace, Lyra recalls these words and puts two and two together: "Now it was plain. Everything she'd heard about the bear-king added up: the mighty Iofur Raknison wanted nothing more than to be a human being, with a daemon of his own."[30] Shortly thereafter, Lyra is ushered in to meet Iofur. She finds him bejeweled like a human. He has a heavy gold chain around his neck, and from it hangs an ostentatious jewel. Even more telling is what he holds on his knee: a stuffed doll with a human face. Humans have animals as daemons, so an animal would have a human as a daemon—if animals had daemons. "He was pretending he had a daemon."[31] Like the witch, Iofur is *pretending* he is human.

Pullman gives us more than ample material for deducing that Iofur symbolizes the witch. To reinforce the Iofur-wants-a-daemon evidence, Pullman introduces Iofur-can-be-tricked evidence. Armored bears can't be tricked—unless they act like humans. In a mock fencing scene with Lyra, Iorek displays his inability to be tricked by false thrusts of Lyra's stick: he ignores them, skillfully parrying only Lyra's genuine thrusts. But earlier Iorek was tricked out of his armor when he became depressed and acted like a human. He drank and got drunk, as humans do.

Because Iofur wants to be human and is pretending to be human, he is tricked twice. First, Lyra tricks him into believing she is Iorek's daemon and can become Iofur's if Iofur kills Iorek in one-on-one combat. In this way she spares Iorek the suicidal task of taking on the whole clan of bears. Second, when Iorek and Iofur have their battle to the death, Iorek wins by tricking Iofur. Iorek pretends his left paw is injured. "You could not trick a bear, but, as Lyra had shown him, Iofur did not want to be a bear, he wanted to be a man; and Iorek was tricking him."[32] Iorek suddenly lunges at Iofur, slashing violently with his "crippled" left paw and tearing off part of Iofur's jaw. Moments later Iofur is dead.

Both Iofur's desire for a daemon and his letting himself be tricked show that he wants to be human and is pretending to be human. This evidence confirms what is already obvious from Iofur's being killed by the Aslan symbol, Iorek: Iofur symbolizes the White Witch, the nonhuman who pretends to be human.

An imaginative interpretation of the name Iofur, probably wrong yet consistent with the subtle humor of "I wreck," flows from the earlier translation of Io-rek into Yo-rek and thence into Yo-wreck, where Yo is Spanish for "I." Pullman pronounces Iofur as Yoo-fur in the *HDM* audio books, giving the *o* a long *o* sound (oo, as in "hoop") that conflicts with the long *o* (as in "go") sound given to it in the name Iorek. There must be a reason. Could that reason have something to do with Pullman's willingness to use backward spellings in his name games, as when he spells "mortal" backward to get Sir Charles Latrom's last name? If you spell the "fur" syllable backward, you get "ruf," pronounced "rough." Yoo-fur becomes Yoo-ruf, which becomes "You [are] rough." Imagine the two armored bears facing each other in caricature. The winner-to-be, Iorek, says, "I wreck." The loser-to-be, Iofur, trepidly replies, "You rough." If nothing else, this interpretation explains why Pullman's audio pronunciation of *Io* switches from "Yo" ("I" in Spanish) to "You" when the name changes from Io-rek to Io-fur.

Will Parry. When the White Witch is getting ready to kill Aslan, she orders the vile creatures who serve her to bind the lion's paws together with cord. Next they shave him, muzzle him, place him on the Stone Table, and bind him tightly so that he seems like a mass of cords. The witch then stabs Aslan, killing him. After the witch and her companions leave, some friendly mice come out and nibble away the cords. Aslan is now unbound but still dead. The children, who have been watching from a hiding place, turn away in sorrow. As they mourn, the Stone Table cracks with a deafening noise, and Aslan comes back to life.

Pullman symbolizes the nibble-away-the-cords part of this event not long after Lyra and Will emerge from the land of the dead. Cliff-ghasts and then armor-clad foot soldiers attack them. Will's knife and a squadron of Gallivespians on dragonflies beat off these two sets of attackers. But then horse-mounted riders wielding scimitars and steel-strong nets move in. Iorek and his armored bears arrive in the nick of time but encounter difficulty. Attackers entangle Iorek in a net too strong for the bear to rip open. Will uses his knife to cut Iorek loose, and Iorek then helps Lyra and Will escape to another world, the *mulefa* world.

Iorek, we know, symbolizes Aslan. In this scene, the horsemen are some of the witch's rabble. The net is the cords they use to bind Aslan. Aslan's death, symbolized previously and perhaps now being resymbolized, is Iorek's entanglement in the net. Will now plays the role of the mice. He "nibbles" away the net—the cords that bind Aslan—with his knife. Iorek's springing back into action may or may not resymbolize Aslan's resurrection. His original death and resurrection occurred when he lost and regained his soul—his armor. The reason Pullman decided to symbolize the event twice, if he did so decide, must be that he wanted to symbolize the previously omitted scene where the mice nibble away the cords that bind Aslan. In any event, Will apparently symbolizes the mice in this scene. (Will plays a more important role in the main allegory.)

The Intercised Children. Mrs. Coulter and her Gobblers have kidnaped scores of children for use in a religious experiment. The Gobblers use a device called the silver guillotine to separate the children from their souls, their daemons. Once separated from their souls, the children are metaphorically dead, just as Iorek was metaphorically dead when separated from his soul, which in Iorek's case was his armor. The separated daemons are kept in glass cages in a confinement building, away from the children. While helping the children escape from the Gobblers, Lyra finds and uncages the locked-up daemons and gets them back to their human counterparts. When the children regain their souls (daemons), they are metaphorically resurrected, just as Iorek was metaphorically resurrected from death when he regained his soul, the stolen armor. Iorek and Serafina's witches help in the rescue by attacking Mrs. Coulter's Tartar guards when the escapees are about to be recaptured. Iorek thereby helps restore the "dead" children to life. The rescue becomes a joint effort by Iorek (Aslan) and Lyra (Lucy and Susan), along with the witches.

Now the pieces are in place. We can see who it is the children symbolize. They symbolize the creatures from *LWW* that the White Witch has turned to stone statues, killing them in effect. The restoring to life of the "dead" children symbolizes Aslan's restoring to life the "dead" stone animals—unicorns, birds, foxes, squirrels, donkeys, satyrs, dwarfs, a giant, and others. Although Iorek has a less prominent role in restoring the children to life than Aslan has in restoring the statues to life, the analogies are unmistakable. The intercised children are the stone statues; the children reunited with their daemons are the statues restored to flesh; and Iorek is Aslan, using his breath to deliver new life to the statues.

The Cliff-Ghasts. The name cliff-ghasts is no doubt derived from "ghastly" and "ghost." According to *The American Heritage College Dictionary*, ghastly means "inspiring shock, revulsion, or horror" and "suggestive of or resembling ghosts." A problem in interpreting the cliff-ghasts is that they are on neither side in the surface story conflict between Asriel and the Authority. Lyra (Lucy, Susan) is on Asriel's side, and Mrs. Coulter and Iofur (the White Witch) are on the Authority's side. Although the cliff-ghasts attack Lyra and her companions on two occasions, they also feast on the Authority in his final moments. They are equal opportunity diners. But in Pullman's story they do spend most of their time terrorizing Lyra and her friends. And their ghastly nature jives perfectly with that of a collection of characters who terrorize the children in *LWW*. In the final analysis, then, the cliff-ghasts are with Mrs. Coulter, the White Witch.

Lucy and Susan witness the torture and execution of Aslan by the witch and her evil followers, although the girls cover their eyes when the witch delivers the fatal stroke with her knife. Afterward, as the girls crouch in some bushes, the whole rabble—"foul" vultures, ogres, giant bats, hags, incubuses, wraiths, wolves, bull-headed men, apes, and others—goes charging past them, intending to find and kill Aslan's followers. The nature of these creatures and Pullman's repetition of Lewis's descriptive word "foul" permit little doubt that the cliff-ghasts symbolize the "vile" rabble who serve the White Witch.

The Four Principal Gallivespians. The individual symbols for the four siblings have been identified, but the royal status of the children as the four kings and queens of Narnia near the end of the C. S. Lewis story has not been symbolized. It should be. And it must be: we can see that Pullman is symbolizing everything significant in the Lewis story. So we are looking for four characters in Pullman's story who can symbolize the two kings and two queens who sit on the four thrones at Cair Paravel. Ideally, these would be two male and two female characters belonging to the same group. Again ideally, they would ride on mounts, just as the grown-up former children do in their hunt for the White Stag.

It isn't hard to find the characters. The tiny Gallivespians operate in male-female pairs, and they ride mounts—three dragonflies and their leader's blue hawk. Although there is a whole army of Gallivespians, only four Gallivespians have names and play prominent roles in Pullman's story. Two are males, the other two are females. Moreover, three of the four explicitly belong to the nobility: Lord Roke, Chevalier Tialys (a chevalier is a French nobleman), and Lady Salmakia flaunt titles describing nobility. Madame Oxentiel outranks the chevalier and the lady, so she implicitly is also of noble rank. Lord Roke is one of Asriel's three high commanders. After he dies in a successful effort to save Lyra from the hair bomb, his companion, Madame Oxentiel, becomes the new high commander. These two senior (higher ranking) Gallivespians symbolize the crowned senior siblings: King Peter and Queen Susan. Tialys and Salmakia, the junior (lower ranking) Gallivespians, symbolize King Edmund and Queen Lucy, the two youngest siblings. The four mounts—three dragonflies and the blue hawk—symbolize the horses ridden by the four siblings.

Indirectly, the four Gallivespians also symbolize the Four

Horsemen of the Apocalypse, who the four mounted children-become-adults symbolize in C. S. Lewis's story. Whether Pullman is aware of Lewis's Four Horsemen symbolism is unknown, but the next symbol—Mary Malone—strongly implies that he is.

Mary Malone. One significant character from *LWW* has not yet been symbolized. That character is Narnia's White Stag, which is said to grant wishes and which leads the children back to the wardrobe. We saw that the White Stag is C. S. Lewis's symbol for the white Lamb of God from the book of Revelation. The Lamb plays a central role in administering the prophesied apocalypse that will culminate in the arrival on Earth of the Kingdom of God. Revelation identifies the Lamb as Jesus, who will share the throne with God. When the four siblings return through the wardrobe to the Professor's house, the apocalypse ends and the children enter the Kingdom of God and its capital, new Jerusalem.

Seeing that Pullman has provided symbols for everyone and everything else of significance, we can hardly doubt that Pullman has a White Stag symbol. The White Stag's main characteristics are that (1) he is white, (2) he leads the children somewhere, specifically, to the Kingdom of God, and (3) he does his good work at the end of the story. Looking for someone overtly white gets us nowhere: the only white characters are the two armored bears—Iorek and Iofur—whose "white" fur is actually yellowish and who are too busy playing the roles of Aslan (Iorek) and the White Witch (Iofur) to play the additional role of the stag.

We must therefore work with the last two characteristics. These do get us somewhere. Characteristic 2: the White Stag *leads* the grown children. So does Mary Malone, except that the children are just emerging into adulthood rather than being fully grown. Mary leads two children to love—and to knowledge. She does this by telling them the story of her first experience with love, which involved tasting marzipan, analogous to the Bible's Forbidden Fruit. When Lyra and Will taste the "sweet, thirst-quenching red fruits" that Mary has packed in their lunch, they fall in love.[33] In doing so, they acquire knowledge, knowledge of their sexuality, which results in their falling in love. So the "leads the children somewhere" analogy does apply to Mary. Mary leads the children to love. A supplemental analogy reinforces the "leads them" analogy. Both the Kingdom of God and love, the respective led-to destinations of the White Stag and Mary, can be characterized as states of bliss.

Does the stag's third characteristic, involvement at the end of the story, also apply? No and yes. Mary is introduced early in the second book of the trilogy, *The Subtle Knife* (*SK*), so she doesn't exactly appear at the end of the story. But her most significant action, playing the role of Genesis's serpent by tempting the coming-of-age youths to discover love, does come almost at the end of the story.

The above analogies do not by themselves constitute a strong case for the proposition that Mary Malone symbolizes the White Stag. But when we consider that Pullman surely must have a White Stag symbol—he is symbolizing just about everything—and that nobody else besides Mary is a suitable candidate, the theory that Mary symbolizes the White Stag strengthens. The theory gets even more vigor from the possibility that Pullman chose the name Mary because of its association with a certain "little lamb [whose] fleece was white as snow." Lewis's White Stag symbolizes Revelation's Lamb of God, whose fleece (we can safely presume) "was white as snow." (Maybe the stag's first characteristic, whiteness, does point to Mary after all.) And when we get to the next symbol, Xaphania, it becomes apparent that Mary is an essential part of a trio of symbols— the four mounted Gallivespians, Mary, and Xaphania—that depict a sequential trio of C. S. Lewis symbols pointing to things from the book of Revelation: (1) the Four Horsemen of the Apocalypse, (2) the Lamb of God, and (3) the lamp in new Jerusalem.

In fact, there is a fourth analogy that further strengthens the tie between Mary and the events of Revelation. As the Lamb of God, the White Stag signifies that Revelation's apocalypse is tearing the world apart. And sure enough, in Pullman's story Mary's act of playing the serpent takes place while an apocalyptic battle between the forces of Asriel and the forces of Metatron is taking place.

Xaphania. Xaphania is the leader of Lord Asriel's angels. Along with Lord Roke, leader of the Gallivespians, and King Ogunwe, leader of the Africans, she is one of Asriel's three high commanders. Her appearance in several scenes and her general importance just about guarantee that she is a symbol. But a symbol for what? Three clues relate her to wisdom. The first is her name. "Xaphania" is clearly based on "Zephaniah," one of the books of the Old Testament. Pullman has (*a*) replaced Z with X, which has the Z sound when used as the first letter of a word, as in "Xerox," (*b*) replaced *e* with *a*, and (*c*) dropped Zephaniah's silent last letter, *h*. Zephaniah is one of the Old Testament's twelve so-called minor prophets. He has no special significance, but the prophets in general were regarded as sources of wisdom. So Zephaniah is an appropriate symbol for wisdom.

The second clue is that Xaphania actually is a font of wisdom. She is, in fact, wisdom-conscious, as this remark of hers suggests: "All the history of human life has been a struggle between wisdom and stupidity [religion]."[34] Xaphania is apparently the wisest angel. Balthamos says that "one of those" angels—just one—who came after the Authority was "wiser" than the Authority and, when she deduced that the Authority was not the Creator, he banished her.[35] That banished angel was Xaphania. We know this because Balthamos then says, "We [Balthamos and Baruch] serve her still."[36] The angel they serve is Xaphania, the leader of the rebel angels, the one and only angel who was wiser than the Authority. Further evidence of Xaphania's wisdom is that she advocates "gaining wisdom and passing it on."[37] Pullman is repeatedly associating the word "wisdom" with her name: she is one of the "followers of wisdom."[38]

The third clue, and the strongest, is that Pullman himself, in his interview with Tony Watkins, seems to connect Xaphania to Sophia, the ancient goddess of wisdom. Explaining his *HDM* mythology, Pullman describes what happened after the first angel, the Authority, formed out of Dust: "As more time went on and more [angels] arose, one of them was *wiser* than him, [who] the early Church and, indeed, the writer of the Old Testament book of Proverbs, knows as wisdom,

Sophia."[39] The angel known in some circles as Sophia, explains Pullman, found out that the Authority was not the Creator and led a rebellion against the Authority. As a result, "she was thrown out of" Heaven.[40] This was the first rebellion against the Authority, the one that preceded Asriel's.

The angel Pullman calls Sophia in the interview sounds almost exactly like Xaphania. In *AS* the angel Balthamos tells Will that the female angel who came after the Authority was wiser than the Authority. She "found out the truth, so he banished her."[41] Let's compare Sophia and Xaphania. Sophia was a wise female early angel who "was thrown out of" Heaven because she found out the truth about the Authority, and Xaphania was a wise female early angel who was "banished" from Heaven because she found out the truth about the Authority. What's the difference? Xaphania can't be a successor to an earlier angel named Sophia, because Balthamos says the original banished angel, the *one* (not one of two) who was wiser than the Authority, is the one he serves. To repeat: "We serve her [the original banished angel] still."

If Xaphania is Sophia under another name, and Sophia is wisdom personified, then Xaphania is wisdom personified. And if this is so, she might be the last character piece in our *LWW* puzzle. That piece is the lamppost that the four siblings find at the entrance to the wardrobe, which leads to the Professor's house, the Kingdom of God. We have seen that, in Revelation, the Lamb of God—both a title and a metaphor for Jesus—becomes a figurative lamp lighting new Jerusalem, the capital of the Kingdom of God. Wisdom can also be construed as a figurative lamp. Wisdom is the lamp that guides our lives, or at least that should guide our lives. (Many people use "the Word of God" as a substitute for wisdom.) So it looks as though Pullman intends that Xaphania, or wisdom, symbolize the lamppost in *LWW*, which symbolizes a different figurative lamp, the one in Revelation.

There can be little doubt that Xaphania represents wisdom, but the connection between wisdom and C. S. Lewis's lamppost needs strengthening. A strong argument supporting the lamppost interpretation is that, if Xaphania is not a lamp of wisdom that symbolizes *LWW*'s lamp of divine wisdom, the *LWW* lamppost has no symbol. It is hard to believe that Pullman, who has symbolized everything else of consequence in *LWW*, would leave something as conspicuous as the lamppost unsymbolized. Another argument for the lamppost interpretation is that Xaphania's big scene comes at the right place. The timing is right. After Lyra and Will fall in love—after Mary (the White Stag) has led them to the state of bliss (the Kingdom of God)—Xaphania appears before them to dispense her wisdom.

But the really convincing argument, the one that leaves absolutely no doubt, is that Xaphania is literally light, brilliant light. When she appears to the children, they are alerted by their daemons. Their eyes turn to the sky. "A *light* was moving toward them: a light with wings."[42] A lamppost is also a light. One light symbolizes another.

The Palmerian Professor and the Cassington Scholar. Two more symbols, though not allegorical ones, warrant our attention. The Palmerian Professor is one of the functionaries who meet with Lord Asriel in the Retiring Room shortly after Lyra foils the Master's attempt to poison Asriel. Now we see Pullman's sense of humor as its best: the Palmerian Professor—Professor Trelawney—symbolizes Philip Pullman. Pullman has decided to insinuate himself into the story as a sort of joke on C. S. Lewis: the atheist enemy is operating under cover in Christendom, hobnobbing there with God and Winston Churchill (symbolized in Pullman's story by the Master of Jordan and Asriel). Can we be sure about this? Five considerations leave no room for reasonable doubt.

1. Palmerian Professor and Philip Pullman both have the initials PP. We all know our own initials too well to fail to recognize them when they show up elsewhere, especially if that "elsewhere" is a name or title we made up. Pullman deliberately gave the Palmerian Professor his own initials.

2. Pullman's alma mater is Exeter College of Oxford University. Exeter's oldest building and its distinctive landmark is

Palmer's Tower. "Palmerian" alludes to Palmer's Tower and Exeter, signifying that the Palmerian Professor is affiliated with Exeter, or at any rate with the Oxford college that in Lyra's world is the equivalent of Exeter—Jordan College. Both Pullman and the Palmerian Professor are tied to Exeter.

3. The Palmerian Professor is the leading authority on armored bears in Lyra's world, just as Philip Pullman is the leading authority on armored bears in our world. Nobody in our world knows more about armored bears than Pullman. He invented them, and he can create new details on demand.

4. In *Lyra's Oxford*, the book-format short story Pullman has written as a sequel to *HDM*, there is a fold-out insert that is a mock tourist map of the town of Oxford in Lyra's world. The map has advertising on the back. One ad is a book publisher's. The ad lists a book by Professor P. Trelawney. Can anyone seriously doubt that the P stands for Philip?

5. At the end of the trilogy, on his acknowledgments page at the back of *AS*, Pullman says he has stolen ideas from every book he has ever read. If we take "stolen" literally, we see that Pullman is facetiously accusing himself of plagiarism. Pullman, according to Pullman, is a plagiarist. And so is the Palmerian Professor. Anyhow, Professor Jotham Santelia, who shares a cell with Lyra after she is captured by the armored bears, calls the Palmerian Professor a plagiarist. One plagiarist symbolizes another. This symbolism is reinforced by its irrelevance to the plot. What is the point of Santelia's accusing the Palmerian Professor of plagiarism? As far as the plot is concerned, there is no point. The remark is purely gratuitous. It sheds no light on anything. The subject never comes up again. The only plausible explanation for Pullman's having Santelia accuse Trelawney of plagiarism is to deliver an ever-so-subtle joke: Philip Pullman is the "plagiarist," the man who stole the name Trelawney from Robert Louis Stevenson's *Treasure Island*. (Squire John Trelawney is the

man who organizes the expedition to the island where the buried treasure lies.)

If you remain skeptical that the Palmerian Professor symbolizes Philip Pullman, consider the initials of the Cassington Scholar, another person attending the meeting in the Retiring Room. His initials are C. S. Those initials identify C. S. Lewis. He was a scholar at Oxford, and Cassington is a good proxy for Oxford: Cassington is a village a few miles northwest of Oxford. Were PP and CS not in the same room, skepticism about the symbolism in CS would be well placed. But given the allegorical connection between *HDM* and *LWW*, hence also between Philip Pullman and C. S. Lewis, we can be reasonably confident that, as a private joke, Pullman is symbolically fraternizing with Lewis. (Because the Palmerian Professor and the Cassington Scholar, viewed as respective symbols for Philip Pullman and C. S. Lewis, do not refer to *LWW* characters, I will not count them as *LWW* symbols at the end of this chapter.)

OTHER SYMBOLS REFERRING TO THE LEWIS STORY

We have looked at the setting's features and the characters that symbolize things from *LWW*. Now we need to look at a prophecy, a "law," a place, and three events in the Pullman surface story. These items symbolize analogous things in the C. S. Lewis story.

The Prophecy about Lyra. When John Faa, Farder Coram, and the rest of the gyptians arrive with Lyra at Trollesund, the main port in the Lapland area of Norroway (counterpart of our world's Norway), they visit the witch consul, Dr. Lanselius. (The name resembles Lancelot, with *s* substituted for *c*. Lancelot means "servant." Dr. Lanselius is a servant of the witches. Does this explain where the name comes from?) From Lanselius they learn certain things about the witches, the kidnaped children, and an armored bear living in the town. More important, they learn of a prophecy about Lyra. "The witches have talked about this child for centuries past," says Lanselius. She "has a great destiny that can only be fulfilled elsewhere—not in this world, but far beyond. Without this child, we shall all die."[43]

Considerably later, after the intercised children at Bolvangar have been rescued, Lee Scoresby is flying Lyra toward Svalbard in his balloon; Serafina Pekkala is flying on her cloud-pine branch alongside the balloon's basket. While Lyra sleeps, Lee and Serafina converse. The witch relates some strange information: "There is a curious prophecy about this child: she is destined to bring about the end of destiny. But she must do so without knowing what she is doing, as if it were her nature and not her destiny to do it."[44]

The witches prophecy about Lyra symbolizes the Narnian prophecy about the two Sons of Adam and two Daughters of Eve who will sit on the four thrones at Cair Paravel. The two prophecies are similar in nature. Each involves bringing something evil to an end. The Narnia prophecy says that the four siblings are destined to bring to an end the reign of the evil White Witch.

The prophecy about Lyra refers to a threatened "destiny" that happens to be the disappearance of all knowledge (Dust) from the multitude of worlds. If knowledge disappears, intelligent life will disappear ("we shall all die").

The Magical Law of Death. People from Pullman's worlds cannot live in worlds other than their own for more than about ten years. After ten years in another world, a person sickens and dies, possibly after a year or two of decline.[45] We might call this phenomenon the Magical Law of Death. (The terminology is not Pullman's.) Will and Lyra learn about this law from the ghost of Will's father, John Parry, who is known as Stanislaus Grumman in Lyra's world. After ten years in Lyra's world, John Parry became seriously ill; he was near death when he was killed by an arrow launched by Juta Kamainen, a witch whose love he had scorned. The Magical Law of Death is the reason that, at the end of the story, Lyra cannot go to live in Will's world. If she does, she can have only ten years or so of happiness; then she will die. The same fate awaits Will if he goes to live in Lyra's world.

Narnia also has a law calling for a person's death. The Narnia law is called Deep Magic. Deep Magic gives the witch the right to kill any traitor. The White Witch invokes the Deep Magic to claim the right to take Edmund's life: Edmund has betrayed his siblings. Aslan accepts the Deep Magic but trades his life for Edmund's. Does *HDM*'s Magical Law of Death symbolize Narnia's Deep Magic? The Magical Law of Death calls for the death of anyone who, figuratively speaking, betrays his world by leaving it. This analogy strongly suggests that the Magical Law of Death symbolizes Narnia's Deep Magic.

The Experimental Station at Bolvangar. Much of *GC* deals with the gyptians' expedition to Bolvangar to rescue the children, many of them gyptian, who have been kidnaped by the Gobblers. Before the rescue party can reach Bolvangar, Lyra is kidnaped by Samoyed hunters. They sell her to men from Bolvangar, agents of Mrs. Coulter and her Gobblers. Soon Lyra is at Mrs. Coulter's Experimental Station at Bolvangar, a captive of the Gobblers. She quickly learns what is going on there. Mrs. Coulter's silver guillotine is being used to separate the kidnaped children from their daemons through the process called intercision.

This dirty work, presided over by Mrs. Coulter, the White Witch symbol, makes it easy to deduce what the Experimental Station symbolizes. It symbolizes the witch's castle. The intercised children are the stone statues Edmund sees in the castle's courtyard—the creatures the witch has turned to stone. And the silver guillotine? It is another symbol for the witch's magic wand, previously symbolized by the poison used to kill Boreal-Latrom.

After the children are rescued, Lyra herself is rescued from Mrs. Coulter, who has briefly recaptured her. Iorek and Lee Scoresby free Lyra, and Lee carries Lyra and Iorek off in his balloon. The good witch Serafina Pekkala soon comes alongside the balloon and fills them in on the details of the gyptian attack on the Experimental Station. "The gyptians have laid waste to Bolvangar," says Serafina. "They have killed twenty-two guards and nine of the staff, and they've set light to every part of the buildings that still stood."[46] Pullman is now symbolizing the ransacking and gate-smashing of the witch's castle by Aslan and the restored-to-life creatures.

The Visit to the Wine Cellars. One day while playing, Lyra inveigles Roger into sneaking down to the wine cellars below the Jordan College kitchen. She has pilfered the butler's spare set of keys for this purpose. Wandering through underground vaults, they inspect the wine bottles and choose one to open. They sip from it. Lyra dislikes the taste, but they keep on sipping because the wine gives them a good feeling inside. Soon both Lyra and Roger are drunk.

Here Pullman is reenacting the hiding hole episode from *LWW*, the time when Mr. Beaver takes the children through a hole in the riverbank into an underground cave. Lyra now symbolizes both Lucy and Susan. Roger symbolizes Peter, the only boy in the episode. (Edmund is off with the witch.) The underground wine vaults symbolize the underground "hiding hole" where the Beavers and the three siblings stop to rest. (Pullman later uses the secret compartment under Ma Costa's bunk to resymbolize the hiding hole.) The wine bottle is Mrs. Beaver's flask. The wine symbolizes the alcoholic beverage in the flask. The bad taste of the wine symbolizes the stinging feeling the siblings feel in their throats. And by getting drunk on the wine, Lyra and Roger do roughly the same thing the children did after drinking Mrs. Beaver's "wine." The children fell asleep.

Note that Peter has now been symbolized by three separate Pullman characters in three separate scenes. In the scene where Lyra and Roger drink wine in the wine cellar, which symbolizes the hiding hole, Roger symbolizes Peter. In the scene where Balthamos kills Father Gomez to save Lyra's life, Balthamos symbolizes Peter, who is saving Susan's life by slaying her attacker, the wolf Maugrim. And in the scenes involving the four Gallivespians, who ride their three dragonflies and one blue hawk, Lord Roke (who rides the blue hawk) symbolizes grown-up King Peter, who is riding his horse in search of the

White Stag: the senior male Gallivespian symbolizes the senior male among the four siblings.

Breaking and Mending the Knife. When Will tries to rescue Lyra from the cave where she is being held in a drugged stupor by Mrs. Coulter, Coulter seems to cast a momentary spell on Will. He looks at Coulter but sees the image of his mother. This causes the subtle knife to break: the knife refuses to be used as a weapon against its bearer's mother. With Will disarmed, Mrs. Coulter temporarily seizes control. Later, after Lyra and Will have escaped from Mrs. Coulter and other adversaries, the children persuade Iorek to apply his armor-making skills to the task of mending the knife. Despite strong misgivings ("They should not have made that knife"), Iorek mends the knife.[47] The breaking and mending of the knife are a pair of events that shout "Symbolism! Symbolism!" These events do nothing to advance the plot. Yes, Will's becoming disarmed does give two Gallivespians a chance to display their combat talents, but Mrs. Coulter has a gun that could just as effectively disarm Will. The knife needn't break for plot reasons. So we must look for symbolism.

But what could be symbolized? The thing that immediately comes to mind, of course, is the breaking of the Stone Table when Aslan's death is "reversed": one breaking symbolizes the other. But this interpretation has three flaws. First, Aslan's overcoming death—the "breaking" of death—has already been symbolized by Iorek's regaining his armor, which is his soul. Second, the timing is way out of kilter. Aslan comes back to life in the middle of book 1, *GC*; the knife breaks about one-third of the way through book 3, *AS*. Third, Iorek, symbolizing Aslan, is not present when the knife breaks, whereas in *LWW* Aslan *is* present when the Stone Table breaks.

Despite these flaws, no better explanation of the knife's breaking exists. Just as Will's being used to symbolize the mice who nibble away the cords that bind Aslan is duplicatory and way out of sequence, the knife's breaking is duplicatory and way out of sequence: the symbolism is definitely not the best. But the breaking of the knife nonetheless does appear to symbolize the breaking of the Stone Table, which in turn symbolizes the breaking open of Jesus's rock tomb—the rolling away of the stone that seals the tomb. The knife, whose two edges include one that cuts anything, is an ideal symbol of death. In fact, Will later (after the knife is mended) uses the knife to kill cliff-ghasts and Specters.[48] The knife signifies death. So the breaking of the knife can symbolize the breaking of death, which is what happens when the Stone Table breaks.

This symbolism definitely duplicates Pullman's earlier resurrection symbolism—but only a previously unsymbolized aspect of Aslan's resurrection. The earlier symbolism was based on the concept that a bear's armor is his soul. Iorek died, metaphorically at least, when he lost his armor, because when a person dies his soul departs from his body. When Iorek later regained his armor—his soul—he metaphorically came back to life. Why, then, did Pullman decide to resymbolize Aslan's already symbolized resurrection? The answer may be that Pullman wanted a broken knife that could be mended. This explanation comes from *Washington Post* book reviewer Michael Dirda. He observes that the mending of the subtle knife echos Siegfried's mending of the sword in Wagner's "Ring of the Nibelungs."[49] Iorek's mending of Will's broken knife, in other words, is some gratuitous nonallegorical symbolism.

Lyra's Return to Jordan College. The last thing the siblings do in *LWW* is return through the wardrobe to the Professor's house, which symbolizes the Kingdom of God. In Pullman's allegory, the intermediate world of Cittàgazze symbolizes the wardrobe, the passage between worlds. (Pullman, we saw, has two wardrobe symbols: the wardrobe in the Jordan College Retiring Room and the world of Cittàgazze.) Since Jordan College in Lyra's world represents the *LWW* Professor's house, Lyra's return to Jordan College represents the return of the siblings to the Professor's house. In the return-to-the-house symbolism, Lyra represents all four children—Lucy, Edmund, Susan, and Peter.

In *LWW* the children reenter the wardrobe right after they pass the lamppost. Similarly, at the end of *HDM*, Lyra returns to the world of

Cittàgazze (the wardrobe) very soon after she meets Xaphania, who symbolizes the lamppost. Pullman offers no surface story rationalization for returning via Cittàgazze. True, Lyra wants a last look at Will's world, but she and Will and Mary could have gone there directly from the *mulefa* world. The reason Pullman sends them via Cittàgazze is that he needs to symbolize the *LWW* siblings' return to the Professor's house via the wardrobe. Lyra's return to Cittàgazze symbolizes the siblings' reentering the wardrobe at the end of the story.

Following an irrelevant side-trip into Will's world, from which Lyra returns to Cittàgazze, she and the gyptians return to her world and to Oxford. The four siblings have returned to the Professor's house.

REVIEW OF THE SYMBOLS

Fully 104 symbols representing persons, things, events, and the like in *LWW* have emerged in *HDM*. The surface story symbol is a character (a person or creature) or a group of characters in the following 41 symbols:

1. Ruta Skadi, the witch = Air Chief Marshall Hugh Dowding of the RAF
2. The witches of Ruta Skaki's clan and cooperating clans = RAF pilots
3. Lord Asriel = Winston Churchill
4. Metatron = German Reichsmarshall Hermann Goering
5. Metatron's angels = the Luftwaffe, or Nazi Germany's air force
6. The Authority = Adolf Hitler
7. The Master of Jordan = the kindly Professor
8. The Master's housekeeper, Mrs. Lonsdale = the Professor's housekeeper, Mrs. Macready, who *makes* the Professor's house *ready*

9– 11. The Master's three servants—steward, butler, and porter = the Professor's three servants—Ivy, Margaret, and Betty

12. Lyra = Lucy, who visits Tumnus

13. Tony Makarios = Edmund, who is ensnared by the witch

14. Lyra (again) = Susan, who goes up in a tree

15. Roger = Peter, in the underground scene where he drinks from Mrs. Beaver's flask

16. Balthamos = Peter, represented by a second symbol, in the scene where he saves Susan by slaying Maugrim

17. Boreal-Latrom = Tumnus, the part-human, part-goat faun

18. Mrs. (Marisa) Coulter = the White Witch in most witch scenes

19. Mrs. Coulter's golden monkey daemon = the dwarf, the witch's servant

20. Serafina Pekkala = the robin, who leads the children to the Beavers

21. John Faa = Mr. Beaver

22. Ma Costa = Mrs. Beaver

23. The children before being intercised at the Experimental Station = the little creatures having a tea party

24. The children after intercision at the Experimental Station = the stone statues (dead creatures) in the witch's courtyard

25. Lee Scoresby, the balloonist = Father Christmas (Santa Claus, traveling in the sky)

26. The other witches from Serafina's clan who tow Lee's balloon = the reindeer who pull Father Christmas's sledge (Santa's sleigh)

27. Iorek, the good bear = Aslan, the lion

28. Father Gomez = Maugrim, Captain of the witch's Secret Police

29. The *tualapi* (huge white sailing birds) = Maugrim's Secret Police

30. The spy-fly that escapes after seeing Lyra = the witch's spy-wolf

31. The cliff-ghasts = the witch's horde of ghastly creatures

32. The netmen who ensnare Iorek = the witch's followers who bind Aslan with cords

33. Will (when slashing the net that entraps Iorek) = the mice who nibble away the cords that bind Aslan

34. Iofur, the bad bear = the witch in the scene where she dies fighting Aslan

35. Lady Salmakia (the Gallivespian) on her dragonfly = grown-up Lucy on horseback

36. Chevalier Tialys on his dragonfly = grown-up Edmund on horseback

37. Madame Oxentiel on her dragonfly = grown-up Susan on horseback

38. Lord Roke on his blue hawk = grown-up Peter on horseback

39. The three dragonflies plus the blue hawk = the four horses ridden by the siblings

40. Mary Malone = the White Stag

41. Xaphania = the lamppost at the Narnia entrance to the wardrobe

In addition to the characters, Pullman uses as symbols sixty-three surface story places, things, events, and the like.

1. The aerial battle between the witches and Metatron's angels = the Battle of Britain (the German bombing of London), which is the reason the children have been sent to live with the Professor during World War II

2. The eight witch clans attacking the angels = RAF squadrons

3. The witches' cloud-pine branches = British Spitfire and Hurricane fighters

4. The witchs' act of diving on the angels = the fighters' diving on German bombers

5. The witchs' flaming torches = the flaming machine guns of the Spitfires and Hurricanes

6. The screams of angels going down in flames = the screaming sound bombers make when plummeting to earth in flames

7. Metatron's angels' spears and swords = the German bombs raining down on London

8. Jordan College = the Professor's house

9. The Retiring Room = the room with the wardrobe

10. The wardrobe in the Retiring Room = the wardrobe in the Professor's house

11. Lyra's hiding in the wardrobe = Lucy's hiding in the wardrobe during a game of hide-and-seek (the second time she enters the wardrobe)

12. Cittàgazze's world = another symbol for the wardrobe in the Professor's house (a gateway between Lyra's world and Will's world)

13. Lyra's going from her world to Will's via Cittàgazze's world = Lucy's going from the Professor's house to Narnia via the wardrobe (the first time she enters the wardrobe)

14. Lyra's adventures = the siblings' adventures in Narnia

15. That part of Lyra's world lying outside of Jordan College = Narnia

16. Boreal-Latrom's two identities = Tumnus's two identities (half goat, half man)

17. Charles Latrom's inviting Lyra to visit him = Tumnus's inviting Lucy to his cave home

18. Latrom's home in Will's world = Tumnus's cave home

19. Mrs. Coulter's sledge = the witch's sledge (sleigh)

20. The chocolatl drink Mrs. Coulter uses to entrap Tony Makarios = the hot drink + Turkish Delight candy the witch uses to lure Edmund into her clutches

21. Tony's being a thief, a sinner = Edmund's being a liar and a traitor, a sinner

22. The witches' prophecy about Lyra = the Narnia prophecy about the four thrones

23. Serafina Pekkala's ability to fly = the robin's ability to fly

24. Iofur's pretending to be human = the witch's pretending to be human

25. The Experimental Station at Bolvangar = the witch's castle

26. Mrs. Coulter's poisoning Boreal-Latrom = the witch's turning Tumnus into stone

27. The poison that kills Boreal-Latrom = the witch's magic wand

28. Ma Costa's houseboat ("narrowboat") = Mr. and Mrs. Beaver's house

29. The Grand Junction Canal = the path along the river that the Beavers follow to take the children to Aslan

30. The trip from where the houseboat was tied up to Trollesund, where Iorek is = the trip from the Beaver's house to the Stone Table, where Aslan is

31. The wine cellars under the Jordan College kitchen = the underground "hiding hole" cave where the Beavers and siblings stop to sleep

32. The wine bottle Lyra and Roger drink from = Mrs. Beaver's flask

33. The wine Lyra and Roger drink = the alcoholic beverage the three siblings (all but Edmund) drink when Mrs. Beaver passes her flask around in the hiding hole

34. Lyra's and Roger's getting drunk on the wine = the siblings' falling asleep after drinking an alcoholic beverage from Mrs. Beaver's flask

35. Mrs. Coulter's intercising the children = the witch's turning the tea partying creatures into stone

36. The silver guillotine = the witch's magic wand (elsewhere symbolized by the poison Mrs. Coulter uses to kill Boreal-Latrom), which turns people into stone

37. Lee Scoresby's balloon = Father Christmas's sledge (Santa's sleigh)

38. Father Gomez's attack on Lyra = Maugrim's attack on Susan

39. Lyra's going up in the air in Lee Scoresby's balloon = Susan's climbing up into a tree with her gift horn when Maugrim attacks

40. Lyra's alethiometer, which she takes with her when she goes up in the balloon = Lucy's gift horn, a proxy for Father

Christmas (who gave it to her), which she takes with her when she is attacked and forced to go up into a tree

41. Balthamos's killing Father Gomez = Peter's killing Maugrim

42. The natural law saying a person must die about ten years after "betraying" their home world by leaving it = the Deep Magic calling for death of traitors such as Edmund

43. The subtle knife, a source of death = the Stone Table (tomb of Jesus), representing death

44. Iorek's being separated from his armor, his soul = both (*a*) Aslan's death, or separation from his soul, and (*b*) Aslan's being separated from his fur when he is shaved just before he is killed

45. The steel-strong net the riders use to "tie" Iorek = the cords the witch's rabble use to bind Aslan

46. Will's cutting away the net that binds Iorek = the mice's gnawing away the ropes that bind Aslan

47. The breaking of the knife = the breaking of the Stone Table

48. Iorek's regaining his armor, his soul = Aslan's resurrection from death, or becoming reunited with his soul

49. Iorek's climbing up out of the priest's cellar, armor-clad again = Aslan's getting up from the Stone Table (a secondary symbol of Aslan's resurrection)

50. Lyra's witnessing Iorek's climbing out of the cellar with his armor = Lucy's and Susan's witnessing Aslan's resurrection

51. The rescue of the children (including the restoration of their daemon-souls) at the Experimental Station = Aslan's restoring the stone statues to life (restoring their souls)

52. The gyptian's destroying the Experimental Station = Aslan's army's ransacking the witch's castle and tearing down its gate

53. Lyra's riding on Iorek's back to where Tony Makarios is dying = Lucy's and Susan's riding on Aslan's back to where Edmund lies mortally wounded after being stabbed by the witch

54. Tony's separation from his daemon (soul), "Ratter" =

Edmund's being mortally wounded, near death (with his soul starting to depart)

55. Lyra's placing a coin inscribed "Ratter" in Tony's mouth = Lucy's pouring her life-saving cordial into Edmund's mouth (returning Edmund's soul to him)

56. The "Ratter" coin, first meaning = Lucy's cordial

57. The "Ratter" coin, second meaning = Edmund's soul, in need of restoration

58. Tony's symbolic regaining of his soul (the coin) = Edmund's miraculous recovery

59. Iorek's killing Iofur = Aslan's killing the White Witch

60. Mary's leading Lyra and Will to love (a state of bliss) = the White Stag's leading the four siblings back to the Professor's (God's) house, which symbolizes the Kingdom of God (a place of bliss)

61. Xaphania's being "a *light* with wings" = the lamppost's being a light

62. Lyra's last visit to the Cittàgazze world before going home = the return of the four siblings to the wardrobe after passing the lamppost

63. Lyra's return to Jordan College = the return of the four siblings to the Professor's house

CHAPTER 5

PARADISE LOST RETOLD

The Hidden Story and Its Themes

The second allegory is the main one, the one where Pullman really gets down to business. This allegory delivers a powerful antireligious message that (*a*) describes the warfare between knowledge and religious superstition and (*b*) emphasizes the falseness of the most basic Christian superstition, the one that promises believers "salvation," or a blissful "eternal life" in Heaven after they die, provided that they have earned the right to be "saved." Most of the material in this allegory comes from John Milton's literary classic *Paradise Lost* (*PL*), which is loosely based on the Bible's books of Genesis and Revelation. Genesis tells the story of Adam and Eve, their eating the Forbidden Fruit from the Tree of Knowledge, and God's expelling them from the Garden of Eden; Revelation offers the story of Satan's abortive revolt against God, the apocalyptic events that follow, Satan's being thrown into a bottomless pit by an angel, and the climactic arrival on Earth of the Kingdom of God and its capital, new Jerusalem. But Pullman goes well beyond these two sources, throwing in material from other parts of the Bible, including the New Testament Gospels, and from Christian creeds, theology, gnosticism, and legend.

This chapter will (1) summarize Milton's *Paradise Lost*, (2) narrate the hidden story that the surface story's symbols will tell, (3) explain Pullman's broad theme of society's warfare between knowledge and religious superstition, and (4) explain Pullman's narrower theme that there is no Heaven—a specific superstition. The next chapter will interpret the bulk of Pullman's symbolism by explaining (5) the hidden story's setting, (6) the surface story characters used as symbols, and (7) places, things, and events used as symbols.

PARADISE LOST SUMMARIZED

In the tradition of epic poetry, John Milton's *Paradise Lost* (*PL*), which tells how Adam and Eve lose Paradise, does not begin at the beginning. It begins with Satan lying in Hell on a lake of fire. He fell there after being shoved out of Heaven by Jesus. It isn't until book V of twelve "books" (chapters) that the reader learns how the story began. Pullman, in contrast, does begin his *PL* allegory at the beginning, so that is where this summary will likewise begin.

At the outset, Lucifer, later renamed Satan, is the highest angel in Heaven, second only to God. Then God creates a son, Jesus, and appoints him the new leader of the angels; all angels must "confess him Lord."[1] Filled with jealousy, Lucifer gathers the angels loyal to him—one-third of all the angels in Heaven—and retreats to his "quarters of the North,"[2] which is a palace. There he plots against God. Only one of Lucifer's angels, Abdiel, opposes the plot. Unable to enlist any support, Abdiel departs and reports the plot to God.

Lucifer begins his war against God. God appoints the angels Michael and Gabriel to lead his loyal angels in the war against Lucifer. Early in the battle, Michael tries to kill Lucifer by splitting him open with a sword. Lucifer, being an angel, doesn't die. He quickly recovers and returns to battle the next day. Soon the fighting gets rather messy, so God sends Jesus out to cast Lucifer, now called Satan, out of Heaven. This Jesus does, unassisted. He drives his mighty chariot at Satan's forces with the roar of ten thousand thunders. Heaven's crystal wall opens wide, creating a gap through which Satan's frightened legions go tumbling down to a burning lake in Hell.

The next thing you know, Satan and his fallen angels, now called demons, are lying on the lake of fire. After a while, Satan decides this isn't the life he wants to lead, so he confers with his second in command, Beelzebub. They decide to break the chains that bind them and to fly to the shore. There Satan calls his other demons to join him, which they do. Before long, they have built a city, Pandemonium, Satan's capital.

Satan calls a meeting of his lieutenants to decide what to do next. He knows of a prophecy that God is about to create a new place and a new race to live there; the race is called *Man*. Wouldn't it be sweet revenge to go to this place, Earth, and corrupt God's new creation? Satan appoints himself to take on the task. He flies to the gates of Hell, which are guarded by Sin and Death. These two creatures happen to be Satan's daughter (Sin) and son (Death). Sin popped out of Satan's head in Heaven when Satan became jealous of Jesus; Death was conceived when Satan raped Sin.

Satan persuades Sin to open the gates. He then begins a torturous journey across the seething maelstrom separating Hell and Earth. He soon encounters Chaos and Night, who reign over this realm. Chaos tells him of another world above that hangs suspended from Heaven on a golden chain. Satan continues on to the new world, Earth. Sin and Death will later follow Satan's track, paving "a bridge of wondrous length" from Hell to Earth.[3]

God sees Satan moving toward Earth and discusses the situation with Jesus. God's omniscience allows him to see that Satan will corrupt man. Man will be to blame, because God created him with free will with which to resist temptation. But, because Man will be seduced by Satan rather than violating God's will out of malice, God is willing to extend grace to Man. He is willing, that is, if someone else is willing to be punished in Man's place. Jesus volunteers. While God and Jesus are conferring, Satan finds stairs leading to Heaven. Disguising himself as a cherub, he climbs the stairs and encounters the angel Uriel. Uriel points to Paradise, where Adam dwells in the world below. Also called the Garden of Eden, Paradise is on top of Mount Niphates. Satan goes to Niphates.

Eden is surrounded by a wall that has only one gate; Gabriel guards the gate. No problem: Satan leaps over the wall, unseen. He finds and spies upon Adam and Eve. From their conversation, Satan learns that God has forbidden the humans to eat the fruit of the Tree of Knowledge. He decides to seduce them into eating the Forbidden Fruit. Meanwhile, Uriel belatedly realizes that the cherub was no cherub. He warns Gabriel, who sends angels to search for Satan. They find him squatting like a toad by Eve's ear, speaking to her dreams. The angels bring Satan to Gabriel. Satan is contentious, but a sign from Heaven persuades him to flee.

When Adam and Eve wake up in the morning, Eve tells Adam of her dream. In it an angel brought her to the Tree of Knowledge, plucked and tasted its fruit, described it as seemingly fit only for gods "yet able to make gods of men."[4] Enticed, Eve in her dream tasted the fruit and then flew up to the clouds with the angel. Adam is bothered by Eve's story but decides that Eve is too pure for the dream to come true. God, watching from above, knows otherwise: he knows that the pair will eat the fruit. But, so as to intensify their ultimate guilt (or so it would seem), he sends the angel Raphael to warn them.

Raphael tells Adam and Eve that Satan will tempt them and that, because they have free will, they can either resist or yield to temptation. Raphael then tells them about their enemy and how he revolted against God and was cast into Hell. At Adam's request, Raphael goes on to tell how Man came into being. Having expelled Satan from Heaven, God took golden compasses (the kind you draw circles with) and used them to prepare the orbits of bodies that would revolve around a new world. He then sent Jesus to create the earth and its contents in six days. Afterward Jesus returned to Heaven.

Satan stays away for eight days, then enters a sleeping serpent's body and returns. That day, Eve suggests to Adam that they can tend the Garden of Eden more efficiently by working apart. Adam reluctantly agrees, warning Eve of the danger of being found alone by Satan. Spying Eve, the serpent approaches, not slithering on the ground but moving upright on his tail. He speaks to the startled woman. Creatures don't speak: she asks how he learned to speak. The serpent replies that he learned by tasting the fruit of a certain tree. Asked by Eve to show her that tree, the serpent brings her to the Tree of Knowledge. Eve tells him its fruit is forbidden, but the serpent is persuasive. At last Eve yields and eats the fruit; it is delicious. Eve later tells Adam what she has done. He knows she is doomed but, out of love, resolves to perish with her: he too eats the fruit. *Having partaken of knowledge, they have thereby become sinners.* Both are suddenly aware of their nakedness and seek to cover it. Then they argue about who is responsible for their sinful condition.

God sends Jesus to Earth to sentence Adam and Eve for violating God's command not to eat the Forbidden Fruit. Somewhat irrationally, Jesus first sentences the innocent serpent, who did not consciously lend his body to Satan and whose body Satan no longer occupies. The serpent will henceforth crawl on its belly and eat dust. He next lays upon Eve two penalties: (1) bearing children in "sorrow"—this alludes to God's pain-of-childbirth penalty in Genesis 3:16—and (2) submitting to her husband's rule. Adam also receives two penalties: (1) having to labor in the dirt for food instead of plucking it freely from plants and (2) becoming mortal, subject to death: "For dust thou art, and shalt to dust return."[5]

Back in Hell, Sin and Death decide to leave. They follow Satan's track across Chaos and pave it, creating *a bridge* from Hell to Earth. (Look for that bridge in *HDM*.) Along the way they meet Satan, flying back to Hell. (He is still an angel and has wings.) He brags of his success, and his children congratulate him. Sin and Death continue on to Earth, where they will live and plague Man until Judgment Day. Then they will be cast into Hell, there to remain forever incarcerated.

Returning to Hell, Satan again boasts of his success to an audience of demons. But, rather than hearing the applause he expects, he hears a response of hisses. The demons, and Satan too, have been transformed into serpents. A grove of trees bearing fruit like the Forbidden Fruit springs up. The demon-serpents eagerly taste the fruit, expecting delicious flavor. But instead of fruit, they find themselves chewing bitter ashes.

Up in Heaven, God hears Adam and Eve pray for forgiveness. Jesus intercedes on behalf of the humans: he will sacrifice his own life if God will let repentant mortals dwell with God in Heaven after they die. God replies that, when he created Man, he endowed Man with two gifts—happiness and immortality. Man, as punishment for his sin, has been condemned to be mortal, but God will grant him happiness beyond the grave. At the same time, though, God shows more of his mean side. He dilutes Man's deferred restoration of happiness by decreeing more unhappiness before the grave: Man is to be thrown out of Paradise. God sends Michael and a band of subordinate angels to Paradise to expel Adam and Eve—whence the words, "Paradise Lost."

Michael goes to Paradise and delivers to Adam the bad news, and the good. Following instructions from God, Michael first plants at the gate of Paradise a flaming sword; it is supposed to frighten off anyone who approaches the garden. This task accomplished, he takes Adam to the top of the highest hill in Paradise. Michael is a loquacious angel and spends most of the rest of *PL* summarizing what will in the future be biblical history. Three future events are relevant to *HDM*. First, Michael says that one of two brothers, sons of Adam, will slay the other. Michael is referring, of course, to Cain's slaying of Abel, though the sons' names aren't mentioned. We learn from Michael an interesting detail not found in Genesis: Cain dispatches Abel by smiting Abel in the "midriff" (belly) with a rock.[6] (In *HDM*, Pullman uses this detail to help identify a certain character as his Cain symbol and another character as his Abel symbol.)

Second, Michael shows Adam all the world's future kingdoms, including the "empire of Negus."[7] Negus was a king who some Christians believed was the legendary Prester John, a priest-king-shaman who supposedly ruled over a prosperous empire in central Asia or Ethiopia. A prester is a priest, and Negus was an Ethiopian emperor. (One of Pullman's characters, a shaman whose first name is John, symbolizes Prester John.)

Third, Michael tells Adam that Jesus will come to atone for Man's sins, thereby annulling Adam's doom. After dying, Jesus will experience "resurrection" and "ascend" to Heaven, where he shall sit at the right hand of God. When "this world's dissolution shall be ripe," Jesus will return to Earth with power and glory "to judge both quick [the living] and dead [the resurrected dead]."[8] Milton is now describing Christianity's Second Coming of Jesus and its attendant Judgment Day, when the virtuous dead are released from ghostly incarceration and taken, along with the virtuous living, to Heaven. (Pullman symbolizes Judgment Day—the judging of the dead and the choosing of those who shall be redeemed—and likewise symbolizes their release to Heaven.)

When Michael is done talking, he and Adam return to Eve. Adam awakens Eve, who Michael earlier put in a state of sleep. Together, Adam and Eve depart from Paradise. Looking back, they see the sword's flames waving over the gate.

PARADISE LOST TURNED UPSIDE DOWN

The symbolism of this second allegory will be grasped more readily if the reader understands the general framework that supports the symbolic details. Accordingly, the exposition will begin, as it did for the first allegory, with a summary of the hidden story. In the first allegory the hidden story buried in the surface story was C. S. Lewis's *The Lion, the Witch and the Wardrobe* (*LWW*). The new hidden story, told in this second allegory, is a radically revised version of John Milton's *PL*. In this section we will look first at the general nature of the revision, which involves borrowing ideas from other sources, and then at the hidden story itself.

The Borrowed-Ideas Approach. It is no secret that Pullman has borrowed from John Milton's *PL* and from William Blake. In his "Acknowledgments" page at the end of the trilogy's third book, *The Amber Spyglass* (*AS*), Pullman writes, "I have stolen ideas from every book I have ever read." He names three authors—von Kleist, Milton, and Blake—from whom he has borrowed ideas, and he challenges his readers to find other examples of borrowings.

One such example can be found in the episode where Lyra explores the vaults where dead former Masters are buried below Jordan College. She finds the skulls of the dead Masters and, inside each skull, a bronze coin on which an emblem of the Master's daemon is inscribed. Deciding to play a trick on the dead, she switches three of the daemon-coins, putting them with the wrong skulls. That night, possibly in a dream (but maybe not), three "night-ghasts" (ghosts) appear at her bedside, throw back their hoods, and reveal bleeding stumps where their heads belong. The next morning Lyra goes back to the vaults, returns the switched coins to their original skulls, and apologizes to the skulls.[9]

It isn't hard to recognize these doings as a combination of three scenes from Charles Dickens's *A Christmas Carol*. Ebenezer Scrooge is being visited by the ghosts of Christmas Past, Christmas Present, and Christmas Yet to Come. The ghosts are concerned about what the miserly Scrooge has and has not been doing with coins, the coins accounted for in his counting-house. Pullman is also stealing from Greek mythology, in which the boatman Charon refuses to ferry any soul across the river Acheron unless that soul's human was buried with a coin (passage money) in its mouth. The coin-switching episode might even borrow from a third source: Washington Irving's famous story "The Legend of Sleepy Hollow," which features a "headless horseman" (only imagined to be headless) who pursues the hero-buffoon, Ichabod Crane.

Another example of borrowed ideas is the kidnaping of children by the Church's General Oblation Board. Its acronym, GOB, is for story purposes the source of the nickname "Gobblers" that people use when referring to the mysterious people who steal children. But the acronym isn't the real source. GOB was almost certainly concocted to exploit the concept of goblins—specifically, the Irish goblins who steal children. Goblins are small, evil or mischievous sprites, related to fairies, elves, brownies, and pixies and sometimes alternatively referred to as fairies. In Irish folklore, fairies and goblins were blamed for stealing the souls of children who inexplicably died during the night. *HDM*'s concept of stolen children has been "stolen" by Pullman from both William Butler Yeats's poem "The Stolen Child" and J. M. Barrie's *Peter Pan*. Yeats's poem includes these repeated lines:

> Come away, O human child!
> To the waters and the wild
> With a faery, hand in hand,
> For the world's more full of weeping
> Than you can understand.[10]

These words describe a fairy's enticing a sleeping child, or rather its soul, to "come away" to living death in fairyland—life in fairyland, death in the crib. Peter Pan does much the same thing when he lures the children off to Neverland, except that he returns the children unharmed. In some Irish folktales goblins substitute for the fairies in luring the children from their cribs and beds. And in Pullman's story, Mrs. Coulter substitutes for the goblins. "Goblins" is really where the name "Gobblers" comes from: Pullman took the GOB from "GOB-lins" and then worked backward to invent the name General Oblation Board as a story source for the nickname he had already decided to use.

A third example of borrowed ideas is Asriel's soldier-spies, the Gallivespians. They are clearly based on the Lilliputians of Jonathan Swift's *Gulliver's Travels*. Like Swift's Lilliputians, the Gallivespians are tiny people. The first seven letters of Gallivespian are identical to the first seven of Gulliver, except for the substitution of *a* for *u* as the first vowel. Letter substitution in borrowed names is a familiar Pullman technique: in chapter 4 we saw that the name *Xaphania* (yet another example of borrowing) is a respelling of the name of the Old Testament prophet Zephaniah, with the Greek initial *X* in Xaphania having the same *Z* sound as the *X* in Xerox. The last three letters of *Gallivespian* are the same as the last three letters of *Lilliputian*, so *Gallivespian* can be seen as a combination of *Gulliver* and *Lilliputian*—plus *vesp*, from the Latin *vespa*, meaning "wasp" (the Gallivespians sting).

The Gallivespian commander, Lord Roke, apparently takes his name from Ursula K. Le Guin's five-novel *Earthsea* fantasy series (1968–2001). The main character, a boy named Ged, travels to Roke Island to study magic. There he studies under the Warder of Roke and nine Masters of Roke. Lord Roke even provides a second literary allusion, one that is consistent with Pullman's penchant for creating humorous names. Roke is a flier: he flies around on his blue hawk. His subordinates are also fliers: they fly on huge dragonflies. Lord Roke is, in effect, the Lord of the Fliers. This surely alludes to William Golding's novel *Lord of the Flies*.

The venomous heel spurs of the Gallivespians are probably borrowed from Ian Fleming's James Bond novel (and the film) *From Russia with Love*. In this story Rosa Klebb, a Russian agent, tries to kill Bond by kicking him with the poisoned tip of a spring-loaded dagger projecting from the tip of her shoe.

Still another borrowed ideas example: Earlier we saw that the Palmerian Professor, one of several Jordan College faculty and staff members who meet with Lord Asriel in the Retiring Room, is Philip Pullman in disguise: his initials, PP, and four other pieces of evidence reveal his hidden identity. We also saw that the Palmerian Professor's last name, Trelawney, is borrowed—or stolen as Pullman would have it—from Robert Louis Stevenson's *Treasure Island*. (In the Harry Potter books Sybil Trelawney is a Professor of Divination at Hogwarts, but Pullman could not have borrowed from this source: Pullman's Trelawney appears in *The Golden Compass* (GC), published in 1995, whereas Sybil Trelawney first appears in the first Harry Potter book, *Harry Potter and the Sorcerer's Stone*, published in 1997, two years later.

Pullman might also have borrowed a detail of his mysterious Dust. Dust exists in two states, potential and actual (realized potentiality). In its potential state, Dust is the elementary particles that roam the sky. In its state of realized potentiality, Dust either coalesces into angels or settles on humans, who absorb it. These two states seem to echo the potential and actual states of Hegel's metaphysical Spirit. A more detailed discussion of the potential and actual states of Pullman's Dust and Hegel's Spirit appears later in this chapter and in a related end-note. The endnote shows how the Spirit fits into the context of Hegelian dialectics, wherein the Spirit progresses from (1) a *thesis* of "potential union" to (2) an *antithesis* of "actual separation," or self-estrangement, to (3) their *synthesis*, "actual union." (The synthesis combines one word from the thesis with one word from the antithesis.)

One other literary allusion not directly identified by Pullman is worth noting. Lee Scoresby's hare daemon, Hester, gets her name from Hester Prynne, the heroine of Nathaniel Hawthorne's novel *The Scarlet Letter*.

Proceeding with his acknowledgments, Pullman identifies "three debts that need acknowledgment above all the rest." Those debts are to (1) Heinrich von Kleist's 1810 essay "On the Marionette Theater," (2) John Milton's epic poem *Paradise Lost*, published in 1667, and (3) William Blake's works, the most relevant of which are his 1790 booklet *The Marriage of Heaven and Hell* and his poem "Milton" (referring to John Milton, the author of *PL*).

The von Kleist essay includes a fictional account of a boy of about sixteen who notices in a mirror a graceful motion he makes. In trying to repeat the motion, he loses his innocence and the grace. The boy is a model for Pullman's Lyra, who is able to read the alethiometer by grace but loses that grace—the ability to read the instrument—when she loses her innocence. Another salient feature of the essay is the tale of a fighting bear who, in a mock duel with a fencer armed with a foil, parries with his paw every true thrust and ignores the fake thrusts. This vignette inspired Pullman's account of Iorek's mock duel with Lyra, who is armed with a stick. In this duel, described earlier under the Iofur symbolism in the *LWW* allegory, Iorek proved that armored bears cannot be tricked.

Pullman's debt to Milton lies in the basic design of Pullman's *His Dark Materials* (*HDM*). *HDM* is a loosely structured retelling of *PL*—extreme variations on a theme, you might say. Countless reviews, articles, books, and Web newsgroup discussions about Pullman and *HDM* have pointed out the obvious: the Authority symbolizes God, and Lord Asriel symbolizes Satan, who is leading a rebellion against God, just as Satan led a rebellion against God in *PL*. What hasn't been publicized, because few if any people are aware of it, is that *HDM* contains far, far more *PL* material and related biblical and theological material than the widely recognized images of God and Satan. Think in terms of more than one hundred symbols, not just the Authority and Asriel.

If God, Satan, and maybe four or five other *PL* characters and things were all the symbolism there were, *HDM* would have no *PL* allegory. At best, it would have what is sometimes called allegorical tendency, or occasional allusion to the antecedent work or ideas. But *HDM* is actually loaded with Miltonian and biblical characters: Jesus, Judas, Abdiel (an underling of Satan's who remains loyal to God), Beelzebub (Satan's second in command), Satan's demons, Michael (the leader of God's loyal angels), Adam, Eve, Cain, Abel, the serpent in Eden, Sophia (the ancient goddess of wisdom), Charon (a boatman from Greek mythology), a fanatical Muslim suicide bomber, the Four Horsemen of the Apocalypse, Lapland witches, Prester John (a priest-king in Christian legend), Sin, Death, Chaos, and Night (the last four are personified by Milton). The things symbolized aren't limited to characters. Pullman also has symbols for Hell, Earth, Heaven, Satan's palace at "the limits of the North" in Heaven (*PL*, book V), Pandemonium (Satan's capital in Hell), Satan's bridge from Hell to Earth, Jesus's chariot (used to push Satan and his followers out of Heaven), Jesus's betrayal, the harrowing of Hell, Judgment Day, a famous gnostic passage from John, a passage from the Apostles' Creed, innocence, guilt (knowledge), the Tree of Knowledge, the Forbidden Fruit, the Temptation, the Fall, Adam's banishment from Eden, Cain's slaying of Abel, Cain's banishment to the land of Nod, churches, faith, religious superstition, and lots of other things. This richness of detail is the stuff of genuine, full-fledged allegory.

Blake was an English artist-poet who, in his self-published illustrated poems, brandished skepticism about Christianity and its teachings about sin, the soul, Heaven, and Hell. Pullman's chief debt to

Blake is Pullman's making Lord Asriel (Satan) a hero of sorts—imperfect, to be sure—rather than the villain. A crucial line from Blake's *The Marriage of Heaven and Hell* (1790) has been quoted in many *HDM* reviews, commentaries, and discussions: "The reason Milton wrote in fetters [restrictive chains or shackles] when he wrote of angels & God, and at liberty [unfettered] when of Devils & Hell, is because he was . . . of the Devil's party without knowing it."[11] Blake is saying that Milton, without realizing it, was on Satan's side. As a Christian, Milton had to and wanted to make God the hero: Milton was bound by figurative chains to God's camp. Yet he unwittingly portrayed Satan sympathetically, making him seem heroic at times. Pullman does the same thing, but deliberately and with much more energy and purpose. He turns *PL* upside down by making God and Jesus sinister villains and making Satan the leader of a noble cause—the cause of knowledge in its war against religious superstition.

A second important debt to Blake involves Pullman's Specters. The concept comes from Blake's poem "Milton."[12] It is full of references to "specters." Pullman has taken the concept of ghostly specters and refurbished it into one of his two most fundamental symbols—Specters and Dust. The *PL* allegory would be impossible to comprehend without the reader's knowing what each of these two coordinate symbols represents.

Before we proceed, a quick review of allegory's characteristics is in order. An allegory, once more, is a surface story—the story you actually read—that uses persons, places, things, and events to symbolize different persons, places, things, and events in a hidden story. C. S. Lewis's *LWW* is allegorical in that it uses characters (e.g., Aslan), places (e.g., the witch's castle), things (e.g., the lamppost), and events (e.g., Aslan's resurrection) to symbolize other persons, places, things, and events, taken mainly from the New Testament. *LWW* is Lewis's surface story, the story of four children and a lion. The hidden story is the New Testament story that the surface story symbolizes—the story of God, the Christ, Satan, the Christ's death and resurrection, the apocalypse that accompanies the Second Coming of the Christ, and the triumphant arrival on Earth of the Kingdom of God. Pullman's *LWW* allegory transforms Lewis's surface story into a hidden story and uses a new surface story, the adventures of Lyra and Will, to deliver the symbols. Pullman's new symbols tell the hidden story about four humans, a lion, a witch, and a wardrobe, and about how the lion dies, returns to life, and kills the witch who earlier killed him, after which a world-shattering apocalypse clears the landscape for the Kingdom of God, which the humans ultimately reach.

The present allegory, the *PL* allegory, uses the same surface story that was used for Pullman's *LWW* allegory. But the *hidden* story is now an augmented and upside down version of *PL*. It is augmented by such non-*PL* characters and themes as Judas, priests, the Christian Church, the resurrection of the dead, Judgment Day, and gnosticism. The hidden story is upside down in the sense that the bad guys are now the good guys and the good guys are now the bad guys. Satan becomes a hero, albeit a flawed one; God and Jesus become villains. Satan's children—Sin and Death—become saviors of mankind rather than bête noires. Sin saves the universe. God becomes mortal and dies. Christianity suffers defeat.

Some of the symbolic characters in the surface story, Lyra and Mrs. Coulter, for example, were also used as symbols in the *LWW* allegory, but here they refer to new people. Some of the other surface story characters—Ma Costa, John Faa, Lee Scoresby, and Serafina Pekkala, for example—were also symbols in the *LWW* allegory but are no longer symbolic, so their scenes contribute nothing to the new hidden story. Jesus, indirectly symbolized (via Aslan, the direct symbol) by Iorek in Pullman's first allegory, is now directly symbolized—but by a different *HDM* character. Satan, indirectly symbolized (via the White Witch) by Mrs. Coulter and Iofur in Pullman's first allegory, is also symbolized directly by a different *HDM* character. God too, formerly indirectly symbolized (via the kindly Professor) by the Master of Jordan, is also symbolized by a different character in the *PL* allegory.

The allegorically told hidden story that results is summarized below. Bear in mind that the hidden story is not going to include a person, thing, or event for every person, thing, and event in the surface story, the *HDM* trilogy. For example, the new hidden story has no characters corresponding to Iorek and Iofur; neither does it have an event corresponding to their fight to the death. Those two characters and the event were part of the previous allegory. Only those surface story characters, things, and events that are symbolic in this particular allegory contribute to the hidden story. This is why the hidden story lacks elements that parallel many of the elements of the surface story. What follows is *not* a summary of the surface story.

The Hidden Story. Once upon a time, a man named Satan lived in a world called Hell. Hell's society was dominated by the Church, a collection of oppressive religious authorities loyal to a remote deity named God. God lived in a place called Heaven, located in the sky above another place called Earth, which was above Hell. The religious authorities of Hell wanted to suppress knowledge, which they equated with sin. They sought to destroy knowledge and replace it with superstition, which was the Word of God. They believed that a life guided by superstition—they thought the superstition was Truth—would lead to an afterlife of eternal bliss in Heaven. And the religious authorities told the people of Hell that they could enjoy an afterlife of bliss—life with God—by observing the Word of God, doing and believing what they were told, avoiding independent thought, participating in Church ritual, and paying money to the Church. By building lots and lots of churches, the authorities were able to flood Hell with superstition. The superstition created a spell that was causing knowledge to gradually disappear.

Satan hated God, rejected his superstitions, and deplored what God and his minions were doing. So he prepared to go to his palace in the North to make plans to overthrow God and to replace God's superstitions with knowledge. Another man, Michael, was afraid that Satan's aggressive ways would bring ruin to society. Michael tried to split Satan down the middle with a sword, but Satan dodged the blow and went on his way. Had Satan met his demise, this story would have ended before it began.

When he went to the North, Satan left behind a daughter named

168 PHILIP PULLMAN'S *HIS DARK MATERIALS*

Sin and a son named Death. He left them in the care of some nice people. Sin and Death had two friends. Their names were Chaos and Night. One day Chaos and Night disappeared. It was rumored that a bad group of Church fanatics had kidnaped them and taken them North to a place not terribly far from Satan's palace. Shortly thereafter, Sin and Death became wards of a chap named Judas. Judas wasn't very nice, because he was a disciple of God's son, Jesus, who was just as bad as God. Maybe worse. Judas happened to be the very person who kidnaped Chaos and Night, although Sin didn't yet know this. Further evidence that Judas was bad is that he worked for the Church, and everyone who worked for the Church was a disciple of Jesus. All the disciples were bad.

Sin didn't like living with Judas, because she found out Judas was going to use her to help kidnap other children. So she and Death ran away. Deciding to rescue Chaos and Night, they went way up North, but not as far as "the limits of the North," where Satan's palace was. Sin and Death found Chaos and Night. Those two and a whole lot of other kidnaped children were being held in a prison camp called Little Hell. The camp was run by Judas, who had gone North ahead of Sin and Death. By going into Little Hell, confronting Judas, and stirring things up, Sin and Death managed to rescue Chaos and Night and all the other prisoners. In later years this bold rescue enjoyed fame as "the harrowing of Little Hell."

After the rescue Sin, Death, Chaos, and Night went farther north to Satan's palace at the limits of the North. There Satan was getting ready to launch his rebellion. Satan had finished his plans for a war against God, the Church, and superstition. His plans called for building a bridge from Hell to Earth. Satan planned to establish on Earth a republic where religion and superstition weren't allowed. But to build the bridge to Earth, Satan needed help. Chaos and Night were very strong, and with their help Satan built his bridge. Unfortunately, Chaos and Night worked themselves to death building the bridge. They died just as the bridge was finished.

With the bridge completed, Satan crossed it to Earth. There he built a capital, complete with lots of nifty towers. He called the place Pandemonium. Fortifying Pandemonium, Satan prepared to make war against God. His army was a motley crew of rebellious angels, demons, Lapland witches, and atheists. The demons included four frightening horsemen who later distinguished themselves in battle and became known as the Four Horsemen of the Apocalypse. The Apocalypse was the terrible war they fought in. The atheists were under the command of Beelzebub, Satan's second in command.

Sin and Death, having nothing better to do and not wanting to go back and live with Judas, decided they would cross the bridge to Earth too. When Sin and Death got to Earth, they met a really nice boy named Cain. He was the son of parents named Adam and Eve. Cain had accidentally killed his brother, a nasty brat named Abel, who really deserved to die. Cain had never met Abel and didn't even know he had a brother, but even so the killing turned Cain into a sinner, technically speaking. That is why he was the perfect companion for Sin.

Cain and Sin also had something else in common: both were from other worlds. Sin was from her home world of Hell, and Cain was from a world with two names, Paradise and Bliss. He was forced to leave Paradise-Bliss when he became a sinner by killing his brother. That is why he came to Earth. The trouble was, Earth wasn't a very hospitable place. It was crawling with superstition. All the grown-ups were so full of superstition that they wandered around like zombies, unable to formulate rational thoughts. Fortunately, neither Sin nor Cain was gullible enough to believe any of that malarky.

Back in Hell, the Church authorities learned of a prophecy: Sin was going to do something—nobody knew just what—that would break the spell of superstition if she wasn't stopped. As it happens, Sin was going to eat some fruit called Forbidden Fruit. This fruit came from a special tree called the Tree of Knowledge. If Sin managed to eat the fruit, she would acquire knowledge, which is another name for sin. (That is why Sin was named Sin.) Knowledge was sin in the eyes of the Church, because knowledge displaces superstition, which is Truth, the Word of God. Sin's acquisition of knowledge would magically burst open the thunderheads of knowledge that were threatening to douse Earth's and Hell's fires of superstition. Knowledge—sin!—would inundate the world, drowning superstition, the Church's crucial source of energy.

The Church leaders hated Sin—not just hated, feared her—and were determined to kill her before she could do whatever she was going to do. Ironically, Sin didn't know she was fated to eat the Forbidden Fruit. Indeed, she didn't even know it existed.

In an effort to stop Sin from fulfilling the prophecy, Judas went to Earth, found Sin, and captured her while Cain was off somewhere meditating. But then Judas changed his mind about killing Sin. Sin was so sweet that he decided to hold her prisoner instead. Judas took Sin back to Hell and hid her in a cave in a remote corner of Hell. Sin didn't remain a prisoner for very long, though. Cain and some demons who were helping him—two of the Four Horsemen of the Apocalypse—found and rescued Sin. (Cain was a real good finder.) Cain then took Sin to the safety of a fourth world.

At this point, Sin and Cain decided to go to still another place. Its name was Hades, and it was under all the above-ground worlds. Sin had learned about Hades in a message from Chaos's ghost that she received in a dream while being held prisoner by Judas. It seems that dead people, instead of going to Heaven to live with God as promised by the Church, went to Hades instead. It was an awful place, a place of suffering. Chaos's ghost wanted out.

Sin and Cain headed for Hades. Upon arriving at the River Styx, which separated the upper worlds from Hades, Sin and Cain had trouble getting the boatman to row them across. Only dead people were allowed to enter Hades. The boatman refused to row Sin and Cain across the river to Hades, because Sin still had her soul. He thought Death was her soul. This meant she was still alive. So Sin left Death behind, thereby convincing the boatman that she was dead. He then agreed to take her. But all the same, he decided to charge her passage money for being such a nuisance: she had to pay him one obol. The boatman didn't see any soul with Cain, so he took Cain along without making a fuss.

On the other side, Sin and Cain found the gate to Hades. Entering the gate and descending into Hades, the two learned that Chaos was right. God was lying to the people of the upper worlds when he told them that, if they behaved themselves, they could come and live blissfully with him in Heaven when they died. God really sent *all* the dead, both the righteous and the wicked, to Hades. There was nothing to do, nowhere to go, nothing to eat, nothing worth seeing, nothing but sheer sitting around in eternal boredom. Even sleep was forbidden. To make matters worse, some cranky overseers screeched constantly at the inmates. Also, the overseers had B.O.

In Hades Sin found the ghost of Chaos, and Cain found the ghost of his father, Adam. Many years earlier, Adam had been kicked out of his home world of Paradise by God. His offense: seeking Truth from a source other than God. God, despite being a liar, wanted to be the only source of "Truth." Adam had gone to Hell and taken over a small anti-Church kingdom populated by Tartars. There he was known as Negus by the Tartars, but Church people who had heard of him called him Prester John. The Church people thought he was on their side. Boy, were they ever wrong! Hearing about Satan's rebellion against God, Adam-Negus had traveled to Earth, where he intended to join Satan's army. Unfortunately, he had died before reaching Satan. The reason he died is that everyone who left Paradise became mortal and had to die before very long. Mortality was God's punishment for people who sought knowledge from a source other than God.

Cain and his father's ghost had a serious conversation. Adam gave Cain some sage advice: "Forget about God's promise of salvation in another world after you die, because God is a liar. There is no blissful life after death. Work to create your own salvation where you live, during your lifetime." Cain recognized Adam's wisdom and added some of his own: "I will always do my own thinking. I will not let any self-appointed religious authorities tell me what to believe and what to do. I will not humble myself before them or before God. I will not submit. I will work to perceive the difference between superstition and knowledge, and I will choose knowledge."

Surveying the depressing situation in Hades, Sin got a bright idea. All the inmates and overseers would get together and create a joyful holiday. They would call it Judgment Day. Sin arranged for the overseers to judge the inmate ghosts by listening to them and releasing those who told the truth. The overseers relished true stories and had an uncanny ability to detect lies. "You shall know the truth," Sin said to the overseers. "And the truth shall make you free," she said to the inmates. So the inmates—all but a few ex-monks and other misfits—told stories to the overseers, who sat in judgment. Those who told the truth were set free; those who lied remained confined. Sin's words—"You shall know the truth, and the truth shall make you free"—endure to this day in a familiar reference book, *John's Gnostic Quotations*, which describes them as the official slogan of Judgment Day.

Sin and Cain led the freed inmates on a journey to the surface. Along the way they had to creep past the edge of a vast, bottomless pit. At that point a still-living Church zealot approached Sin wearing a vest filled with explosives and intent on murder-suicide. Fortunately, Cain recognized the threat and shoved the zealot into the pit a few seconds before he blew himself up. Nobody except the zealot got hurt. When the party finally reached the outside world, the former inmates (but not Sin and Cain, who weren't dead) dissolved into atoms and became part of nature. That was the end of God's phony "Salvation" and the beginning of our modern Era of Recycling. Ever since, everyone who dies dissolves into atoms that rejoin the earth, the air, and the water and ultimately reassemble into flowers, trees, birds, squirrels, lakes, mountains, clouds, breezes, and other natural things.

Meanwhile, back at Pandemonium, Satan received some useful information. An angel named Abdiel had snuck into Heaven. There Abdiel learned that God was sick and had delegated all his authority to his son, Jesus. Jesus was planning to attack Pandemonium and wipe it out. Then he was going to go down to Hell and launch a Christian inquisition. Heretics—people who don't go to church—would be tortured into confessing that they were heretics, or maybe even witches. Then they would be burned in "the eternal fire"—the fire of superstition—for their heresy. Abdiel spoke his Testimony of Truth to Satan. Satan responded by getting his defenses ready.

Pretty soon Jesus attacked from the sky with his war machine, a deadly chariot. A fierce and prolonged battle took place. On Jesus's side were his chariot, God's loyal angels, some of Hell's witches (fewer than Satan had), the Church's Swiss Guard Army (sent by the pope), and lethal Dogma Cannons firing shells laden with insidious superstition gas that could cloud the minds of intelligent beings. On Satan's side were the rebel angels (half as many angels as God had), demons, an army of atheists led by Beelzebub (this unit effectively took on the Swiss Guard), most of Hell's witches, and powerful Darwin Cannons firing projectiles of superstition-blasting knowledge.

For a long time the war's outcome was uncertain. But luck was with Satan, more or less. Jesus's previously loyal disciple Judas came over to Satan's side and double-crossed his former master. Judas told Jesus that Jesus could find Satan in Hades, sneak up on him, and kill him. As part of a trap, Satan went down into Hades and waited near the edge of a pit. (This was the very pit Sin and her gang had crept past on the way out of Hades.) Anticipating an Apostles' Creed that would be written about his action, Jesus descended into Hades. He was unaware that Satan knew he was coming. Jesus planned to ambush Satan, but instead Satan ambushed Jesus. Judas, who had descended with Jesus, joined Satan in attacking Jesus, who was stronger than Satan. Jesus tried to throw Satan into the pit, but Satan and Judas, working as a team, managed to drag Jesus over the edge. All three fell to their deaths, with Satan and Judas clinging to Jesus. With Jesus and his chariot out of the way, the forces of knowledge began to get the upper hand in the apocalyptic battle upstairs.

While all the fighting was going on, God died of old age and Alzheimer's disease. Not everyone gets Alzheimer's, but God was particularly vulnerable because his body and mind never had any real substance. Vultures began eating him alive in his final moments—a fitting end to a lying, vicious, cruel, sadistic, arbitrary, might-makes-right, vain, pompous, egomaniacal tyrant.

But the Church and its superstition were not yet vanquished. Religion was still dominant back in Satan's home world of Hell. There superstition was consuming knowledge, which people needed for making Hell a decent place in which to live. Sin, with help from Cain, accidentally solved this problem by living up to her name. She met a friendly talking serpent who suggested that she try some delicious fruit called Forbidden Fruit. Remember that prophecy? It turns out that the serpent and the fruit were what the prophecy was all about.

The Forbidden Fruit came from the Tree of Knowledge and contained lots of nutritious knowledge, although Sin didn't know this. Sin and Cain, not realizing the implications of what they were doing, both ate the fruit. This was the very thing the Church had feared was going to happen. And—talk about good luck!—by partaking of knowledge, the two Innocents learned about love. This knowledge made them fall in love, an event now known to historians as the Fall. The Fall was an act of magic, sort of like a princess kissing a frog. It broke superstition's spell, causing knowledge to start raining down all over the place. Knowledge quenched the fires of superstition, the churches went to pot, and mankind gained genuine salvation—the victory of knowledge over superstition.

One other development cemented the victory of knowledge. Until she fell in love, Sin had a faculty for knowing Truth intuitively, without thinking, without appreciable effort. She had been like an innocent child who was always told what was true by her parents or her priest, without having to think and figure things out for herself. Suddenly, after eating the Forbidden Fruit, she found she had lost that intuitive, Truth-finding faculty. This loss bothered her to no end.

Then a wise angel named Wisdom came to Sin with comforting information. Wisdom was the wisest being in the universe, so she knew what she was talking about. She told Sin that Sin was no longer an innocent child. She was now a grown-up, which is the same as being a sinner, so she could no longer receive Truth by grace. By acquiring knowledge, Sin had lost her innocence and had become a sinner. Sinners had both the need and the ability to think for themselves. Consequently, Sin could start learning Truth the hard way: by observing and testing and thinking and reasoning as intelligent people do, and by rejecting claims and beliefs that are unsupported, irrational, preposterous, or contrary to evidence and experience. Wisdom explained that this thoughtful, effortful approach to Truth was the only certain way to discern what is genuine knowledge and what is mere superstition. Real knowledge rests on conscious understanding; superstition rests on faith, the lazy person's way of perceiving "Truth." Real knowledge comes from effort; superstition is received by grace.

Cain, poor fellow, had to return to his world, Bliss-Paradise, in order to take care of his mother, Eve. Sin wanted to go with him and be with him forever. She wanted to depart from her home world of Hell and spend an eternity in Bliss with Cain. She longed for life in Paradise. But Sin and Cain remembered something Adam's ghost had told them back when they were in Hades. According to the Law of Death, Sin could not go to Bliss. Far from offering her a long, blissful life, Bliss's environment would kill her within ten years. This distressing news meant that Sin could not depart from her world to live in Bliss. Where Sin was concerned, the other world of Bliss didn't exist.

Fortunately, Sin's adventure ended on a happy note. Adam had also told Sin and Cain that they could find bliss in their own worlds by working to make those worlds better. Hell could be transformed into a Republic of Heaven, a far better place than the phony Kingdom of God that God and his Church had promised when God was alive. This knowledge gave Sin the courage to put aside wishful thinking, to accept reality, and to live her life joyfully and productively without leaning on the crutch of superstition.

THE BROAD THEME: KNOWLEDGE VS. RELIGIOUS SUPERSTITION

With the hidden story in hand, let's turn to the symbols Pullman uses to tell that hidden story. Pullman's underlying theme, largely but not entirely hidden in symbolism, is that we live in a world where knowledge and religious superstition are at war. Superstition can be defined as any false belief in the supernatural.[13] If you believe in Zeus or Hades or magic or astrological determination, and if that entity actually exists, your belief is not a superstition. But if the supernatural entity—say, Zeus—does not exist, is not Truth, your belief is a superstition. The churches seek to replace knowledge with superstition; religion and religious superstition are the enemies of knowledge.

You could say a remarkable parallel exists between A. D. White's two-volume 1896 classic, *A History of the Warfare of Science with Theology in Christendom*, and Pullman's *HDM* trilogy. White's well-marshaled facts and Pullman's imaginative, tendentious fiction deliver the same message: religion is the enemy of knowledge. Another fine book developing this theme is Homer W. Smith's 1952 treatise, *Man and His Gods*. Pullman uses the angel Xaphania to deliver his own version of the message: "All the history of human life has been a struggle between wisdom and stupidity [religion]."[14] Mary Malone puts it this way: "The Christian religion is a very powerful and convincing mistake, that's all."[15]

John Parry, Will's father, is less pithy in his description of the struggle: "Every advance in human life, every scrap of knowledge and wisdom and decency we have has been torn by one side [knowledge, science] from the teeth of the other [superstition, religion]. Every little increase in human freedom has been fought over ferociously between those who want us to know more and be wiser and stronger [advocates of knowledge], and those who want us to obey and be humble and submit [advocates of religious superstition]."[16]

In Pullman's surface story, celestial "Dust" *symbolizes* knowledge. (Dust is not knowledge in the abstract in the surface story; it has a more complicated meaning there, a meaning involving tiny particles of matter that are particles of knowledge—knowledge in physical form. This meaning will be explained later.) Evil, Dust-eating, soul-devouring Specters symbolize religious superstition. The Specters "grow by feeding on Dust."[17] That is, religious superstition grows by destroying and replacing knowledge. Each time a new window between parallel worlds is opened—Will's subtle knife opens windows—a new church or sect is created: the windows are churches. Simultaneously, two things happen. First, a new Specter (a new superstition or syndrome of superstitions) is created: "Every time we open a window with the knife, it makes a Specter."[18] Second, Dust—knowledge—leaks out of the world. In short, superstition replaces knowledge when a new church or sect arises.

Lord Asriel, who is Lyra's father and the leader of the rebellion against the Kingdom of Heaven, is "trying to preserve the Dust."[19] Rebel angels are among the forces that gather under his command. The highest rebel angel, Xaphania, in words paraphrased by Serafina Pekkala, alludes to Dust when she says, "The rebel angels, the followers of wisdom, have always tried to keep open minds [open to knowledge]; the Authority [God] and his churches have always tried to keep them closed."[20]

Dust. To better understand this Specters-replace-Dust symbolism, we must examine Dust and the Specters separately. Pullman's hidden story is about the need to preserve knowledge (Dust) by eliminating the superstitions (Specters) that destroy (eat) it. As already mentioned, each time a new window opens, a new Specter is created and Dust escapes. This means that each time a new church or sect arises, its unique superstitions replace knowledge and lead to erosion of human wisdom. In the surface story plot, Dust is constantly escaping, because open windows are everywhere: Dust is literally going out the windows. At the end of the story, the windows are all going to be closed by Xaphania's angels. The Dust will no longer escape. Symbolically, this means that, in an ideal world, the churches and their superstitions would vanish.

How do we know that Dust symbolizes knowledge in the hidden story? The evidence is compelling. Consider the following:

1. Near the end of *AS*, Pullman's metaphorical retelling of the Bible's Garden of Eden myth very nearly declares openly that

Dust is knowledge. The Cave (Mary's computer) tells Mary she must "play the serpent" (the tempter in Eden).[21] Pullman twice explicitly refers to Mary as "the tempter."[22] Father MacPhail agonizes about what will happen if "the child [Lyra] is tempted as Eve was."[23] Lyra, according to MacPhail, is "in the position of Eve, the wife of Adam" and is "Eve, who is going to be tempted and who, if precedent is any guide, will *fall* [an allusion to the Christian doctrine of "the Fall" of Adam and Eve, who fell from God's grace when they disobeyed God and ate the Forbidden Fruit]."[24] Mrs. Coulter tortures the witch Lena Feldt into confessing that "Lyra is Eve."[25] Mary actually does tempt Lyra, both with Mary's marzipan story about falling in love and with the little red fruits Mary packs in Lyra's lunch. The little red fruits Will and Lyra eat are obvious representations of the Forbidden Fruit Adam and Eve ate. The Bible's Forbidden Fruit, in turn, was from the Tree of *Knowledge*; the Forbidden Fruit delivered *knowledge* to Adam and Eve. The little red fruits do the same thing for Lyra and Will: the fruits deliver *knowledge*. Only this time the delivery mechanism is different. Adam and Eve got knowledge directly from the fruit. But with Lyra and Will, the fruits are just a supernatural triggering device. The knowledge arrives indirectly—*from the sky*. When the two eat the fruits, the Dust stops flowing out of the world and drifts down onto Lyra and Will, and onto all the worlds. And when the two return to Mary covered with Dust, the symbolism proclaims that the come-of-age former children are saturated with knowledge. The metaphorical event's meaning is so clear, so crystal clear, that we cannot reasonably doubt what Dust is. Dust is knowledge.

2. The Church's Magisterium, or ruling body, "decided that Dust was the physical evidence for original sin."[26] Original Sin refers to Adam's and Eve's eating the Forbidden Fruit from the Tree of Knowledge. This first (original) act of sin was

therefore the acquisition of knowledge. If Dust is the "physical evidence" of sin, Dust must be knowledge—knowledge in the form of the surface story's physical particles. These particles symbolize the abstraction we call knowledge, which is not physical. The abstraction called knowledge belongs to the hidden story. Sex-fixated theologians have interpreted original sin's knowledge narrowly as knowledge of sexuality. But sexual knowledge and feelings are but one small aspect of knowledge, not to be mistaken for the essence of Dust. How do we know this? The other evidence being summarized here points to knowledge in a much broader sense than sexual knowledge. Are we to assume that *sexual* knowledge enables the alethiometer to respond truthfully to questions having nothing to do with sex?

3. Lord Asriel says, "Dust is what makes the alethiometer work."[27] Lyra's alethiometer is a truth-telling instrument. The device's name comes from the Greek word "aletheia," which means truth. Asked a question, the alethiometer answers with the truth. You can't tell the truth without knowledge: to tell the truth the alethiometer must have knowledge—Dust. Asriel's daemon can therefore say, "She can read the alethiometer; she has access to *knowledge*."[28] Conclusion: "Dust is what makes the alethiometer work" means knowledge is what makes the alethiometer work.

4. Human skulls dated about 33,000 years ago had "a lot more Dust around them" than skulls dated earlier.[29] The reason is that the more recent skulls were from the time when *Homo sapiens* had just evolved and had begun producing knowledge. "There were shadow particles [Dust] around before then, . . . but there was no physical way of amplifying their effects. . . . And then something happened . . . [and] it involved evolution. . . . Around that time [33,000 years ago], the human brain became the ideal vehicle for this amplification process."[30] In other words, knowledge couldn't develop to a significant degree until the human

brain came along to produce it. That is why human skulls had more Dust—knowledge—than prehuman skulls.[31]

5. The *mulefa* (intelligent wheeled animals) had no knowledge until Dust entered their bodies. Whereas Dust enters humans by falling on their bodies, Dust enters the *mulefa* circuitously: it lands on the upturned wheel-pod tree blossoms, which deliver it to the pods (huge seeds), whose Dust-saturated oil enters the *mulefa* through the claws with which the *mulefa* grip the pods. *Mulefa* civilization, which arose from knowledge of how to use wheel-pod tree seedpods for wheels, began 33,000 years ago. According to *mulefa* mythology, a snake (analog of Eden's serpent) asked a pre-*mulefa* creature, "What do you know? What do you remember? What do you see ahead?" The reply: "Nothing, nothing, nothing." No knowledge, no memory, no foresight. The snake told the creature to put its foot through the hole in the seedpod "and you will become *wise*." The creature did so, "and the first thing she saw was the sraf." Dust is sraf in *mulefa* language. At that moment, the *mulefa* were born. "Ever since we have had the sraf, we have had memory and wakefulness [perception]. Before that we remembered nothing." When the *mulefa* acquired sraf (Dust), they acquired knowledge, because Dust *is* knowledge.[32]

6. The Dust that falls from the sky is attracted to adults, but very little falls on children until they reach puberty, which is when their daemons assume a fixed form. Then Dust settles on the adolescents as heavily as it does on adults.[33] What does this mean? Passage to adulthood marks the beginning of creativity, or contribution to human knowledge. Intelligence reaches a level sufficient to permit the development of new knowledge. Viewed in the language of the Adam and Eve myth, puberty is when knowledge replaces innocence—adult knowledge replaces childish innocence. We can be sure Pullman equates puberty with the beginning of knowledge

because, in a discussion with the Archbishop of Canterbury, Pullman surprisingly explained the significance of puberty, despite his general unwillingness to interpret *HDM*. "Understanding of things . . . [and] the beginning of intellectual inquiry . . . happens typically in one's adolescence, when one begins to be interested in poetry and art and science and all these other things."[34] In a separate interview, Pullman amplified this point: "Falling in love . . . is linked with the coming of wisdom . . . at the age of adolescence . . . [because] that's also the age at which we become passionate intellectually too. We develop a passionate interest in mathematics or chess or art or science or biology or whatever it might happen to be."[35] This means that, when children reach puberty and begin acquiring Dust, they are acquiring knowledge.

7. Xaphania tells Lyra and Will: "Dust is not a constant. There's not a fixed quantity [of knowledge] that has always been the same. Conscious beings make Dust—they renew it all the time, by thinking and feeling and reflecting, by gaining wisdom and passing it on."[36] Pullman, using Xaphania as his mouthpiece, is saying that new Dust—new knowledge—is constantly being generated through thought and reflection. Humans generate knowledge.

8. If the Dust vanishes, "everything good will fade away and die."[37] The implication: if knowledge disappears, all that will be left is superstition.

9. Specters eat Dust.[38] Once you understand that the Specters represent superstition (explained under the next subheading), you can see that *superstition* is what devours Dust. Superstition is the enemy of Dust. If this is so, what must Dust be? What is superstition the enemy of? Superstitions—false beliefs that assume supernatural reality—are the enemy of knowledge. The Christian fundamentalist superstition called creationism (the belief that God created the world in six days and directly created man) is, for example, the enemy of scien-

tific knowledge of evolution. The belief of many Christians, particularly Christian Science adherents, that illness and disease can be cured by prayer is the enemy of scientific knowledge of the causes of and treatments for various ailments.

10. Searching for Lyra, Father Gomez goes to Cittàgazze. It is full of Specters, but they don't attack him. He thinks his "sacred task" is "protecting me [Gomez] against these—Specters."[39] But what is really protecting him is a paucity of knowledge. This religious zealot is so stuffed with superstition that his mind holds no more knowledge than a child's. Once more: *Specters eat Dust.* The Specters don't attack children and zealots, because those persons have too little knowledge for a Specter to feed on.

11. Dust is the enemy of the Church, the enemy of religion. Stanislaus Grumman (a.k.a. John Parry) says, "The Oblation Board fears and hates Dust."[40] Why is this? Why is Dust a threat to religion? Religion is, among other things, an institutionalized effort to provide supernatural explanations of things for which no natural explanation is known. When the ancients couldn't understand how man came into existence, religion provided the answer: God created man—out of dust, and in his own image.[41] When the towns of Sodom and Gomorrah were destroyed by an erupting volcano, religion told the people that God caused fire and brimstone to rain down on those places to punish their men for being wicked.[42] When insane people displayed weird behavior, religion explained the problem: insane people are possessed by demons.[43] Then knowledge arrived and shamed the Church for its superstitious ideas. Darwin's theory of evolution, reinforced by abundant subsequent evidence, showed that evolution, not God, created man. The science of geology explained the subterranean forces that cause volcanic eruptions formerly attributed to God. Modern medicine has shown that insanity results not from demons but from biochemical disturbances in

the brain and by brain "miswiring" (some of it genetically programmed)—although popes and priests continue to exorcise demons from the insane. In all of these cases, knowledge—Dust—has undermined religion by lessening the willingness of people to accept on faith what the Church tells them to believe. Knowledge undermines religion. That is why the Church fears Dust.

12. The final item is almost a dead giveaway. As this is being written, Pullman is writing another *HDM* book that will be a prequel to his trilogy. It will develop a mythology starting with creation and leading up to the beginning of *The Golden Compass* (*GC*). The new book's title will be *The Book of Dust*. That title is a play on words or, you could say, a play on titles: *The Book of Dust* is a reworking of the title of *The Book of Knowledge*. *The Book of Knowledge* is a widely popular and respected encyclopedia for young children, first published in 1910 and retitled *The New Book of Knowledge* in 1966. Pullman has pointedly substituted "Dust" for "Knowledge" in the encyclopedia's title. Pullman is boldly hinting—practically telling us—that Dust represents Knowledge; "Dust" can be substituted for "Knowledge" without changing the title's meaning.

In the hidden story Dust is knowledge as we understand the word, an abstraction. In the surface story, the story that appears in print, Dust is slightly different. Surface story Dust is an elementary form of matter, tiny pieces of knowledge with magical properties. Whereas knowledge in the hidden story is a nonphysical (abstract) concept like confidence or hatred or desire, the surface story's Dust is something physical. It is "shadow particles" that roam the sky and drift down onto humans. These particles, in addition to being attracted to humans—primarily adults—and to wheel-pod tree blossoms, are attracted to each other. The Authority and all the other angels condensed out of Dust. Angels, who describe themselves as "structures" or "complexifications" made of Dust, talk to Dr. Mary Malone by printing words on her computer screen. Similarly, they communicate with Lyra through her alethiometer. These angelic "complexifications" are knowledge personified, just as Bunyan's Giant Despair is despair personified and Milton's Sin is sin personified.

Dust conveys knowledge to both humans and the *mulefa* (wheeled animals). It conveys knowledge to these intelligent beings in various ways: (*a*) by falling on them and implicitly being absorbed, (*b*) through the alethiometer, (*c*) through Mary's computer screen, and (*d*) via wheel-pod oil, which the *mulefa* absorb through their claws.

Pullman seemingly is, but really isn't, inconsistent in describing Dust as an elementary particle. An elementary particle is a subatomic particle (something smaller than an atom) that can't be broken down further: it has no parts, no smaller constituent particles. An atom is not elementary, because it can be broken down into electrons, protons, and sometimes neutrons. Electrons are elementary—they can't be broken down further—but protons and neutrons can themselves be broken down into smaller constituents called quarks, so protons and neutrons are not elementary. But quarks, which physicists believe include six types or "flavors," are elementary; they can't be broken down. Also elementary are particles called leptons, which again have six types: electrons, muons, tau particles, and three kinds of neutrinos.

In *GC* Pullman lets Lord Asriel explain Dust, originally named Rusakov particles after its discoverer. Rusakov discovered "a new kind of elementary particle," comparable to "electrons" and "neutrinos." Are you sure, Lord Asriel? "This new kind of particle was elementary all right, but it was very hard to measure because it didn't react in any of the usual ways."[44] Here Dust is elementary particles, not agglomerations of particles.

Yet in his interview with Tony Watkins, Pullman seems to tell a different story. Now Dust is *formed*, indirectly, from truly elementary particles. In Pullman's mythology, elementary particles link up to form organized structures. We can infer that this linking up is comparable to what happens when quarks link up to form protons and neutrons, and when those higher particles link up with electrons to form atoms, which in turn link up to form molecules. "At some point when the complexity of the organization becomes sufficient, matter begins to become conscious. And when matter becomes conscious of itself and is able to be self-reflective, *then* [only then] it generates Dust, you see, and so Dust comes to life. At some point early in time a being arose of Dust, and he was the first thinking creature. He was the one I call the Authority. . . . Inevitably, other beings of Dust arose in time."[45]

Pullman is subtly expressing a point: knowledge couldn't exist until a conscious being, a being who could think, came into existence. Knowledge can't exist without minds that create and perceive it. In making this point, however, he partly contradicts what he says about Dust being "a kind of elementary particle." The Authority and other angels arose "of Dust"—they formed from Dust particles—yet each one "generates Dust." So is Dust the chicken or the egg?

I think Pullman, if he were willing to explain his symbolism, would say that Dust has two related meanings, both of which are knowledge. In most contexts Dust's original description applies: Dust is elementary particles, not something generated by angels that coalesce from particles. It certainly isn't angels that drift down from the sky onto humans and onto wheel-pod tree blossoms. But when Pullman speaks of angels who form from Dust and yet generate Dust, the generated Dust is not the symbol—elementary particles—but what is symbolized. The elementary particles symbolize knowledge as we understand the term, knowledge that arises from "thinking."

You could say that the elementary particles of Dust are *potential* knowledge and that the Dust that results from thinking is *actual* knowledge. Accordingly, in the final pages of *GC*, Lyra senses "the presence of the Dust . . . like the forms of thoughts *not yet born*" (my italics).[46] Something "not yet born" is merely potential, still maturing, not yet actual. When the Dust matures into knowledge, formed from "thoughts," knowledge is born and becomes actual. Pullman might have borrowed the potential-into-actual concept from Hegel.[47]

By overtly employing the concepts of potential knowledge and actual knowledge, Pullman could easily rationalize the apparent contradiction between (*a*) the idea that Dust creates intelligent beings, angels, and (*b*) the idea that intelligent beings such as angels and humans create Dust. He could say that Dust and intelligent beings enjoy a symbiotic relationship. The magical elementary particles of surface story Dust, representing *potential* knowledge, ripen into *actual* knowledge when they either (*a*) attach themselves to, and get absorbed by, intelligent beings or (*b*) coalesce or "complexify" into thinking angels. Contact with Dust gives intelligent beings, including humans and *mulefa*, the ability, the curiosity, and the motivation needed to think, to apply themselves diligently to tasks of understanding, and thereby to develop and perceive knowledge. Contact with intelligent beings allows Dust to be "born" from potential knowledge into actual knowledge. Symbiosis.

The same transformation—potential into actual—occurs, and symbiosis is again seen, when Dust coalesces into conscious, thinking, perceptive angels who produce knowledge. The angels benefit by coming to life as wise, conscious beings who generate knowledge in the usual sense of the word, not in the sense of particles. The Dust again benefits by becoming actual knowledge.

Dust in the form of elementary particles becomes actual knowledge, which is knowledge in the everyday sense of the word, when it is absorbed and enters the mind. Pullman ambiguously uses "Dust" to refer to both potential knowledge (the particles) and actual knowledge (the product of thinking). The physical particles of visible, golden Dust *symbolize* what we call knowledge. The latter—the abstraction—is what is *symbolized*, what Dust is in the hidden story. Abstract knowledge is also part of the surface story. There it is the surface story's actual knowledge that enters, or is produced by, the minds of humans when Dust in the sense of elementary particles accumulates on humans.

So fundamental to the story is Dust that the trilogy's title, *His Dark Materials*, alludes to it. The phrase "his dark materials" comes from book II of *PL*. Satan is preparing to cross the vast chaotic gulf between Hell and Earth. Milton expounds:

Into this wild abyss,
The womb of Nature and perhaps her grave,
Of neither sea, nor shore [earth], nor air, nor fire,
But all these in their pregnant causes mixed
Confus'dly, and which thus must ever fight,
Unless the Almighty Maker them ordain
His dark materials to create more worlds,
Into this wild abyss the wary Fiend [Satan]
Stood on the brink of Hell and looked a while,
Pondering his voyage; for no narrow frith [firth, ocean inlet]
He had to cross.[48]

Here Milton's poetry—verse marked by a tangled, convoluted, syntactically scrambled, stop-in-midstream-and-restart style and a hard-to-digest Elizabethan vocabulary—is a nightmarish puzzle for those of us who try to comprehend. But the essential idea is that the void Satan is about to cross is a chaotic mixture of water, earth (land), air, and fire—God's dark materials of creation. The ancient Greeks, and possibly Milton too, regarded water, earth, air, and fire as nature's four elements.

Pullman adapts the phrase by using "his dark materials" as a metaphor for Dust. The metaphor actually has an element of literalism, because the mysterious matter known as Dust or Rusakov particles in Lyra's world is called dark matter or Shadows in Will's world, which is our own world. Dark matter, in turn, is a concept actually used by today's astrophysicists. They think it accounts for most of the mass of the universe and for the behavior of galaxies and other stellar features. Dark matter can't be seen, because it emits hardly any light or radiation, maybe none. But its gravitational pull, added to the gravitational pull of visible matter, is the glue that keeps galaxies and the universe from flying rapidly apart. Naturally, Pullman is giving this real material fictional characteristics.

Pullman might or might not also be reading a secondary metaphor into "his dark materials." In *PL*, "His" refers to God. But in Pullman's *HDM*, "His" could very well refer to Lord Asriel. He and his followers are the defenders of Dust, which the Church regards as evil and wants to get rid of. To be sure, near the end of *GC* Asriel tells Mrs. Coulter that he wants to destroy the Dust. But he is lying. In *AS* the truth comes out much later when Mrs. Coulter speaks to Asriel: "But you didn't mean it. You meant the very opposite, didn't you? I see it now. . . . Why didn't you tell me you were really trying to preserve Dust?"[49] Asriel then acknowledges his intent to preserve the Dust. Preserving the Dust is *his* cause. The Dust is "his dark materials."

Specters and Their Windows. The Specters are the opposite of Dust and are the enemies of Dust. In the hidden story, the Specters are religious superstitions, just as Dust is knowledge. Nicholas Tucker, though he fails to recognize that Pullman's Specters are superstitions, nevertheless gets half way to the truth in his summary of Blake's concept of specters: "The principal enemies of the individual when it comes to making the spiritual journal through the fallen world [of Christianity] from darkness to light are what Blake described as the various spectres that haunt us and which we must always learn to cast away. For Blake, such spectres are *the creation of oppressive religion* backed up by the state" (my italics).[50] Those words come close to abstractly describing Pullman's Specters, which are also the creation of religion, although Pullman's surface story is foggy where any role of the state is concerned.[51]

Having gotten half way to the truth, Tucker drifts far off course when he rashly claims that "there can never be a definitive answer as to what exactly Spectres, or indeed *any other* characters in Pullman's work, are intended to symbolise" (my italics).[52] Translation: "If I can't interpret a Pullman symbol, nobody can. So if I can't deduce who Asriel and Lyra symbolize, nobody can." This bizarre, not to mention immodest, idea almost amounts to a denial that Pullman uses symbols, even though in the same sentence Tucker acknowledges Pullman's intent to symbolize. If a symbol has no "definitive" meaning, a meaning intended by the symbol's creator, then the so-called symbol isn't really a symbol: no symbol exists.

Why is this so? The answer takes us straight to the definition of a symbol. A symbol is something used by someone—an author, a poet, a playwright, an auteur, or an artist—to represent something else: Dust represents knowledge, Iorek represents Aslan, C. S. Lewis's White Witch represents Satan, and the Experimental Station is the witch's castle. There can be no symbol unless its designer, an author in Pullman's case, intends to use something as a symbol and gives the symbol a specific meaning. Once an author creates a symbol it, by definition, represents something—a person, a place, an object, an event, or whatever. The symbol necessarily has a definitive meaning or referent, namely, whatever the author is using the symbol to represent. If the author weren't using, say, Lord Asriel to represent someone or something else (Satan, as it happens), Asriel wouldn't be a symbol. Yet Tucker insists that there can be no "definitive answer," which means Pullman doesn't intend that his symbols represent anything in particular. That insistence constitutes a self-contradictory denial that what Tucker himself called a symbol, Specters, is really a symbol.

By way of qualification, a symbol occasionally has two or three meanings, especially when two allegories are going on at once in the same surface story. In Stanley Kubrick's film *2001: A Space Odyssey*, both Homer's *The Odyssey* and Nietzsche's *Thus Spake Zarathustra* are being allegorized. The hero, Dave *Bowman*, represents Odysseus (who was a *bow-man*, an archer) in the first allegory and the prophet Zarathustra in the second.[53] Likewise, in Pullman's double allegory, Mrs. Coulter represents the White Witch in the first allegory and somebody else in the second. A symbol may even represent two things in the same allegory. In the Kubrick film, Heywood Floyd represents both Paris (the seducer of Helen of Troy) and Menelaus (Helen's husband) in different scenes, and in Pullman's *LWW* allegory Lyra represents both Lucy and Susan in different scenes. And since Lyra represents a third entity in the *PL* allegory, she symbolizes three things altogether. But these anomalous cases of multiple referents don't validate the notion that a symbol can have as many meanings as there are intelligent interpreters. The genuine multiple meanings—the "definitive answers"—arise not from multiple interpreters but from the one author who created the symbol and gave it two or three meanings, depending on context.

Tucker is dead wrong about "there can never be a definitive answer." Where the Specters are concerned, the answer isn't even hard to find. We know from the allegorical context, from the *PL* allegory's unifying theme of religion, and from the Specters' fighting for the Authority that the Specters have something to do with religion. We also know that the Specters are something evil and that, in Pullman's story, the worst evils are manifestations of or creations of the Church, or religion; hence, the Specters are something belonging to religion, contrasted with irreligion, atheism, or science. Again, we know from their importance in the surface story that the Specters are an essential aspect of religion, not something minor or incidental. (As it happens, the Specters represent the very essence of religion.) We know too that the Specters are a multitude, not just one thing such as Heaven or faith or the Holy Spirit. And because Specters eat Dust, we know that Specters and Dust are enemies, polar opposites: the Specters are to religion as Dust is to atheism.

Now all we have to do is figure out what multitudinous facet of religion is the enemy of knowledge (Dust). The answer is obvious: Specters are religious superstitions, false supernaturalistic beliefs that supplant and destroy ("eat") knowledge. Specters are religion's concept of Truth, just as Dust is atheism's concept of Truth. Religious superstitions have all of the Specter characteristics identified in the above paragraph. Superstitions are (1) something evil, (2) creations of the Church, or religion, (3) an essential aspect of religion, not just a minor feature, (4) a multitude—a vast multitude—not just one thing like the Holy Spirit, and (5) the opposite of, and the enemy of, knowledge (symbolized by Dust).

These characteristics aren't the only evidence that the Specters symbolize religious superstitions. Specters take over the mind, while leaving the body intact. People possessed by Specters behave as though mindless, acting irrationally: a possessed father indifferently watches his son drown. Yet these possessed people remain physically unimpaired. Religious superstitions do the same thing. They take over the mind, causing people to behave and think irrationally, while the body remains unimpaired (with rare exceptions, as when a snake cultist dies from a rattlesnake bite, other cultists participate in mass suicides, and Christian Scientists die because they irrationally rely on prayer instead of medical science). Superstition-possessed people engage in such irrational acts as self-flagellation, blaming hurricanes on homosexuals, burning "witches" at the stake, chanting Hindu mantras and Catholic Hail Marys, eating their savior's body (represented by bread) and drinking his blood (represented by wine), taking horse-drawn buggies out on high-speed highways because God forbids using cars, declaring that we are predestined to receive our fates, claiming the earth is only about six thousand years old, also claiming that the "original sin" of two imaginary humans (Adam and Eve) required punishing innocent future humans, and believing that Jesus's suffering on the cross vicariously punished those future humans for the crime they didn't commit. Yes, superstition-possessed people, like Specter-possessed people, are irrational.

Something Will says reinforces the deduction that the Specters symbolize religious superstitions. Will: "I think maybe they come from my world after all, the Specters." Lyra: "But you don't have Specters in your world! You never heard of them, did you?" Will: "Maybe they're not called Specters. *Maybe we call them something else.*"[54]

Pullman is hinting at something that truly exists in our own society, which is also Will's. That something is not anything supernatural—Pullman does not believe in the supernatural—but it definitely is something related to supernaturalism, and to religion. That something is not hard to find. *Our "we call them something else" word for Specters is "superstitions."*

Although the Specters are religious superstitions in the hidden story, they are something else in the surface story. There they are formless spirit creatures, visible to adults but invisible to children, that attack and devour the souls of humans. Specters don't kill people but do deprive them of their essential humanity, the ability to think and act rationally. Humans who have been overpowered by Specters turn into mindless zombies. Their minds have been clogged with superstition, which has squeezed out knowledge.

Religious people—people who are receptive to superstition—are vulnerable. But not atheists. When Dr. Mary Malone leaves her world (which is also Will's, and ours) and goes to the intermediate world of Cittàgazze, where Specters rule, she is somehow immune to the Specters. The computer, which she has rigged to let the Dust speak to her, has told her she need not fear the Specters. Why is she immune? Pullman doesn't say, but we can reasonably infer that it is because she has become an atheist. A former Catholic nun, she has left the Church and no longer believes in God. Consequently, she no longer harbors, and is no longer receptive to, religious superstition. More precisely, superstition—Specters—can no longer attack her: she is immune to it.

For a clearer understanding of what Pullman's Specters symbolize, and what Will's "we call them something else" means, we need to dig beneath the abstract word "superstitions" to learn more concretely what these superstitions are. Only by thoroughly understanding what religious superstition is can you understand what the Specters are—and what Will rightly suspects can be found in his own world, our world. And only by understanding the depth, breadth, absurdity, and frequent reprehensibility of religious superstition can you really appreciate what Pullman is attacking. He isn't just attacking religion in the abstract. And he isn't just attacking the atrocities committed in the name of religion. He is attacking a detailed complex of bizarre, fantastic religious beliefs.

From an atheist's perspective, which is Pullman's perspective (and mine), religious superstitions can be grouped into five categories: (1) supernatural beings, (2) sin, (3) salvation, (4) practices that establish a friendly relationship with the deity, and (5) miracles and other supernatural occurrences.

We begin with supernatural beings and related supernatural entities. These include

- Gods, including God, Allah, other good gods such as the Hindu gods, and evil gods such as Christianity's Satan and Zoroastrianism's Ahriman (Satan's prototype)
- Goddesses, including such favorites as Mary (a saint to Catholics—first among equals—but definitely a goddess to religious scholars), Isis, Astarte, and Athena
- Angels, which populate Heaven and occasionally come to Earth to deliver messages or do good deeds
- Demons, which cause all sorts of illness and mischief and which even today are being exorcised from insane people by some Catholic priests and even by popes
- Spirits, including Christianity's Holy Spirit, Zoroastrianism's Holy Spirit, the evil spirits to which Jesus attributed and the Bible and the pope still attribute illness and insanity, and the spirits of primitive animism, which inhabit natural objects such as trees and rocks
- Souls, a special type of spirit that inhabits human bodies and lives on in Hell, Limbo, Purgatory, or Heaven after the mortal body dies
- Ghosts, variant souls that hang around Earth instead of going to an afterworld, or else that come back from the afterworld, after the mortal body dies. The Old Testament's ghost of Samuel is an example. A ghost sometimes is amorphous (shapeless) and invisible but other times (e.g., in Dickens's *A Christmas Carol*) has the shape, and even the clothing, of the person who died
- Witches, women who have the ability to perform magic or sorcery (often for evil purposes) and who, in the past, were often burned at the stake or otherwise killed in response to the biblical injunction, "Thou shalt not suffer a witch to live"[55]
- Saints, demigods who are the souls of beatified humans and who serve as intercessors (pleaders) between man and God, sometimes having limited powers of their own
- Valkyries, maidens who serve the god Odin in Norse religion by bringing the souls of worthy slain warriors to Valhalla
- An impersonal metaphysical "force" with which (not whom)

certain Buddhist mystics and other mystics commune in trance-like states of religious "ecstasy." Ecstasy is produced by intense concentration and apparently involves self-induced biochemical changes in the brain, changes that may relate to the brain chemical serotonin

- A somewhat different universal "force" or "higher power" accepted by some Christians and "spiritual" people who no longer believe in a personal God, where God is defined as a rational, self-conscious deity who takes an interest in human affairs, wields power, responds to prayer, and grants or withholds favors. The "force" is an ineffable supernatural entity—not a godlike being—whose role in the universe believers do not understand but that they think might have been involved in the creation of the universe and of life within it. In essence, the "force" is an excuse for believing in a "higher power"—and thereby avoiding the label "atheist"—without believing all the absurdities associated with belief in God and salvation

The second set of religious superstitions concerns sin, defined as a violation of a divine law or command. H. L. Mencken wrote: "Men do not derive their ethical ideas from the powers and principalities of the air; they simply credit those powers with whatever laws they evolve out of their own wisdom or lack of it."[56] Religion nevertheless insists that there exist divine laws written, so to speak, among the stars. A complete recitation of these laws is an impossible task; a limited set of examples must suffice. Assorted divine laws and commands found in the Bible or recognized by various religions, denominations, and congregations (guided by priests, ministers, and rabbis who can read God's mind or interpret ambiguous passages in the Bible and the Torah) include the following:

- You shall not kill.[57]
- Kill any child who curses his father or mother.[58]
- If a man commits adultery with his neighbor's wife, kill both adulterers.[59]

- If a man seduces his daughter-in-law, kill both parties.[60]
- Treat every woman who is divorced on grounds other than unchastity as an adultress.[61]
- Treat every man who marries a divorced woman as an adulterer.[62]
- Stone to death any bride who is not a virgin.[63]
- Burn to death any harlot who is the daughter of a priest.[64]
- Kill any farm boy who is guilty of sodomy with pigs or sheep.[65]
- Kill both of two homosexuals who commit sodomy with each other.[66]
- Do not practice witchcraft.[67]
- Kill every witch (as the good people of Salem did).[68]
- Stone to death any friend who tries to convert you to Islam or Hinduism or Buddhism.[69]
- Kill any prophet or preacher or dreamer who tries to persuade you to worship a god other than God.[70]
- Kill anyone who does any work on the Sabbath, the day of worship.[71]
- Do not educate girls; kill anyone who tries to educate girls (Muslim fundamentalism).[72]
- Teach nothing except religion to schoolboys (Muslim fundamentalism).[73]
- Do not worship Allah, Vishnu, or other non-Judeo-Christian gods.[74]
- Do not use birth control.[75]
- Do not have or perform an abortion.[76]
- Do not have premarital sex.[77]
- Do not have sex with your wife if the world is about to end.[78]
- Do not under any circumstances file for divorce.[79]
- Rule over your wife if you are a husband; be subordinate to your husband if you are a wife.[80]
- Cut off the hand of any woman who, to rescue her husband who is fighting with another man, seizes the private parts of a man who is beating her husband.[81]
- Do not allow any bastard to enter your church or synagogue, and

don't allow any of the next ten generations of his descendants to enter either.[82]

- Do not allow a man whose enemies crushed his testicles or cut off his penis enter your church or synagogue.[83]
- Do not admit widows under sixty years old membership in your church or synagogue.[84]
- Tear down the temples and shrines of conquered people.[85]
- Enslave conquered people, unless they have resisted, in which case kill the men and enslave just the women and children.[86]
- Keep your slaves for six years, but free them in the seventh year.[87]
- Bore a hole through a slave's ear with an awl if he refuses to accept his freedom without being allowed to take his wife and children with him.[88]
- If you are a slave, obey your master.[89]
- Do not gamble, even for small stakes such as pennies.[90]
- Do not drink alcoholic beverages.[91]
- Do not heat your house or other residence on the Sabbath, the day of worship.[92]
- Do not work on the day of worship.[93]
- Do not take God's name in vain (don't say "God damn" or "God dammit").[94]
- Do not call anyone a fool, unless you are Jesus (else you will burn in "the hell of fire").[95]
- Do not tattoo yourself.[96]
- Do not be a homosexual.[97]
- Do not wish for something that belongs to someone else; refraining from stealing or forcefully taking what you wish for isn't enough.[98]
- Do not accumulate material goods—cars, TVs, stoves, books, woolens, toys, tennis racquets, china sets, jewelry, and so on.[99]
- If you lend money to your brother, do not charge interest; your lost earnings on investments belong to your brother.[100]
- Do not hybridize cattle by crossing two breeds—for example, a Guernsey with a Holstein.[101]

- Sacrifice sheep and oxen to God upon an altar.[102]
- Sacrifice your first-born son to God.[103]
- If you are a woman, do not wear skirts shorter than ankle length.[104]
- If you are a married woman whose brother-in-law has been living in your house, and your husband dies, and the brother-in-law refuses to become your husband and take you to bed, publicly spit in his face.[105]
- Do not wear a wool or wool blend suit, dress, skirt, jacket, or coat that has a lining or collar made from a different fabric such as silk, cotton, nylon, polyester, or any combination of these; and do not wear a down-stuffed nylon or polyester jacket with a wool collar.[106]
- If you are a woman, do not wear jeans, slacks, or pants suits.[107]
- If you are a woman, do not go out in public without an appropriate head or face covering, such as a bonnet or white mesh piece (Amish, Mennonite), hijab (Muslim), or burka (Muslim).
- If you are a man, do not go out in public unless you are wearing a black hat (Amish) or yarmulke (Jewish).
- Do not eat rabbit stew, turtle soup, or bacon.[108]
- Do not eat nonkosher food.[109]
- Do not eat beef (Hindu).
- Do not drive cars (conservative Amish)—use buggies instead—or else drive only black cars with black bumpers ("black bumper" Amish and "black bumper" Mennonites).
- Do not touch a corpse or a menstruating woman (Zoroastrianism, ancient Judaism).

A related subset of sin-related superstitions consists of things that do not define sin but instead are beliefs relating to sin. This subset includes

- Original Sin, defined as Adam's and Eve's eating the Forbidden Fruit in violation of God's command. All subsequent generations of mankind are tainted by Original Sin, because it is passed on from generation to generation by the act of fornication. We are all sinners, no matter how guilt-free our personal behavior has been.

- The Immaculate Conception, a Catholic belief holding that Mary, alone among humans (not counting the quasi human Jesus, conceived without fornication), was conceived free from Original Sin. (The Immaculate Conception is often confused with the Virgin Birth.)

- The Atonement, or "He died for our sins"—the belief that Jesus's death on the cross was *necessary*, not just a quirkish act of God, in order that deserving people could be "saved," or admitted to Heaven. (Implicitly, God was not omnipotent—he lacked the power to admit people to Heaven—before the crucifixion; he magically acquired that power by means of the crucifixion.)[110]

The third set of religious superstitions involves salvation in a life after death. These superstitions are closely related to those involving sin, because sin is a barrier to salvation. Sin, or at least venial (forgivable) sin in the case of Catholicism, can be overcome by such means as priestly absolution or prayerful repentance, but unrepented sin— say, by nonreligious persons—and mortal (unforgivable) sin in the case of Catholicism can lead to damnation in the afterlife. The afterworlds, afterstates, and related rewards and punishments of religion's human soul include

- Heaven
- Virgins in Heaven (often seventy-two), awarded to Muslim male martyrs
- Purgatory
- Hell
- Agonizing, unending torture by fire—an eternity of being burned alive—in Hell
- Limbo, a place for blameless persons excluded from Heaven

because they either (*a*) were unbaptized infants too young to make moral choices or (*b*) died before the Christ's crucifixion and therefore had no chance to become Christians

- Sheol, the Hebrew netherworld, a dreary underground place where the ghosts of the dead reside without reward and punishment, except that later Judaism sometimes viewed Sheol as a place where the wicked were punished
- Hades, the Greek equivalent of Sheol, a gloomy subterranean residence of the dead
- Valhalla, in Norse religion the hall of Odin, where the souls of warriors slain in battle are received by their deity
- Reincarnation in a higher human (Hindu transmigration of souls)

The religious superstitions in a fourth group are related to the salvation superstitions in that these new superstitions involve practices believed to enhance the believer's chances of salvation. But the objectives go beyond salvation: these superstitions seek to propitiate the deity, to avoid offending him, to harness his magic, to generally establish a friendly relationship with him, and by these means to obtain services, favors, and protection in the present life as well as salvation in the next life. Examples include

- Formally worshiping God through prayer, invocations, litany, hymns of praise, the doxology (more praise), the gloria patri (still more praise), cross-led processions, bowing and kneeling (humbling oneself), benedictions, candles, monetary offerings, listening to preaching, and various other forms of ritual
- Displaying piety through more prayer (outside of church), blessings before meals (said with palms pressed together), regularly reading the Bible, wearing crucifixes, giving up things for Lent, tithing, ostentatiously expressing one's religious beliefs and devotion to God in Christmas card and telephone answering machine messages, and strictly adhering to religious law, including dress codes and dietary codes

- Eating the deity's body (symbolized by bread in Christianity) and drinking his blood (symbolized by wine or grape juice in Christianity) to absorb desired traits of the deity
- Proselytizing (especially valued by Mormons and Jehovah's Witnesses)
- Confessing sins to a priest, receiving absolution, and doing whatever penance the priest prescribes (a Catholic and Eastern Orthodox practice)
- Manipulating a rosary (formularized praying and prayer counting by Roman Catholics), sometimes—not always—as a form of penance
- Turning prayer wheels (mechanical praying by Buddhist monks)
- Tearing off and folding enough strips of toilet paper to provide for an entire family during the twenty-four hours of the Sabbath, when such "work" is forbidden (Orthodox Jews)
- Being baptized, or using water to cleanse oneself of sin (especially valued by Baptists, who emphasize baptism by immersion)
- Ritually cleansing oneself with cow's urine six times a day over several days to remove defilement caused by contact with a tabooed object (Zoroastrianism)
- Washing away the sins of a religious initiate by slaying a bull on a grate above a pit where the initiate stands and bathes and self-baptizes himself in the bull's warm blood that flows down through the openings in the grate (worshippers of Attis and Mithras)
- Ritually transferring the sins of the people onto a goat (the Hebrew scapegoat) and then sending the sin-bearing goat away into the wilderness (ancient Judaism)[111]
- Seeking the application of holy water
- Crossing oneself
- Burning incense
- Wearing or carrying amulets or talismans
- Having a priest smudge one's forehead with ashes on Ash Wednesday
- Chanting Hindu mantras

- Reciting the Apostles' Creed or the Nicene Creed
- Prostrating oneself facing Mecca
- Self-flagellation, practiced by many Muslims
- Erecting crosses beside highways
- Nailing "The Lord Is Coming" signs on trees beside highways
- Making pilgrimages
- Sacrificing humans

The fifth group of religious superstitions involves miracles and other supernatural happenings. The following beliefs are prominent examples:

- God created the world in six days, making man out of dust in the process.[112]
- God created the first woman (Eve) out of a rib from the first man (Adam).[113]
- God created daylight, together with separate periods of day and night, on the first day, before he created the sun, the moon, and the stars on the fourth day.[114]
- A serpent spoke to Eve in the Garden of Eden.[115]
- God turned Lot's wife into a pillar of salt for disobeying God's arbitrary command not to look back at the volcanic destruction of her home.[116]
- The scattered bones in the valley of dry bones assembled themselves into skeletons, took on flesh, and came back to life when spoken to by the prophet Ezekiel.[117]
- Shadrach, Meshach, and Abednego survived unharmed, along with an angel sent by God to protect them, when cast into the fiery furnace by King Nebuchadnezzar.[118]
- A disembodied hand appeared out of nowhere and frightened King Belshazzar by writing "Mene, Mene, Tekel, Parsin" on the wall.[119]
- The Witch of Endor conjured up the ghost of Samuel, who spoke to Saul.[120]
- God spoke to Moses from a burning bush.[121]

- Moses and Aaron performed several miracles to impress the Pharaoh, but the Pharaoh's magicians were able to duplicate some of the miracles—turning their rods into serpents, turning water into blood, and bringing forth swarms of frogs. Only when Moses and Aaron brought forth a swarm of gnats from the dust were the magicians unable to duplicate the miracle.[122]
- The Red Sea's waters parted for Moses and his people when Moses, following instructions from God, lifted up his rod, stretched out his hand, and "divided" the water.[123]
- Jesus was born of a virgin.[124]
- Jesus went up onto the Mount of Transfiguration, and there the ghosts or reincarnations of Moses and Elijah appeared to him and talked with him.[125]
- Jesus walked on water.[126]
- Jesus placed a curse on a fig tree, causing it to wither and die, when the tree had no figs for the hungry prophet.[127]
- Jesus cast out demons from the infirm and the insane, curing them.[128]
- Jesus gave sight to a man who had been blind since birth by making a paste of clay and spit, rubbing it in the man's eyes, and having the man rinse his eyes in a pool.[129]
- Jesus brought the dead back to life.[130]
- Jesus arose from the dead and walked on earth again three days after dying on the cross.[131]
- After his resurrection, Jesus walked through a solid wall to join and speak to his eleven loyal disciples, who were meeting in a room with the doors shut.[132]
- The resurrected Jesus appeared to the disciples "during forty days," and then, "as they were looking on, he was lifted up, and a cloud took him out of their sight" to Heaven, which is in the sky, above Earth.[133]
- Jesus will have a Second Coming at a time in the near future.[134]
- The resurrection of the dead, a concomitant of the Second Coming, will occur on a future Judgment Day.[135]

- The Assumption (a Catholic doctrine) took place: Mary's physical body—not just her soul as with everyone else except Jesus and Elijah—was lifted up into Heaven.
- Protestant fundamentalist preachers have successfully performed faith healing and obtained laying-of-hands cures.
- Registered second-party Christian Science "practitioners" have healed the sick by praying for them, often at locations hundreds or even thousands of miles from the sick persons.
- Roman Catholic priests and popes have cured insanity (the usual affliction) by performing exorcisms to cast out the demons responsible for the afflicted person's condition.
- After Jesus's death, his disciples Peter and John gave the ability to walk and leap to a man "lame from birth" who "was being carried." They did this by directing their gazes at him while Peter took the man's hand and said, "In the name of Jesus Christ of Nazareth, walk."[136]
- Witches have caused bad weather.[137]
- Snake cult snake handlers receive divine protection from snakebite.
- Glossolalia ("speaking in tongues") uttered by Pentecostal sect members ("Holy Rollers") is the result of being possessed by the Holy Spirit.
- Spiritualist sect members can speak to the spirits of the dead, and vice versa.
- Voodoo priests can harm or kill people by sticking pins in voodoo doll effigies of the victims.
- European witch cultists could harm or kill people by making wax images of their enemies and slowly melting the images near small fires.

You might believe that some or even most of these beliefs embody truth, should be accepted, and therefore are not superstitions. And you might be right, if whatever supernaturalistic beliefs you accept really do represent Truth. But the point here is that these are the type of

204 PHILIP PULLMAN'S *HIS DARK MATERIALS*

beliefs that *Pullman*, an atheist, would regard as superstition. To accept any one of the above beliefs is, from an atheist's point of view, to accept a superstition, a false belief in something supernatural. These superstitions are found *in our world*, Will's world. They are our world's Specters, the images Will sees dimly when he says, "Maybe we call them [the Specters] something else." We call them superstitions (but only when we don't believe them ourselves).

One more consideration supports the idea that the Specters symbolize religious superstition. It is well known that Pullman does not believe in God and that he wrote the *HDM* trilogy as a rebuttal to C. S. Lewis's *LWW*. At the end of Pullman's story, there exist myriads of windows that must be closed. In the context of an atheistic story, what is it that needs to be closed? The logical answer is that the windows represent something atheists would be happy to see disappear. In the story context, this something can't be God, because he died a little earlier in the story. Besides, God is just one entity, whereas the windows are a multitude. It is hard to imagine a more persuasive "multitude" needing to be closed than the multitude of churches, the purveyors of superstition.

The windows and the Specters are closely related in the hidden story; they go hand in hand. The windows are churches, sects, and religions. These organizations are our society's "windows" through which superstitions are seen and accepted as Truth. The Specters are the superstitions seen through churches. Each time the subtle knife cuts (opens) a new window, a new Specter is created: each time a new sect appears, it brings with it (*a*) new superstitions that distinguish the new sect from others, (*b*) old superstitions being delivered to new worshippers, or (*c*) both.

THE NARROW THEME: THERE IS NO HEAVEN

Within Pullman's broad theme of warfare between knowledge and superstition, the chief superstition needing to be destroyed is the belief in Heaven. Like Islam but unlike Judaism, Christianity is what scholars call a salvation religion. The overriding purpose of Christianity is to prepare people for salvation—life with God in the next world. Those who worship God, obey his laws, engage in the proper rituals (e.g., baptism and Communion) and other religious practices (e.g., prayer and dress), and ask God or Jesus for forgiveness can be "saved." Different churches have different requirements for salvation but, in general, "every little bit helps." After death, the people who are saved can enter the Kingdom of God, more commonly called Heaven. There the "saved" are reunited with loved ones and enjoy eternal bliss in a life beyond the grave. In this afterlife they can fraternize with angels, saints, and perhaps even God and Jesus. But *most people are not saved*. In Jesus's words, "Enter by the narrow gate; for the gate is wide . . . that leads to destruction [Hell]. . . . For many are called, but *few are chosen*."[138] Those not chosen by the Christ for salvation will be cast into the "furnace of fire" where, Jesus warned, "men will weep and gnash their teeth."[139] Christianity is a tool—an essential tool—for enabling believers to be among the chosen few.

The Surface Story's Message. Pullman's message that there is no Heaven is visible in both the literally told surface story and the surface story's symbolism. The surface story is about the adventures of Lyra Belacqua and Will Parry; Will is in only the last two books. Will is twelve years old when the story begins, and Lyra is "about his own age"[140] when she meets him and about eleven when her adventures begin. But time passes. The two children reach puberty and fall in love at the story's end. In between, conversations in the surface story openly challenge the Christian belief in Heaven. At one point, the angel Baruch tells Will that "the churches . . . tell their believers that they'll live in Heaven, but that's a lie."[141]

How big a lie? The two children visit the world of the dead and discover its horrors. There is no separation of the good and the wicked. Upon dying, *everyone* goes to the same place, the world of the dead. It is a wasteland, a dismally oppressive place where the ghosts of the dead just stand or sit in gloom. There is no running or jumping or laughing. Harpies occasionally attack "with gusts of rotten stink, battering wings, and those raucous screams."[142] The angel Balthamos calls the world of the dead "a prison camp."[143]

One of the ghosts describes how the Church has spread falsehoods about life after death: "When we were alive, they told us that when we died we'd go to Heaven. And they said that Heaven was a place of joy and glory and we would spend eternity in the company of saints and angels praising the Almighty, in a state of bliss. That's what they said. And that's what led some of us to give our lives, and others to spend years in solitary prayer, while all the joy of life was going to waste around us and we never knew. Because the land of the dead isn't a place of reward or a place of punishment. It's a place of nothing. The good come here as well as the wicked, and all of us languish in this gloom forever, with no hope of freedom, or joy, or sleep, or rest, or peace."[144]

To emphasize the message, Pullman metaphorically describes what really happens when we die. What really happens, of course, is that we get buried, we decay, and the decay gets taken up by the roots of trees and other vegetation. Or our ashes are scattered and dissolve in the wind, the earth, and the waters. Or, under less favorable circumstances, our bodies are consumed by vultures, bears, ants, other scavengers, fungi, and bacteria and are recycled that way. Pullman's metaphor is Lyra's description of what will happen when the ghosts emerge from the world of the dead and experience genuine death: "When you go out of here, all the particles that make you up will loosen and float apart. . . . All the atoms . . . [will go] into the air and the wind and the trees and the earth and all the living things. They'll never vanish [they'll just be recycled]."[145]

The surface story also attacks the Heaven-related belief that a supernatural soul lives on and goes to Heaven or Hell after the physical body dies. In Pullman's story it is the soul that vanishes and the body that, in the form of a ghost, goes to the afterworld. Each human and witch has a daemon (pronounced "demon"), usually of the opposite sex. The daemon is that person's outside-the-body soul and is an essential part of the person. It shares that person's intelligence and talks to its human. But the daemon has the form of an animal: cricket, snake, mouse, ermine, cat, dog, skunk, pine marten, monkey, bear, lion, firefly, moth, bat, sparrow, goose, or other creature. A child's daemon changes from one animal to another constantly, mostly in response to shifts in the child's mood or situation. But at puberty the daemon "settles": it assumes a permanent form that reflects the person's supposedly stabilized personality or status (servants have dog daemons).

The essential points here are that, rather than being an inner spirit like theology's soul, the daemon (*a*) is external and (*b*) has the physical substance and form of an animal. External, not internal. Physical substance, not spirit. When a person dies, that person's daemon vanishes. Poof! The soul does not go to Heaven or any other afterworld. This bit of irony—the body, not the soul, lives on—is Pullman's way of saying that we have no supernatural, spiritlike souls that survive after we die.

The Hidden Story's Message. The symbolically told hidden story repeats the surface story's attack on the belief in Heaven. Recall that the universe of Pullman's surface story has three main worlds; these don't count some other worlds of secondary importance and still other "interpenetrating" worlds, numbering in the millions, that exist but have little to do with the story. The three main worlds are (1) Lyra's and Asriel's home world, (2) Will's and Mary's home world, which is our own Earth, and (3) Cittàgazze's intermediate world, which serves as a passageway between the first and second worlds. As explained in the opening paragraphs of my chapter 1, Will's and Mary's world symbolizes Paradise—the Paradise of *PL*—in this allegory.

At the end of the story, Lyra longs to go to Paradise with Will, who must return there. But she can't: people who go to another world and stay there die in about ten years. Although Lyra could theoretically go and then return to her world through a window before the ten years were up, that isn't a practical possibility. Keeping a window open would allow Dust to escape. Nor could Will use his knife to open and close a new window periodically, allowing Lyra to travel back and forth occasionally to regain her health. The knife must be destroyed lest it fall into the wrong hands. The knife let in the Specters that laid ruin to the world of Cittàgazze. In the hands of Church people, it would bring ruin. Specters would run wild, as they did in Cittàgazze. This means Lyra must remain in her own world. And Will must return to his, to care for his mentally ill mother—and to stay alive for more than ten years.

So the two lovers must part. Lyra must live in her world and Will in his. Lyra cannot go to Paradise. For her, there no Paradise. There will be no life of bliss in another world. Lyra's inability to enjoy a blissful life in the symbolic Paradise is Pullman's way of saying that there is no Heaven. Earlier, the ghost of Will Parry's father stated the message directly: "We can only live in our own [world]. . . . We have to build the Republic of Heaven where we are, because there is no elsewhere."[146] Translation: There is no supernatural Heaven.

For emphasis, Pullman repeats this message in the concluding lines of the trilogy. Lyra's daemon recalls Will's saying "there isn't any elsewhere." Lyra interprets: "I remember. He meant the Kingdom was over, the Kingdom of Heaven, it was all finished. We shouldn't live as if it mattered more than life in this world, because where we are is always the most important place." Lyra might have gone to Will's world, a figurative Paradise, for ten years before dying, "but then we wouldn't have been able to build it." Lyra's daemon asks, "Build what?" "The *Republic* [not God's Kingdom] of Heaven," replies Lyra.[147]

CHAPTER 6

PARADISE LOST RETOLD

Setting, Characters, and Events

The preceding chapter summarized the second allegory's hidden story (not to be confused with the surface story) and presented the allegory's main themes. Those themes include a broad theme and a narrow one. The broad theme is that knowledge (Dust) and religious superstition (Specters) are at war. Superstition is a threat to knowledge: Specters grow by eating Dust. The narrow theme emphasizes a particular superstition, life in Heaven after death. "The life everlasting" is basic to Christianity, so Pullman is especially hostile to it. In this chapter we shall see how Pullman uses surface story places, characters, things, and events to tell the hidden story and develop his antireligious themes.

THE HIDDEN STORY'S SETTING

In the opening lines of *Paradise Lost* (*PL*), Satan gathers his wits after being cast into Hell by Jesus. He soon gets organized and builds his capital, Pandemonium. Then he decides to get revenge against God. He will go up to Earth and lead astray Adam and Eve, God's new creations. To do this, Satan must cross a great void, a chasm of darkness and chaos, between Hell and Earth. With incredible difficulty, he struggles upward. Sin and Death (personified) later follow him, paving the path blazed by Satan to create "a bridge of wondrous length" from

Hell to Earth.[1] This is the bridge over which countless sinners will follow Sin and Death back to Hell in the future.

At the end of *The Golden Compass* (*GC*), Lord Asriel uses an incredible burst of energy, released from Roger's body the instant Roger and his daemon die, to build a "bridge to the stars."[2] The bridge actually leads from Lyra's world across the aurora borealis to the world of Cittàgazze. Asriel, who is Pullman's Satan symbol, crosses over into Cittàgazze, a coastal city in the new world. Lyra and Pantalaimon—Sin and Death—follow. Here (1) the home world of Asriel and Lyra symbolizes Hell, (2) the world of Cittàgazze symbolizes Earth, situated above Hell and below Heaven in *PL*, (3) the aurora borealis is the chaotic void separating Hell and Earth, (4) Asriel's crossing the bridge symbolizes Satan's crossing from Hell to Earth, and (5) Lyra's and Pantalaimon's crossing symbolizes "Sin and Death . . . following his track."[3]

Now we need to inspect the above two worlds—Lyra's and Cittàgazze's—from a different perspective, bringing a third world into the picture and omitting Heaven. The three main worlds of *His Dark Materials* (*HDM*) are these:

- *The world Lyra and Lord Asriel come from.* This world loosely resembles early twentieth-century (and earlier) Earth: there are zeppelins, transport balloons, rifles, and crossbows, as well as— surprisingly—cars and vans. The world is populated not only by humans but by supernatural creatures—daemons (pronounced "demons"), witches, armored bears, cliff-ghasts, and evil spirits (inside the spy-flies). There is also a man—a shaman—with supernatural powers. The supernaturalism ties in with this world's allegorical identity: Hell.
- *The world Will Parry and Mary Malone come from.* This is a world with Rolls Royces, cell phones, computers, floppy discs, microfilm, ballpoint pens, movies, Burger Kings, Coca Cola, chewing gum, credit cards, ATMs, PINs, and a *former* Soviet Union. It is our own Earth, set in the 1990s. Nothing is super-

natural except the angels in Mary's computer and a window to Cittàgazze. In the *PL* allegory, this world symbolizes Bliss, Paradise, and Eden, all of which amount to the same thing. Although there is a sense in which this world also represents Heaven, the afterworld where most of today's Christians expect to go when they die, it should not be interpreted as Heaven: Heaven in this allegory is the Clouded Mountain, a place in the sky above the other worlds. In *PL* there is a clear distinction between Heaven (where God dwells and Jesus drives his chariot) and Paradise (Eden, the place where humans dwell, located on Earth, below Heaven).

• *The world of Cittàgazze (City of Magpies).* This is an intermediate world that must be passed through to get from Will's world to Lyra's and vice versa. Among the Cittàgazze inhabitants are supernatural Specters. The intermediate world is modeled after both (1) the wardrobe from *LWW*, which is an intermediate place or passageway between the children's home world and Narnia, and (2) the Earth of *PL*, which is an intermediate place situated below heaven—Earth is suspended from Heaven on a golden chain—and above Hell. In this allegory we are concerned with only the second model.

HDM also features fourth, fifth, sixth, seventh, eighth, and ninth worlds, best described as secondary worlds. The fourth world is the world where Asriel builds his fortress. The fifth is where the *mulefa*, or wheeled animals, live. The sixth is the one to which Lyra and Will go temporarily when they escape from the cave and from which they return to Lyra's world to have Iorek mend the broken knife. (This is also the world that Will briefly entered earlier to find a place to cut his way stealthily into the cave where Lyra was being held prisoner by Mrs. Coulter.) The seventh world is the one Will cuts his way into from Lyra's world to achieve safety after Iorek mends the knife. The eighth is one Will and Lyra go to next and from which they escape to the suburbs of the dead when they hear soldiers coming. The ninth is the suburbs of the dead, from which they enter the land of the dead by crossing a lake to an island with the entry gate.

The land of the dead is not a separate world in the sense that the other worlds are. It is instead an underworld that lies below all the other worlds and that, unlike the upper worlds, does not have the same geography as all the other worlds. It can lie below all the other worlds because all of the upper worlds are "interpenetrating":[4] they occupy the same space but belong to different dimensions, which means they don't physically interact or interfere with each other and which also means that a person can be in only one world at a time.

PULLMAN'S *PARADISE LOST* ALLEGORY'S SYMBOLIC CHARACTERS

The characters who symbolize persons and things from *Paradise Lost*, the Bible, theology, and other religious and mythological sources are the Authority, Metatron, Lord Asriel, the Master of Jordan, Lyra Belacqua, Pantalaimon (Lyra's daemon), Lyra's "death" spirit (her guide to the land of the dead), Roger Parslow, Salcilia (Roger's daemon), Will Parry, John Parry and Mrs. (Elaine) Parry, the upstairs intruder in Will's house, Mrs. (Marisa) Coulter, the witches, the Gallivespians, Baruch, Father MacPhail, King Ogunwe, Mary Malone, Xaphania, the intercised children, the "zombies" who have been possessed by Specters, the dead being ferried across the lake to the land of the dead, the aged boatman who ferries the dead, and Metatron again, in a second role. Most will be interpreted in this section; some are bound up with events interpreted in the following section and will be discussed there.

The Authority. We begin with "the Authority." He is so obviously a symbol for God that not much need be said about him. The Authority was the first angel to form from Dust. In a monumental lie, he told the later angels that he was the Creator of the universe and of the angels. He has become the Supreme Being that the churches of the various worlds worship. But he is now extremely old, feeble, senile, and moribund. He has delegated his power to his Regent of Heaven, Metatron.

As explained by the angel Balthamos to Will, the Authority goes by many names: "The Authority, God, the Creator, the Lord, Yahweh, El, Adonai, the King, the Father, the Almighty—those were all names he gave himself."[5] Most of those names except the first—it comes from Pullman—are easily recognizable as names applied to the God of Judeo-Christian religion. *Father* can be found in the opening words of the Lord's Prayer: "Our Father, who art in Heaven." A well-known hymn features three of the names in a row in its first line: "Holy, Holy, Holy! Lord God Almighty!"[6] So do the opening words of the Apostles' Creed: "I believe in God, the Father Almighty . . ." *Yahweh* comes from God's ancient Hebrew name, usually rendered in English as YHWH, spelled without vowels in early Hebrew writing. The vowels *a* and *e* were added in the Hebrew Bible much later, in the seventh century AD, to agree with the usual oral pronunciation, "Yahweh." (Look up "Tetragrammaton" and "Yahweh" in your dictionary.) *Adonai*, originally DNY before the addition of vowels, is the Hebrew word for "Lord." In Baalism, an ancient nature religion of the Middle East, *El* was the father god who begat all the other gods; the goddess Asherah was the mother. Baal, who is better known, seems to have been their grandson and was a rival of Yahweh. A longer form, *El Shaddai*, was an earlier name for Yahweh, as was *Elohim*.[7]

By giving the Authority all these names and appellations that are associated with God, Pullman removes all doubt that the Authority is God. The only issue is whether we have symbolism or literalism. Pullman has come very close to not just symbolizing God but literally saying that the Authority is God. He even includes "God" in the list of names by which the Authority is called. The only differences between Christianity's God and the Authority are that (*a*) God is immortal whereas the Authority is mortal and (*b*) God is the Creator of the universe and man whereas the Authority only claims to be the Creator.

Pullman introduces these two differences because he knows God can die (as a belief) and because he knows God is not really the Creator of the universe and man. (In Friedrich Nietzsche's magnum opus, *Thus Spake Zarathustra*, higher man "kills" God by ceasing to believe, not by literally killing a living being.)

Metatron. In Jewish mythology, Metatron is a high-ranking angel who was formerly the prophet Elijah[8] (but formerly Enoch in Pullman's story) and who is now the only angel permitted to remain seated in the presence of God. Who, if anyone, does Metatron symbolize in Pullman's story? A possible clue, but a misleading one, appears in the Bible's book of Revelation and again in Milton's *PL*. Revelation 12:7–9 tells of a war in Heaven between rebellious angels led by Satan and angels loyal to God, led by Michael. Pullman reprises this conflict by providing another war between loyal angels and rebellious ones. The loyal angels are led by Metatron, the rebellious ones by Lord Asriel. At first glance, then, Metatron would seem to symbolize Michael.

But Michael is just a minor character in the Bible, whereas Metatron is far more important in Pullman's trilogy. Evidence from *PL* permits no doubt that Pullman is using Metatron to symbolize Jesus, the Christ (messiah). In *PL*, Michael and Gabriel initially lead God's loyal angels in the fight against Satan's rebel angels. But when Michael and Gabriel encounter difficulty, Jesus takes over. Driving his "fierce chariot," Jesus herds the rebels to the wall of Heaven.[9] The wall opens, and Jesus forces Satan and his rebels over the edge of Heaven, sending them cascading into Hell.

In Pullman's trilogy, Metatron moves across the sky in a floating "Clouded Mountain," also called "the Chariot" in three places.[10] The Chariot moves "with the Regent at the reins."[11] Metatron uses this Chariot in attacking Asriel's Republic of Heaven. Metatron's "driving" the Chariot and his using it to attack the rebel angels affirm that Metatron symbolizes the Christ, as depicted in *PL*. Identifying Metatron with the Christ is the whole point of calling the Clouded Mountain "the Chariot." Were "Chariot" not an allusion to the Christ's chariot from *PL*, there would be no reason to give the Clouded Mountain two names.

As the clincher, Metatron descends into a symbolized Hell, thereby reenacting the line from the Apostles' Creed that says Jesus "descended into Hell" after his crucifixion. Metatron's descent into Hell (beneath Asriel's fortress) will be discussed in more detail in this chapter's next section, "Places, Things, and Events as Symbols."

Lord Asriel. Once you figure out who Metatron symbolizes, it's easy to deduce who Lyra's father, Lord Asriel, represents. In both Revelation and *PL*, Jesus and God's loyal angels are opposed by Satan and his rebellious angels. Correspondingly, in *HDM*, Lord Asriel and his rebel angels have gone to war with the Kingdom of Heaven. The conclusion is inescapable: Asriel, leader of rebel angels, symbolizes Satan, leader of the earlier rebel angels.

Further, and absolutely conclusive, evidence of who Asriel symbolizes is the "bridge to the stars" symbolism presented earlier in connection with the setting. Asriel's bridge from Lyra's world across the aurora borealis to the world of Cittàgazze plainly symbolizes Satan's bridge from Hell to Earth. When Asriel crosses his bridge, Pullman is symbolizing Satan's crossing the *PL* bridge. This means that Asriel symbolizes Satan. (In *PL* Satan really just blazes a "track" through the void that separates Hell from Earth; Sin and Death, following Satan's track, then "pave a broad highway or bridge over Chaos."[12] But we cannot doubt that Pullman is attributing the bridge to Satan, who provided the bridge's substructure.)

You might ask: how can Satan be on the side of good, the side of knowledge? That question is easily answered. Pullman is writing an antireligious opus. In it the forces of religion are evil and the opponents of religion are good. Metatron, symbolizing the Christ, is evil. Asriel, symbolizing Satan, the enemy of the Christ, is therefore good.

The idea that Asriel is Satan does seem to conflict with explicit statements by Pullman identifying Mary Malone as "the serpent." Mary introduces Lyra, the "new Eve," to knowledge—specifically, knowledge about love, which represents knowledge in the abstract.

Dust, symbolizing knowledge, begins to fall from the sky onto Lyra and Will when they fall in love. According to both *PL* and popular theology, the serpent in the Garden of Eden was Satan. But in Genesis the serpent, or tempter, in Eden is not identified as Satan. This fact allows Pullman to treat Satan and the serpent as separate entities. A further consideration is that Mary's role as the serpent is explicit and is presented as a figure of speech, a metaphor, whereas Asriel's role as Satan involves subtlety and must be recognized through deduction. We can be sure that Mary, though she is a figurative serpent or tempter, is not the Satan symbol. Asriel is Satan.

Lord Asriel's name comes from that of Asriel (also spelled Azrael), an angel who is one of Islam's six most important angels and who personifies death. Lord Asriel brings death to Metatron (Jesus). In the Old Testament, Numbers 26:31, Asriel is a human, the founder of the Jewish family of Asrielites. In the Bible's apocryphal book of Tobit, Asriel is again an angel.

Asriel's daemon is a snow leopard named Stelmaria. Stelmaria is apparently not a symbol. Her name's origin is uncertain. *Stella*, as in *stellar*, is Latin for "star," so *Stel* could be based on Asriel's "Bridge to the Stars." *Maria* might then be nothing more than a device to feminize the name: daemons and their humans are generally opposite in sex. A feminine name with religious connotations—say, a name mentioned in "Ave Maria"—goes best with the allegory's religious subject matter. A more intriguing possibility is that *Stelmaria* is based on, and a mockery of, "Ave Maria." *Ave Maria* is Latin for "Hail Mary" (both a salutation and a popular Catholic prayer, customarily said multiple times with a rosary). If we switch from Latin to Greek, *stel* and *stele* mean an upright inscribed slab of stone, a gravestone, or a pillar. *Gravestone* fits—in a perverse sort of way. *Gravestone Maria* can be loosely translated as "the Virgin Mary is dead," which is certainly consonant with Asriel's (and Pullman's) views on religion.

The Master of Jordan. The Master of Jordan is one of several *HDM* characters who are symbols in both allegories, representing different persons or things in different allegories. In the first allegory, the

Master symbolizes the kindly old Professor whose house the children are living in while London is being bombed. In the *PL* allegory he plays, as you would expect, the role of a character from *PL*.

The key to interpreting the Master is found in his big scene. At the very beginning of the trilogy, in chapter 1 of *GC*, the Master performs the act represented in the chapter's title, "The Decanter of Tokay." He puts poison in a decanter of Tokay wine he expects Lord Asriel to pour a drink from. The attempt to poison Asriel is unsuccessful, because Lyra, hiding in the wardrobe, sees the Master put the poison in the wine and soon thereafter warns Asriel. When the porter comes into the room—Lyra is still hiding—Asriel knocks the decanter to the floor and blames the porter.

The unsuccessful attempt to poison Asriel has "symbolism" written all over it. And the symbolism necessarily relates to the *PL* allegory: the Master symbolizes the Professor in the first allegory, and the Professor doesn't try to kill anyone—besides which Asriel is, in the first allegory, offstage playing Churchill, whom nobody tries to kill. The question is: where in *PL* does someone try to kill Satan? In book VI of *PL* the answer appears. Book VI describes the war in Heaven between Satan's rebel angels and God's loyal angels. (Like earlier epics such as Homer's *The Odyssey*, Milton's epic does not begin at the beginning. It begins with Satan lying in Hell on a lake of fire, having been cast out of Heaven. This is why the war in Heaven isn't presented until book VI, where the angel Raphael describes to Adam what happened earlier.)

During the first day of fighting, God's forces are led by the archangel Michael; Jesus has not yet taken charge. Michael and Satan, both armed with swords, meet on the battlefield. Both raise their swords to strike. Michael's sword is so tempered that it will cut through anything. (This may be where Pullman got the idea for a "subtle knife" that cuts through anything; the knife's edge that kills—one of two edges—is like the edges of Michael's sword.) Michael and Satan strike simultaneously, but Satan's sword is no match for Michael's. Michael's sword cuts Satan's in half and then, reversing, slices through Satan's right side. Poor Satan. He is convulsed with pain. But, being an angel, he can't be killed. He soon recovers and returns to action on the second day of fighting. That's when Heaven really gets messed up, with both sides throwing hills and mountains at their opponents. God decides to stop the tearing up of Heaven. He sends Jesus out, unassisted, to put an end to the revolt. Using his chariot, Jesus does just that.

The point here is that Michael tries unsuccessfully to kill Satan. Asriel symbolizes Satan. Who is it that tries unsuccessfully to kill Asriel? The Master of Jordan. So the Master symbolizes Michael. And the Master's unsuccessful attempt to poison Asriel symbolizes Michael's unsuccessful attempt to kill Satan. The poison symbolizes Michael's sword. Don't be fooled by the fact that Michael didn't use poison. To repeat, one good analogy is all it takes to create a symbol. In the previous allegory, Mrs. Coulter (the witch) used poison to kill Boreal-Latrom (Tumnus, the faun). That was good symbolism even though, in *The Lion, the Witch and the Wardrobe* (*LWW*), the witch "killed" (turned to stone) Tumnus with her wand, not with poison. In that allegory, the poison symbolized the wand.

Lyra Belacqua. Lyra Belacqua is the heroine and central character of the trilogy. Who or what, if anything, does she symbolize? Many reviewers have assumed she symbolizes Eve, because in several places the surface story refers to her as a new "Eve." Lyra is "the one who came before" and who will "come again" and who is "Eve, again."[13] She "is in the position of Eve, the wife of Adam, the mother of us all" and is also "Eve, who is going to be tempted and who . . . will fall," and she will "somehow, sometime soon, be tempted, as Eve was."[14] Not only that, Mary Malone's computer, wired for communication with angels, tells Mary she "must play the serpent," implicitly a new version of the serpent that tempted the original Eve in the Garden of Eden.[15] Lyra's "tempter" will "play the serpent," which again implies that Lyra will be a new Eve.[16] But this new Eve is merely a figurative Eve, not the literal Eve of Christian theology and not a reincarnation of the original Eve. Pullman does have a genuine, nonfigurative Eve symbol, but that symbol is Will Parry's mother, as will be explained later in this chapter.

Although Lyra is a figurative Eve, she has this role only *in the surface story*. In the allegory's hidden story she is someone else. That person personifies something abstract, something the Bible's Eve does. Moreover, Lyra's "fall" involves falling in love; she does not fall in theology's sense of falling from God's grace—sinning by disobeying God.

What Lyra symbolizes in the *PL* allegory is Sin. She symbolizes Sin in two different ways. The first relates to *PL*, the second to the Genesis myth of Adam and Eve.

(1) THE *PL* BASIS FOR LYRA = SIN: The earlier discussion of the *PL* allegory's setting revealed that Sin and Death, personified, follow Satan over the bridge from Hell to Earth. This event now demands closer inspection. In book II of *PL*, Satan prepares for his trip from Hell up to Earth: he flies to the gates of Hell. The gates are guarded by Sin and Death, both of whom are personified curses that will soon be inflicted on mankind. Death, more of a "shape" or "goblin" than an anthropomorphic being, advances "with horrid strides" to block Satan's way. Satan scornfully rebukes Death, who responds by threatening to kill Satan with his "mortal dart" (arrow);[17] Satan too radiates mortal intent.

At this point Sin rushes between them. Her hideous appearance will be described when we get to the witches. For now, suffice it to say that she reveals to the unsuspecting Satan that she is his daughter: she addresses him as "father." Back in Heaven, she sprang from his head when he became filled with envy of the newly arrived Jesus. Sin also reveals that Death is her son and Satan's, the consequence of Satan's having incestuously raped her while they were still in Heaven. Sin holds the key to Hell's gates and has been forbidden by God to unlock them. But Satan tells her he has come to set her and Death free from their "house of pain." Sin seems to think this is a swell idea and, besides, she is already mad at God for having thrust her down into Hell's gloom. She decides to disobey God. Sin decides to sin! Taking her key to the gates, she opens them for Satan. He then begins his arduous climb to Earth. Sin and Death eventually follow. When they get to Earth, they will bring sin and death to Adam and Eve and to their descendants.

Lyra is Asriel's daughter.[18] Asriel is Satan. Therefore, Lyra is Sin, Satan's daughter. If those facts don't convince you, consider this incontrovertible evidence: Lyra and Pantalaimon follow Asriel (Satan) across his "Bridge to the Stars" when he proceeds from his world (symbolizing Hell) to Cittàgazze's (symbolizing Earth). Who do you suppose symbolizes Death? Who accompanies Lyra across the "Bridge to the Stars"?

The child of Satan part is clear enough: Lyra is the daughter of Asriel (Satan) and Mrs. Coulter. But in what sense is Lyra the mother of Death? She is the mother of Death in two senses, the second of which is the more important. First, in Pullman's story, the dead do not really die, at least not at first. Whether good or bad during their mortal lives, all humans live on as ghosts in the land of the dead. Without dying—without becoming a ghost—Lyra goes to the land of the dead and finds a way to lead the dead out of their prison. Once outside, the ghosts truly die: they joyously dissolve into atoms and become part of the night, the air, the leaves, the grass, and all else that is nature. So delightful is their vanishing that Will is reminded of "the bubbles in a glass of champagne."[19] Pullman is saying, symbolically, that when we die our bodies decompose, or are converted to smoke and ashes, or are eaten by scavengers, so that our atoms are recycled into trees, rivers, air, and other things in the natural world; we do not go to Heaven, Hell, or Purgatory. The immediate point, though, is that Lyra brings genuine death to the suffering ghosts, the *living* dead. So she is the metaphorical mother of Death, the genuine death that replaces the semidead status of ghosts. As such—as the mother of Death—she is, according to Milton, Sin.

(2) THE GENESIS BASIS FOR LYRA = SIN: The second way Lyra symbolizes Sin relates to the Adam and Eve story from the Bible's book of Genesis. In Christian theology, sin is bad. Not just bad,

horrible: it can send you to Hell. Why is sin so horrible? Because sin is disobeying a command or law of God, the worst possible offense. But in Pullman's hidden story, sin is good. It is partaking of the fruit of the Tree of Knowledge: it is acquiring knowledge—knowledge in the broadest sense, not just the narrow knowledge of sexuality that Adam and Eve acquire when they eat the Forbidden Fruit.

Let's compare Lyra's sin with Eve's. Eve was the first person to sin. God had forbidden Adam and Eve to eat fruit from the Tree of Knowledge. But after being tempted by the serpent, Eve sinned by eating the Forbidden Fruit. Adam then followed suit. Theologians call Eve's Original Sin, along with Adam's, "the Fall." Adam and Eve fell from God's grace and were expelled from Eden when they disobeyed him and ate the Forbidden Fruit.

Lyra is similarly tempted by a serpent, a figurative one. In Lyra's case, the "serpent" is explicitly identified as Mary Malone. Mary tells Lyra how she, Mary, once fell in love. Mary's "fall"—her falling in love—symbolically "tempts" Lyra to fall herself. Soon afterward, Lyra eats red fruit from a new Tree of Knowledge. Just as the original Eve fell, the second Eve, Lyra, "falls": she falls in love with Will. She thereby acquires knowledge of love, which represents knowledge in a broader sense. To the Church, knowledge is sin. By acquiring knowledge, and by experiencing the new "fall," Lyra has become a sinner.

Thus does Lyra become Pullman's symbol for Sin, redefined as acquiring knowledge. As soon as Lyra eats Mary's fruit, Dust (knowledge) begins falling from the sky on her—and on the *mulefa*'s grove of Dust-starved wheel-pod trees. Lyra's becoming covered with the falling Dust symbolizes her acquisition of knowledge. She is no longer innocent; she has graduated to the state of "guilt." She is a sinner. Satan's daughter, Sin, has become a sinner—someone who has acquired genuine knowledge. In Pullman's scheme, this is good. But in the eyes of the Church, becoming a sinner is the epitome of evil.

Why does the Church think it is evil to lose your innocence and become sinful? The answer is that, when a person sins, knowledge replaces superstition. Knowledge is Falsehood, whereas the superstition is Truth. Earlier, Father MacPhail, president of the Church's Consistorial Court, correctly stated that "if this temptation does take place, and if the child [Lyra] gives in, then Dust [knowledge] and sin [acquisition of knowledge] will triumph."[20] He then declared, referring to "Dust," that "we must destroy it altogether."[21] Dust brings sin, and "better a world with no Church and no Dust than a world where every day we have to struggle under the hideous burden of sin."[22] (This may be the best line in the entire trilogy!)

Now we can understand why Lyra, in love and consequently covered with the falling Dust, symbolizes Sin. The Church wants to destroy Lyra because, in doing so, it will destroy Sin. Lyra symbolizes Sin.

Where does the name Lyra Belacqua come from? Lyra is a northern constellation containing the fifth brightest star in the heavens, Vega. *Lyra* is pronounced LIE-ra. Is it a pun, alluding to Lyra's habit of telling lies? (Lyra: "I'm the best liar there ever was."[23]) Or does the name Lyra, like the title *Northern Lights* (the European title of *The Golden Compass*), point to the northern location of the aurora borealis, where Asriel has photographed the Dust? Most likely, the name is intended to suggest both. We can also ponder the already discussed likelihood that the initial *L* and the *y* in Lyra come from "Lucy," the youngest of the four *LWW* siblings. (See the "Lyra" subheading in chapter 3, where it is shown that there is less than 1 chance in 500 that "Lyra," compared with "Lucy," would (*a*) have four letters, (*b*) begin with *L*, and (*c*) have a second letter in common with "Lucy.") All three allusions—lying, the North, and Lucy—seem to be deliberately incorporated in the name.

As for Belacqua, *bel* is a Latin root meaning "pretty" or "beautiful." *Acqua* could be a disguised respelling of *aqua*, the Latin word for "water" (as in "aquatic" and "aquarium"); the *c* reinforces the *q*, putting more *k* in the *kw* sound of *q*. Combining "pretty" and "water" gives us "pretty water," which makes no sense as a description of Lyra or Sin.

A more persuasive interpretation is that *acqua* is being used as an abbreviation for Aquarius, a southern constellation. *Belacqua* would then mean "pretty southern constellation." This meaning complements one of the meanings of Lyra's first name, namely, the northern constellation Lyra. The first-last name combination gives us a north-south constellation combination. The complementary pairing of north and south could be intended to symbolize two complementary human-daemon pairings: (1) the pairing of human and animal and (2) the pairing of female and male. The "southern constellation" meaning could also be intended to confirm that Lyra's first name comes from a constellation.

Pantalaimon. Lyra's daemon (out-of-body soul, in the form of an animal), Pantalaimon, is surely one of the most inspired symbols in Pullman's story. It wasn't too hard for Pullman to make Lyra the daughter of Satan. He could even make her the metaphorical mother of Death by having her bring genuine death to the living dead in the dismal land of the dead. But how could he handle the genealogy of making Death the offspring of an incestuous relationship between Satan and his daughter, Sin? *HDM*, though really adult stuff at the allegorical level, is partly for children (young adults) at the surface story level. That rules out incest.

Pullman solved the problem by inventing daemons. The humans of Lyra's world, and for that matter the witches too, are dual entities. They have a human body and an external, material soul. The external soul is the daemon (pronounced "demon"). The human and its daemon, usually a creature of the opposite sex, are essentially a single entity. When the human dies, the daemon dies at the same instant. Human and daemon are born together. Though physically separate, the daemon is a part of its human. So if Lord Asriel is Lyra's father, he is also the father of her daemon. No incest needed. Lyra, in turn, is the metaphorical mother of her daemon because, when she is born, she brings her daemon with her. Note that Pullman has made human and daemon opposite in sex so that Lyra, like Sin, is female, whereas Pantalaimon, like Death, is male.

So much for parentage. How does Pantalaimon substantively

qualify as Death? When Lyra tries to enter the land of the dead, she learns that only the dead can enter. But she gets in anyhow—on a technicality. A crippled, "aged beyond age" boatman is in charge of rowing the dead across a lake to an island where the gate to the land of the dead is. He will take Lyra only if she leaves her daemon (soul) behind: "If you come, he must stay."[24] Lyra argues, but the boatman is adamant: "He [Pantalaimon] can come in the boat, but if he does, the boat stays here."[25] It seems that the boatman defines death as separation from one's soul, which for Lyra is Pantalaimon. In Christianity, the soul departs at death. Human daemons, of course, are always physically separate from their human bodies, but the daemon must remain close by. What Lyra does is undergo the unprecedented (for humans, but not for witches) agony of extreme spatial separation from her daemon. She reluctantly—nay, despairingly—agrees to leave Pantalaimon behind. Leaving him behind qualifies her as "dead." By separating, Pantalaimon becomes Death for Lyra.

The source of the name Pantalaimon—Pan for short—is debatable. Some commentators believe the name is based on the Greek word *Panteleimon* (note in "Pantalaimon" the substitution of *a* for *e* in two places).[26] *Panteleimon* means "all merciful." One of the Christian saints, St. Panteleimon, adopts the Greek word as his name and is said to be all merciful. But despite the phonetic and spelling similarities in the names, this Greek derivation invites extreme skepticism. Pullman's names are generally relevant to the character. Describing Pan as all merciful goes beyond irrelevant, beyond arbitrary; the description is downright inappropriate. Nowhere does Pan do anything that can be described as merciful. About the only thing that can be said for the idea that *Pantalaimon* is merely a respelling of *Panteleimon* is that the allusion to a religious figure, St. Panteleimon, is appropriate for an allegory about religion.

If we go beyond Patalaimon's surface story identity (an animal) and consider his hidden story identity, Death, a name that means "all merciful" goes beyond inappropriateness to absurdity. In *PL*, Death is the very antithesis of mercy. He is vile tempered, threatening, and homicidal—besides being ugly. He treats Satan scornfully and is preparing to kill Satan when Sin intervenes. When he gets to Earth, he will kill every human being ever born, often in cruel and painful ways. No, Death is not merciful, and Pullman cannot have intended to give *Pantalaimon* that meaning.

A far more convincing explanation is that *Pantalaimon* comes from *Pandemonium*, the capital of Hell in *PL*. We know Pullman is symbolizing and borrowing heavily from *PL*, so a Pandemonium connection constitutes a highly relevant tie-in. It is all the more relevant because Sin and Death (Lyra and Pantalaimon) come from Pandemonium in Milton's epic. The name *Pandemonium* combines *pan* (Greek for "all"), *demon* (from the Latin *daemon*, spirit, and the Greek *daimon*, divine power), and *ium* ("place of" in this context): Pandemonium is the "place of all demons," the place where all of Satan's demons live. Let's now focus on the *demon* in Pan-demon-ium. Pan is a daemon (demon), but a particular kind of daemon. He is a dae-mon belonging to a girl whose name is pronounced Lie-ra. That makes him a Lie-mon, which can also be spelled Lai-mon (from *daimon*, the Greek spelling of demon) without changing the pronunciation. Now both names have the "lie" sound, alluding to Lyra's propensity to tell lies. To summarize, we have an etymological evolution from demon to daemon to lie-mon to lai-mon. Phonetically speaking, Lie-ra the liar and her Lie-mon are a pair.

Add *Panta* as a spelling variant of *Pande* (from "*Pande*monium") and you have Pantalaimon. The *pan*, meaning "all," suggests all the different animal forms a daemon can assume. But can changing the *de* to *ta* be rationalized? Yes, we can rationalize this spelling change just as easily as the opposing interpretation can rationalize changing the two *e*'s in *Panteleimon* to the two *a*'s in *Pantalaimon*—and just as easily as we can rationalize changing the spelling of *Zephaniah* (Old Testament prophet and book) to *Xaphania*. With these little spelling changes, Pullman plays name games and makes his puzzle more challenging.

Lyra's "Death" Spirit. In the boatman scene, Pullman seems to digress from *PL* by throwing in some symbolism from Greek mythology. But he really isn't digressing, because that Greek mythology pops up in *PL*. Describing Hell, Milton names "four infernal rivers that disgorge into the burning lake." The rivers include "abhorred Styx, the flood of deadly hate, and sad Acheron of sorrow, black and deep."[27] In Greek mythology, the souls of the dead are ferried across the river Styx to get them to Hades. Pullman's lake that separates the land of the dead from the upper worlds symbolizes the river Styx. The dead rowed across the lake represent the souls being ferried to Hades. Also separating Hades from the upper world in the Hades-Styx myth is a different river: the river Acheron, the river of woe. An aged boatman rows the ghosts of the dead across Acheron's waters. His name is Charon. Pullman's boatman symbolizes Charon; he has been relocated to the symbolized river Styx. Charon will ferry the ghosts of only those people who (*a*) have had a proper burial and (*b*) have passage money. Passage money is a coin called an obol, placed in the mouth of the deceased. Pullman's boatman's refusal to take Lyra without her being properly separated from her daemon symbolizes Charon's refusal to ferry ghosts who have not been properly buried.[28]

But what about the passage money? Pullman solves that problem by inventing a spirit companion, usually invisible (invisible until a person reaches the suburbs of the dead), called a death. Nobody enters the land of the dead without a death. When the Gallivespian Tialys gets angry with Lyra and is on the verge of stinging and killing her, Lyra's death— a man with a kindly smile—suddenly becomes visible and stands beside her. He promises to guide her to the land of the dead. He symbolizes her obol, her passage money. Pullman previously symbolized the obol in both (*a*) the scene where Lyra teases the skulls in the vault below Jordan College by switching their coins and (*b*) the scene where Lyra puts the "Ratter" coin in the mouth of Tony Makarios before he is cremated. The likely reason Pullman decided to symbolize the obol a third time is that he wanted to make his crossing-to-Hades scene complete in its Greek mythological detail. There really isn't any other good excuse for inventing Lyra's "death" and putting him in the story.

Lyra's "death" spirit is Pullman's least inspired symbol. It has four problems. The first, already mentioned, is that Pullman is overdoing it when he symbolizes the obol coin a third time. The second problem is that the idea of giving each human not just one but *two* spiritually linked companions or "familiars"—a daemon and a "death"—is too much of a good thing. Like the daemon, a person's "death" is with the person throughout life; it just can't be seen, and nobody is aware of "deaths" until they reach the suburbs of the dead. One supernatural soul or alter ego is enough for any fictional character. The third problem, related to the second, is that terrible ambiguity and confusion result when not only does Lyra have two companions but both of them represent death. In the hidden story, Pantalaimon symbolizes Death, Sin's companion. Death in this instance is Milton's personified death, which relates to the whole human race: when Satan crosses his bridge from Hell to Earth, Sin and Death tag alone and become plagues on humanity. Putting a second "death," a personal one spelled with a lowercase *d*, in the surface story gives us one death companion too many. You have to wonder which death is the one that counts.

The fourth problem is that giving Lyra two companions introduces confusion about which death symbolizes a proper burial and which symbolizes the obol. If Lyra had no "death" spirit, the separation of Pantalaimon—Lyra's soul—from Lyra could easily be seen as symbolizing burial: the soul departs (according to theologians, who believe these things) when a person is buried. But since Lyra's "death" spirit also resembles a soul—it is with her throughout life, is invisible, and is a spirit—and is also separated from her at the lake, that second act of separation could just as easily symbolize burial. We can recognize the "death" spirit as the obol, not the proper burial, only by judging which death's separation makes the better burial symbol and which makes the better obol symbol—and then uncertainty remains concerning whether the judgment was correct. Only the boatman's negative attitude toward Pantalaimon belies the idea that he represents the obol, passage money. Greek boatmen (and Italians too) always like to get paid for their services.

Roger Parslow and Salcilia. Lyra's playmate, Roger Parslow, is Jordan College's kitchen boy. He symbolized Peter in the *LWW* allegory's scene where Lucy, Susan, and Peter drink from Mrs. Beaver's flask in the hiding hole. Is he also a symbol in the *PL* allegory? Yes. Roger and his daemon, Salcilia, like Lyra and Pantalaimon, operate as a symbolic pair. In the climactic events of *GC*, where Asriel uses the flash of energy from Roger's life to build his Bridge to the Stars, Pullman is symbolizing the end of book II of *PL*. After exiting from Hell, Satan struggles to cross the dark, chaotic void that separates Hell and Earth. He is buffeted up and down by unseen forces. Eventually he reaches the thrones of Chaos and Night, who reign over the abyss. Satan addresses the pair:

> Chaos and ancient Night, I come no spy,
> With purpose to explore or to disturb
> The secrets of your realm, but by constraint
> Wand'ring this darksome desert, as my way
> Lies through your spacious empire up to light,
> Alone and without guide, half lost, I seek
> What readiest path leads where your gloomy bounds
> Confine [join] with Heav'n; or if some other place
> [other than Heaven, alluding to Earth] . . . direct my course.[29]

Pullman reenacts this encounter in the scene on the cliff near Asriel's northern residence at Svalbard, the island where the armored bears live. The scene is the one where Roger dies and the energy released when he separates from his daemon creates Asriel's "Bridge to the Stars," the bridge across the aurora borealis. In this scene, Asriel is Satan. Lyra and Pantalaimon are Sin and Death. But where are Chaos and Night? Those two have to be Roger and Salcilia, who are also present. Appropriately, Roger and Salcilia constitute a pair, like Chaos and Night.

But one pair's symbolizing another is almost as far as analogy can take us. We must stretch our imaginations to see any analogy between Roger and Chaos, or between his daemon and Night. Satan does put Chaos before Night when addressing the pair: he calls them "Chaos and ancient Night." That suggests that Roger, the first member of the symbolic pair, symbolizes Chaos, the first member of the symbolized pair—just as Lyra (first member of Sin and Death) symbolizes Sin (first member). Roger, though, is not a noticeably chaotic person.

Pullman probably intends to base a Roger = Chaos analogy not on Roger's personality or behavior but on the chaos that unfolds when Asriel kills Roger by killing his daemon. First there is a chaotic battle in which Pantalaimon and Roger's daemon fight Asriel's snow leopard daemon. Pantalaimon snatches Roger's daemon from the jaws of the snow leopard. The leopard leaps after him, and Pantalaimon releases Roger's daemon. Then "both young daemons, changing flick-flick-flick, turned and battled with the great spotted beast . . . [which] slashed left-right with needle-filled paws."[30] The snow leopard is too powerful. Roger's daemon dies. Roger's life-ending separation from his daemon releases a blinding jet of pure energy that zips skyward like reverse lightning along a wire trailing down from the sky. The wire is held aloft by a witch who is helping Asriel, and the energy is the life torn from Roger's body.[31] The chaotic result: "The sheets of light and color that were the Aurora tore apart; a great rending, grinding, crunching, tearing sound reached from one end of the universe to the other."[32] These two chaotic events—the daemon battle and the aurora's tearing apart—are acceptable evidence that Roger symbolizes Chaos. Therefore, the other half of the Roger-daemon pair must symbolize the other half of the Chaos-Night pair, Night.

Pullman's source for the name *Parslow* is probably Joseph Parslow, the butler and close friend of Charles Darwin, famous for his theory of evolution. The theory of evolution amounted to a devastating attack on Christianity's creation doctrine, so we can see a rationale for using the Parslow name: its antireligious connotations agree with the antireligious themes of Pullman's trilogy. Also, Roger's status as the Jordan College kitchen boy, a servant of sorts, agrees with Joseph Parslow's status as a servant.

Roger's daemon's name, *Salcilia*, is much more of an enigma. *Salcilia* is suggestive of salicylic acid, used in making aspirin (acetyl salicylic acid), with *i* substituted for *y*. But if Pullman has in mind a metaphor that makes Roger's daemon a figurative aspirin tablet, that metaphor is invisible. An alternative approach breaks the name into *sal* and *cilia*. *Sal*, as in *saline*, is Latin for "salt"; it could mean "salty." *Cilia* are hairlike extensions found on some cells and, in the case of a paramecium (a one-celled microorganism), used for propulsion. The result of this combination, "salty hair," is another dead end.

The "salt" part of the name, however, might relate to kitchens: Roger is a kitchen boy. Pullman could be marrying "salt" to the girl's name *Cecilia*, because the daemon is female. Or, as a private joke, he could be memorializing some child's (his son's?) mispronunciation of "Cecilia." (Pullman does have jocular tendencies: Asriel's manservant at Svalbard is named Thorold, which transposes the syllables of "Old Thor," Thor being the Norse god of thunder and Norse country being where Svalbard is. Thorold's Doberman pinscher daemon is named Anfang, the *fang* part of which might come from Jack London's novel *White Fang*, whose wolf-dog hero shares Thor's preference for arctic locales. Earlier examples of humorous names are MacPhail = "make fail," Makepwe = "make pew," Trollesund = "sound where trolls live," and possibly Iorek = Yo-wreck = "I wreck" and Iofur = Ioruf = "you rough.")

Will Parry. You might think that, because Lyra is a new Eve or second Eve, Will is a new Adam or second Adam, the second Eve's mate. And in a sense he is. But, we have seen, Lyra's role as a second Eve—Eve "come again"—is too explicit to be regarded as symbolism. Most allegorists, and certainly Pullman, are more subtle than that. Lyra's being the new Eve is really a figure of speech and is part of the surface story, not part of the hidden story. The same is true of Will's role, implied, as the new Adam. Just as Lyra does not symbolize Eve, Will does not symbolize Adam.

Then who does he symbolize? He symbolizes Adam's son, Cain. In Genesis, Cain is the first son of Adam and the murderer of his brother Abel. Seven arguments build a powerful case affirming that Will represents Cain.

1. Will accidentally kills an intruder in his house, an act that could, and surely does, symbolize Cain's slaying of Abel.
2. The method by which Will kills the intruder resembles the method by which Cain kills Abel. Will slams into the intruder's belly; Cain slams a rock into Abel's belly.
3. Becoming a killer made Cain a figurative companion of Sin. Becoming a killer results in Will's finding Lyra, who becomes his companion and who symbolizes Sin.
4. After Cain killed Abel, God made him "a wanderer" and sent him away to the land of Nod. After Will kills the intruder, he becomes a wanderer and goes off to another world, the world of Cittàgazze. He then wanders through many worlds.
5. Both Cain and Will are sinners—killers—and in that sense are agents of Satan. Sure enough, in Pullman's story Will actually is allied with Satan, symbolized by Lord Asriel.
6. Cain does have a minor role in *PL*. His story from Genesis is retold in book XI. And he is famous in Christian theology for murdering his brother Abel and for then asking, "Am I my brother's keeper?" This fame augments his importance.
7. Lyra's being a figurative "second Eve" makes Will a figurative "second Adam." (The words "second Adam" can actually be found in *PL*, although they do not refer to a son of Adam.)[33] "Second Adam" can easily be interpreted as meaning Will is the first son of Adam. First sons are often named for their fathers, so "second Adam" is equivalent to "first son of Adam." Cain is indeed the first son of Adam.

Pullman conceivably provides yet another clue to Will's symbolic referent, Cain, when he has Will and his mother switch places in the child-adult relationship. Will's mentally ill mother displays childlike behavior, while Will assumes the adult role, caring for her and assuaging her fears. This role reversal could be intended to signify that Will has advanced precociously beyond the stage of innocence, where adults tell the child what to think and do. He has advanced to a state the Church construes as guilt or sin, the opposite of innocence. Will's living in the state of post-innocence guilt would then symbolize Cain's living in a state of guilt after slaying his brother Abel. A strong argument for accepting this interpretation is that Pullman has no other compelling reason for making Mrs. Parry mentally ill, dependent on Will.

The trouble with this role reversal symbolism, if such it is, is that Pullman doesn't follow through with it. Once Will leaves his mother with Mrs. Cooper, he goes back to being innocent. In the world of Cittàgazze, where the Specters rule, children who have not reached puberty, hence who are still "innocent," can neither see the Specters nor be harmed by them. And sure enough, neither Lyra nor Will can see the Specters, and neither one is attacked by Specters. This means that Will is still innocent (as is Lyra). Will remains innocent until the story is almost over. Then he and Lyra eat the new Forbidden Fruit, fall in love, and thereby gain knowledge of sexual attraction, which represents knowledge in the broadest sense. Knowledge destroys Will's innocence and makes him a sinner: knowledge is sin in the eyes of the Church. So either (*a*) Will's playing the adult vis-à-vis his childlike mother is not intended to represent post-innocence guilt—the guilt of Cain—or (*b*) Pullman is moving Will in and out of "guilt" according to the allegory's needs of the moment. Probably the former. A related problem is that Will plays the adult role—he is "guilty"—long before he kills the intruder.

The surname *Parry* in *Will Parry* raises two possibilities. The better one focuses on Will's father, John Parry. His last name is apparently borrowed from William Edward Parry, the British explorer who searched for a Northwest Passage through the arctic from the Atlantic to the Pacific. John Parry is likewise an arctic explorer. Before accidentally leaving his world, he went to an arctic region in search of Dust. The second possibility is that Will's knife is being treated as a small sword. In dueling, to parry is to ward off an opponent's sword. *Parry* might allude to Will's being the knife bearer, a person who parries.

Will's first name probably comes from the short form of William

Edward Parry's first name. Another source, suggested by Michael Chabon in the *New York Review of Books*, is dubious. Chabon speculates that the character Mrs. Cooper, the piano teacher Will enlists to care for his mother, takes her name from Susan Cooper, author of *The Dark Is Rising* children's fantasy novels, and that Will takes his name from Will Stanton, the protagonist of those novels.[34] Chabon fails to say, however, why a name as common as Cooper was taken from that particular Cooper, Susan Cooper, so this derivation is immediately implausible. The presence of the word "Dark" in both titles—*His Dark Materials* and *The Dark Is Rising*—is a mighty slim connection. Besides, Pullman says he hasn't read Susan Cooper's books.[35] That just about rules out the Susan Cooper idea. A more plausible, but not necessarily correct, derivation of the name Cooper recognizes that Mrs. Cooper is the person who is keeping Mrs. Parry *cooped up* for the duration of Will's absence. This derivation becomes more plausible when we notice that it applies also to the trilogy's second character named Cooper. A Dr. Cooper invented the silver guillotine at the Experimental Station at Bolvangar and later invented the guillotine-activated hair bomb at Geneva. Both devices require putting a human and its daemon in a guillotine's two cages—*coops*—during the severance process.

John Parry and Mrs. Parry. John Parry, known in Lyra's world as Stanislaus Grumman, is Will's father. He is an important character, important enough to be a symbol. Since John Parry is not a symbol in the *LWW* allegory, it seems likely that whomever he symbolizes is from *PL* or the Bible. Two of his attributes suggest an Adam-and-Eve link with both sources. John Parry is (1) the father of Will and (2) a man with two identities, and two worlds to go with them. Those two attributes are the keys to interpreting John Parry. Since Will symbolizes Cain, there can be no doubt whatsoever that his father, John Parry, symbolizes Adam, Cain's father. This relationship squares with the earlier observation that Will, as the "second Adam," could be interpreted as the son of Adam. It also squares with Pullman's demonstrated respect for *PL*'s paternal relationships: he earlier made Lyra the daughter of Asriel because Sin (Lyra) is the daughter of Satan (Asriel) in *PL*.

When Adam and Eve ate the Forbidden Fruit, they fell from God's grace, inspiring the Christian doctrine of the Fall. Punishment was an aspect of the Fall. As part of Adam's punishment, God expelled him from Eden, putting him in a new land. John Parry "fell" when he walked through an unseen hole in the fabric of his world into a new world, Cittàgazze's world, from which he continued through another hole to Lyra's world. His "fall" put him in a new land and symbolizes Adam's expulsion from Eden.

Another part of Adam's punishment was being made mortal, destined to die. In Genesis God imposes this punishment by reminding Adam that he was formed from dust and then declaring, "to dust you shall return."[36] In *PL* Milton retells the story of the Fall by having God send Jesus to the Garden of Eden to sentence Adam and Eve. Jesus tells Adam, "For thou out of the ground wast taken; know thy birth, for dust thou art, and shalt to dust return."[37] Pullman symbolizes Adam's becoming mortal by having John Parry (Adam) become ultramortal when he leaves his world (Paradise, Eden, Bliss): Parry learns that he can live in the new world (Lyra's) for only about ten years. Then he will die.

John Parry's last name comes from the same source as Will's: William Edward Parry, the arctic explorer. The source of his first name, John, will be revealed in the discussion of John Parry's alter ego, Stanislaus Grumman, coming up next.

John Parry's wife is Elaine Parry.[38] Since John Parry symbolizes Adam, Mrs. Parry must symbolize Eve, Adam's mate. Mrs. Parry's insanity might be construed as a flaw in the symbolism—Eve was not insane—but it agrees with the questionable role reversal symbolism discussed in connection with Will. This symbolism holds that, by taking care of his mother, instead of vice versa, Will assumes the adult role and thereby advances from the child's state of innocence to the adult's state of sin or guilt. If this interpretation is correct, Will needs the state of guilt to accommodate his guilt for the "murder" of the upstairs intruder.

Mrs. Parry's failure to move to the new land with Mr. Parry is another minor flaw in the symbolism. But it really isn't necessary that she accompany Mr. Parry: one good analogy—being the wife of the man symbolizing Adam in this case—is all it takes to create a symbol. Pullman, moreover, may have an explanation for the failure-to-move-out-of-Eden flaw. For plot reasons, Will's mother must remain in her home world. Her insanity, and her resultant status of childish innocence vis-à-vis Will, could be Pullman's excuse for not having her depart from the world that symbolizes Eden, or Paradise. Before her husband disappeared, Mrs. Parry was mentally an adult: her husband's letters make this clear. Her regression to a state of innocence may be intended to explain why she is still in Eden, her home world and Will's. That explanation, unfortunately, fails to acknowledge that she should have been kicked out of Eden when she was still "guilty" (sane, and an adult).

Stanislaus Grumman. Like Boreal-Latrom, who symbolized Tumnus in the *LWW* allegory, John Parry has different identities in different worlds. His real name, the name by which he went in his own world (and Will's), is indeed John Parry. But after passing through the Cittàgazze world and taking up residence in Lyra's world, he adopted the name Stanislaus Grumman. He became a scholar, affiliated with the Berlin Academy, and began studying the Tartar culture. Some Tartars made him an adoptive member of their clan. Apparently as part of the adoption process, Grumman had a hole drilled part way through his skull, a process known as trepanning. He also acquired a Tartar name, Jopari. ("Jopari" results from the botched efforts of the Tartars to pronounce the name "John Parry.") He then became a Tartar shaman, a sort of combination medicine man, priest, and sorcerer.

When we finally meet him he has somehow acquired paranormal powers, possibly as a result of the trepanning. He demonstrates these to Lee Scoresby on four occasions—first, when he mysteriously obtains a ring belonging to Lee's faraway mother and uses it to draw Lee to him; second, when he conjures up lightning to bring down a pursuing zeppelin; third, when he directs a Specter into the cockpit of another zeppelin; and fourth, when he commands the birds of the forest to attack and bring down yet another zeppelin. Grumman is also able to enter into trances, during which his mind can visit distant places and gain information. He apparently uses this faculty to learn about the hair bomb aimed at Lyra: his warning, delivered in the land of the dead, enables Lyra to escape the bomb. As a shaman, Grumman implicitly is a Tartar leader.

What is the point of making Grumman not only a Tartar but a Tartar leader? Pullman is developing some more symbolism describing things in *PL*, obscure things as it happens. Book X of *PL* has a Tartar simile: "As when the Tartar from his Russian foe by Astrakhan over the snowy plains retires."[39] Pullman might be alluding to this passage. Book XI has a more fertile passage referring to "all earth's kingdoms," including the empire of Negus: "Nor could his [Adam's] eye not ken th' empire of Negus."[40]

The empire of Negus alludes to a legendary man named Prester John. A prester is a priest or presbyter. The legend of Prester John— John the Priest—arose in the twelfth century. Christians heard rumors of, and believed that there existed, a priest-king called Prester John. He supposedly ruled over an ideal, incredibly prosperous Christian empire somewhere in central Asia, Tartar country. John's Christian name and geographic location can be interpreted as implying that he was an adoptive Tartar, although this is not specifically a part of the legend. In the fifteenth century a Portuguese man named Pedro Covilham visited a Christian kingdom near the Red Sea. The kingdom was ruled by someone called Negus, a title used by Ethiopian emperors. Covilham decided that Negus was Prester John (a strange notion implying that Negus looked like he was around three hundred years old). Milton's reference to Negus could be interpreted as alluding to Prester John.

John Parry's Grumman-Jopari persona seems, then, to symbolize Prester John. That interpretation can account for Parry's first name, John. It can also account for Pullman's decision to make him an adoptive Tartar and a priest of sorts: a shaman is, loosely speaking, a priest. And it agrees with the indisputable fact that Pullman is trying to do a reasonably thorough job of symbolizing as many things in *PL* as possible.

The name Stanislaus Grumman seems devoid of hidden meaning. Extensive Google searches on the Internet produced no associations between (*a*) either *Stanislaus* or *Grumman* and (*b*) Sir William Parry, the arctic, Tartars, shamans, magic, prester, or Prester John. Pullman evidently chose a name that John Parry might have chosen—a German name—as a step toward gaining membership in the Berlin Academy. Grumman is a German surname, and Stanislaus is German, Polish, Czech, and other Slavic. Pullman might well have found the name in the Berlin telephone directory, just as he found the name Serafina Pekkala in the Helsinki directory, although it is more likely that he simply made it up.

The Upstairs Intruder. The event that causes Will to flee from his world into Cittàgazze's begins when two intruders come into his house, shortly before dawn. They are looking for a green leather case containing his missing father's letters. Will has already found the green case but is trapped upstairs. One of the intruders comes upstairs, flashlight in hand. As the man opens the door to the room at the top of the stairs, the room where Will is hiding, Will explodes out of the dark and *slams into the intruder's belly* (à la Cain's slamming a rock into Abel's belly in *PL*). Stepping backward, the startled man trips over Will's cat and plunges down the stairs, cracking his head on the hall table. He is dead. Will has murdered him. At least that is how Will and Pullman and Lyra's alethiometer view the situation. (The alethiometer tells Lyra that Will is a murderer.)

Since Will is Cain, and Cain kills his brother Abel, the upstairs intruder necessarily symbolizes Abel. The alethiometer's labeling Will a murderer is particularly significant in supporting this conclusion. Will isn't really a murderer: that is absolutely clear. The intruder's death was accidental. Will wasn't even trying to harm him; Will was simply trying to escape. For that matter, the intruder didn't have to die from his fall. A broken leg or a concussion would have enabled Will to escape. Pullman chose to have the man die in order to make Will, like Cain, a murderer. The alethiometer came up with the ridiculous pronouncement that Will was a murderer for the same reason: Pullman needed to justify calling the accident murder.

Mrs. Coulter. Just as Metatron's symbolic identity (the Christ) leads to that of his adversary, Asriel (Satan), so does it lead to that of Lyra's mother, Mrs. Coulter. During most of the story, Mrs. Coulter is one of religion's most fervent zealots. She runs the Church's General Oblation Board. Its acronym, GOB, is for story purposes the source of the nickname "Gobblers" that people use when referring to the mysterious people who kidnap children. (We saw in chapter 5 that "goblins" is the real source, Pullman's source.) Though the public in *HDM* doesn't know it, the kidnaped children are taken north to Mrs. Coulter's Experimental Station at Bolvangar for intercision. Intercision is a process whereby a child is separated from its daemon, without killing the daemon (this would kill the child), before the daemon has "settled" into its final, immutable form. After the daemons are cut away, they are placed in glass cages in a building that is well separated from the one where the intercised children are housed.

The purpose of intercision is to block the intellectual, but not the physical, transformation that occurs at puberty and that allows Dust to be attracted to the emerging adult. The Church believes that Dust is a manifestation of Original Sin and that contamination by sin might be prevented by keeping adults in their Dust-free juvenile state of innocence. Dustproofed adults would theoretically remain in the same child-like state of innocence that Adam and Eve enjoyed before they ate the Forbidden Fruit and became tainted with knowledge (from the Tree of Knowledge), or Original Sin. A successful experiment, in other words, will mean that the intercised children can never become corrupted by knowledge (Dust); they will always be in the grip of superstition.

(We can see that, in this allegory, the intercised children represent children who have been brainwashed by priests, Sunday school teachers, and their own previously brainwashed parents to such an extent that they will never be able to think for themselves. In this respect they symbolize much the same thing as the zombies in Cittàgazze's world. The zombies are adults who are so deeply corrupted by blind faith that they are unable to function as thinking adults.)

Mrs. Coulter's work with the Gobblers makes it clear that she is, in effect if not literally, a disciple of Metatron. She is a warrior in the battle against sin. But then she turns against Metatron, betrays him, and brings about his death. She goes to Metatron, proposes a sneak attack on Lord Asriel, and leads Metatron to where Asriel waits near the edge of the abyss. There she betrays Metatron by joining Asriel in a two-party attack on the regent. Battling desperately against a stronger foe, Coulter and Asriel drag Metatron over the edge of the abyss. Metatron and his two attackers then fall to their deaths.

Metatron, remember, symbolizes Jesus, the Christ. Who was it that betrayed Jesus and brought about his death?

Correct! Mrs. Coulter is Judas. The *HDM* character who symbolizes Judas is the one who betrays the character who symbolizes Jesus. Now, it might seem implausible that a woman symbolizes a man, but that is the way symbols sometimes work. To repeat, one good analogy, betrayal of Jesus in this case, is all it takes to make a symbol. After all, if George Orwell in *Animal Farm* can use a pig (Napoleon) to symbolize Joseph Stalin and another pig (Snowball) to symbolize Leon Trotsky, and if Aesop can use a hare to symbolize a talented but lazy human, and if C. S. Lewis can use a lion to symbolize the Christ, and if Jesus can use weeds growing among the wheat to symbolize human sinners (destined to be separated and burned at harvest time), and if Nietzsche can use a camel to symbolize lower man (creator of God and bearer of God's burdens), why can't Pullman use a woman to symbolize a man? If those examples haven't convinced you, here's an even better one: If C. S. Lewis can use the White Witch, a female, to symbolize Satan, a male, why can't Pullman also use a female to symbolize a male? Again: If Pullman himself used a male, Iofur, to symbolize a female, the White Witch, in the *LWW* allegory, why would he hesitate to use an opposite-sex symbol in this allegory? And once more: If Pullman used the Master of Jordan's three male servants to symbolize the Professor's three female servants from *LWW*, why wouldn't he use an opposite-sex symbol for Judas?

Have you wondered why Mrs. Coulter's instrument is called a *silver* guillotine instead of, say, a *Sin-tercisioner*? Could it be that she is attracted to silver? And could it be that, by introducing the word *silver* in context with Mrs. Coulter, Pullman is hinting at the Gospel scene where Judas accepts thirty pieces of silver as a bribe for betraying Jesus?[41] This is not to suggest that the silver guillotine symbolizes the thirty pieces of silver. But Pullman may well have chosen the device's name as a way of planting the word *silver* in the minds of his readers, thereby helping them to recognize the Judas symbolism.

The Witches. The witches are important figures in the surface story and in the *LWW* allegory but get short shrift the *PL* allegory. *PL* has a fleeting reference to witches. Satan flies to the gate of Hell shortly before crossing the bridge to Earth. On either side of the gate stand Sin and Death. Sin is woman, fair of appearance, from the waist up. But from the waist down she is a serpent, armed with a mortal sting. Barking, howling Hellhounds surround her middle and creep into and out of her womb, still barking even when inside. Milton compares her ugliness to that of a "night-hag . . . called in secret," who comes "riding through the air . . . lured with the smell of infant blood, to dance with Lapland witches."[42]

Those same two words, "Lapland witches," appear in Pullman's text when Lyra and the gypsies approach Trollesund, Lapland's main port. Trollesund is where they hope to meet and gain the assistance of witches. John Faa says, "Now, Farder Coram knows these Lapland witches."[43] Here Pullman is doing nothing more than work into his allegory a small, inconsequential detail from Milton's epic.

The Gallivespians. Lord Asriel's soldier-spies, the Gallivespians, are very likely a collective symbol for Satan's demons. The Gallivespians are tiny people, a hand-span tall. As such, they resemble the tiny Lilliputians of Jonathan Swift's *Gulliver's Travels*. We saw in chapter 5 that Pullman derived the name *Gallivespians* by combining

(1) *Gallive* from "Gulliver," spelled with *a* substituted for *u*, (2) *vesp* from "vespa," which is Latin for "wasp," and (3) *ian* from "Lilliputian." Venomous spurs protrude from their heels. They fly around on seagull-sized dragonflies—or a blue hawk for their leader—leap onto their enemies, and fatally or disablingly sting them. The wasp metaphor, *vespa*, comes from their wasplike stings. In the world the Gallivespians come from, humans "regard them as diabolic."[44] This characterization ("diabolic"), the harassing-of-humans behavior, and the fact that the Gallivespians work for Lord Asriel (Satan) are strong evidence that the little people symbolize Satan's demons.

Beyond their roles as demons, four of the Gallivespians symbolize something else. These four are the featured ones: Lord Roke, Madame Oxentiel, Chevalier Tialys, and Lady Salmakia. Mounted on their dragonflies and blue hawk, they are the Four Horsemen of the Apocalypse, from Revelation. Pullman may or may not intend this symbolism: it could arise accidentally from his C. S. Lewis allegory's parallel use of the four mounted Gallivespians as symbols for the four horse-mounted siblings from *LWW*. We saw earlier that, after Aslan slays the White Witch, the four children become kings and queens of Narnia. After many years on their thrones, they go horseback riding in search of a White Stag. Here it is C. S. Lewis who is using the mounted siblings to symbolize the Four Horsemen. Pullman, in turn, uses the four mounted Gallivespians (two males, two females) to symbolize the four mounted siblings (also two males and two females), thereby indirectly symbolizing the Four Horsemen of the Apocalypse. Most likely, Pullman intends both the direct and the indirect symbolism. In that case, he is borrowing again: borrowing from the book of Revelation.

Baruch. The angels Balthamos and Baruch operate as a pair. Pullman uses Balthamos as a symbol in his *LWW* allegory, where Balthamos symbolizes Peter. (When Balthamos kills Father Gomez, Peter is killing the wolf Maugrim, chief of the witch's Secret Police.) That makes it almost inconceivable that Baruch is not also a symbol, though not necessarily in the same allegory. In fact, Baruch bears a striking resemblance to one of the angels in *PL*.

In *PL* Satan, originally known as Lucifer, begins as the highest angel, God's closest associate. But when God creates his son, Jesus, and makes him the new number two person in Heaven, God ordains that all others must "bow" to Jesus and "confess him Lord."[45] Satan is filled with "envy against the Son of God."[46] He withdraws his legions—angels under Satan's command—to his northern palace. There he organizes his rebellion. One of his subordinates, the Seraphim (high-ranking angel) Abdiel, speaks out against Satan's plan. Abdiel argues that God has justly decreed that every soul in Heaven should kneel before Jesus. When none of the other angels supports Abdiel, he returns to God and tells God what Satan is up to. God praises him for his loyalty to "the cause of truth" and for his "testimony of truth."[47]

In *The Amber Spyglass*, Balthamos and Baruch have managed to find their way into the heart of the Authority's citadel, the Clouded Mountain. They have learned that the Authority has delegated his power to Metatron. Metatron plans to turn the Clouded Mountain into an "engine of war," destroy Asriel's Republic of Heaven, and establish "a permanent inquisition in every world."[48] Balthamos and Baruch find Will while traveling to Asriel's fortress to warn Asriel. Balthamos stays behind to guard Will; Baruch continues on to Asriel and reports what he has learned about Metatron's plan.

The similarities between Baruch and Abdiel are easy to see. Like Abdiel, Baruch has been to the enemy camp and learned about a plot that is afoot. Also like Abdiel, Baruch reports that plot to the leader of the forces of Good. Lord Asriel's "truth"—knowledge—is the genuine truth, so Baruch serves "the cause of truth" when he brings his "testimony of truth" to Asriel. You could argue, of course, that Abdiel served God, whereas Baruch serves God's enemy, Asriel (Satan). But as part of the process of turning *PL* upside down, Pullman has decided to have Abdiel stay with the other rebelling angels in Satan's camp instead of remaining loyal to God. The evidence is not quite conclusive, but it strongly suggests that Baruch represents Abdiel. Who else could he represent?

The name Baruch comes from the Old Testament, where it appears in several places in the books of Nehemiah and Jeremiah. Baruch is also one of the apocryphal (rejected) books of the New Testament. These biblical sources give the name appropriate religious connotations but offer no analogies relating to the characteristics of Pullman's angel. Well, there is one analogy, but it is weak. Baruch is the faithful scribe of the prophet Jeremiah. His faithfulness to Jeremiah is analogous to Abdiel's faithfulness to God. But the biblical Baruch's faithfulness really consists of little more than doing his job and being a friend.

Father MacPhail and His Court. In *AS*, Mrs. Coulter steals an intention craft from Asriel and flies to her world's Geneva, the former seat of the Papacy and now the location of a tangle of Church organizations collectively known as the Magisterium. Coulter intends to spy on the Church, which she now opposes. At Geneva she foolishly seeks out Father MacPhail, president of the Consistorial Court of Discipline, the most feared body of the Church. He makes her a prisoner, then uses her in designing a plan to kill Lyra. He orders one of his lackeys to steal a lock of Lyra's hair from Coulter's locket while Coulter sleeps. MacPhail intends to use the hair as part of a homing device for directing the force of the blast from an incredibly powerful hair bomb he intends to make. The blast will supernaturally transport itself from the bomb's location to wherever the rest of the snipped-off lock of Lyra's hair is, specifically, on Lyra's head. Lyra will be atomized, even though her location is remote from the bomb and in another world.

The bomb requires enormous amounts of power, so MacPhail goes to a rural "anbaric" (electric) power station, where he uses heavy cables to hook up the bomb to generators. The bomb gets its energy in much the same way Asriel got his energy for building his "bridge to the stars"—from severing the human-daemon link. Asriel did this by killing Roger's daemon and somehow transferring the resulting burst of energy to a wire trailing down from the sky; MacPhail plans to use intercision, severing a human from its daemon while the silver guillotine is attached to a detonating device. Why are *two* power sources—

anbaric power generators and intercision—necessary? "Just as an atomic bomb needs a high explosive to force the uranium together and set off the chain reaction, this device needs a colossal current [from the power station's generators] to release the much greater power of the severance process."[49] In other words, the power station powers a triggering device, and the silver guillotine powers the bomb itself.

MacPhail brings Mrs. Coulter along to fuel the silver guillotine. She will be severed from her daemon—poetic justice. But then Coulter escapes. MacPhail resolves to give up his own life to supply the bomb's energy. He and his daemon climb into the twin "coops" of Dr. Cooper's silver guillotine. Releasing the silver blade, he severs himself from his daemon, deliberately sacrificing his own life. (Pullman seems to have forgotten that intercision seldom kills children. Are adults, being contaminated by Dust, supposed to be an exception to the rule?) The bomb explodes—in another world. Fortunately, it misses Lyra, because Will, advised by his psychic father, has put his subtle knife to good use. He has sliced off the rest of Lyra's shortened lock of hair, cut an underworld window, put the residual hair into a small cavity carved with his knife in the subterranean rock, and closed the window.

Father MacPhail symbolizes the worst sort of religious zealot: the Muslim suicide bomber who sacrifices his own life in order to kill perceived enemies of his religion. In creating MacPhail, Pullman was presumably inspired largely by the Muslim suicide bombers who were targeting Israelis in the 1990s, when *AS* was written. As noted earlier, MacPhail = MacFail = Make Fail. The name describes MacPhail's failure to achieve his objective.

Before we leave Father MacPhail, a few extra words need to be said about his Consistorial Court of Discipline. The court has twelve members.[50] No, these don't symbolize Jesus's twelve disciples. If they did, Mrs. Coulter—Judas—would be a member. But then why did Pullman decide to give the court twelve members? He did so because courts often work with juries, and juries consist of twelve persons. The twelve members of the Consistorial Court represent the twelve members of a jury. (This is not symbolism, because it has nothing to do with the allegory's unifying theme of religion.)

Father MacPhail's Consistorial Court of Discipline symbolizes John Calvin's court of the same name that was established in Geneva, Switzerland, during the Protestant Reformation. Calvin was a French theologian who, after converting to Protestantism and fleeing from persecution in France, established what amounted to a theocracy in Geneva. There, from 1536 until his death in 1564 (except for a 1538–41 exile in Strasbourg), he imposed his system of religious institutions, worship, and morality on the citizenry. The chief institutions of Calvin's system were a College of Pastors and a Consistorial Court of Discipline. The court had the power to excommunicate persons who deviated from doctrinal consistency.

Pullman might secondarily intend that the Consistorial Court of Discipline (CCD) symbolized a present-day Catholic organization named the Confraternity of Christian Doctrine (CCD), which has the same initials. This extant CCD is a Catholic layman's association established by Pope Pius IV in 1562 to provide religious instruction in parishes. It quickly became widely implanted in Italian, French, and German parishes, but it has only a few chapters in England. The Catholic Church's CCD's mission of providing theologically consistent instruction in the Catholic doctrine roughly parallels, except for the enforcement aspect, the mission of Father MacPhail's CCD.

King Ogunwe. The leader of Asriel's conventional military force, the army of Africans (humans), is King Ogunwe. Along with Xaphania and Lord Roke, he is one of Asriel's three top commanders. He is also the most difficult of the three to interpret—if we assume he really is a symbol. A reasonable guess, and "guess" is the appropriate word, is that he symbolizes Beelzebub. In *PL*, Beelzebub is Satan's second in command, the "one next [to] himself in power."[51] And in *HDM* Ogunwe is Asriel's second in command, provided that we somewhat arbitrarily limit the competition to persons belonging to Asriel's species, human beings. The rationale for doing so, not a particularly good one, is that Beelzebub was a member of Satan's species, the fallen angels, known as demons. (The counterargument would be that Lord Roke, commander of the demons, symbolizes the demon Beelzebub. But Roke has been accounted for—he symbolizes Peter, the oldest of the four mounted siblings near the end of the *LWW* allegory—so the likelihood is that Pullman is giving the job of symbolizing Beelzebub to someone who otherwise lacks a symbolic role, Ogunwe.)

An additional reason for suspecting that Ogunwe symbolizes Beelzebub is that Beelzebub is an important character in *PL*. If Abdiel, who ranks below Beelzebub among Satan's original underlings, has a symbol (Baruch), Beelzebub should have one too. Ogunwe is the only Pullman character having enough analogical resemblance to Beelzebub, and also having nobody else to symbolize, to merit consideration as the Beelzebub symbol.

Xaphania. The first allegory, which depicts *LWW*, uses the angel Xaphania as a symbol for the lamppost at the Narnia entrance to the wardrobe. The symbolism is partly indirect. Xaphania directly represents Sophia, the ancient goddess of wisdom, who becomes a metaphorical lamp that guides people. As such—as a metaphorical lamp—she is analogous to the lamppost outside the wardrobe. Direct symbolism is also present, because Xaphania is described literally as "a light with wings."[52] A lamppost is a light.

In the *PL* allegory, we must work with the first analogy, which is based on Xaphania's directly symbolizing Sophia. Pullman, we saw, has created an *HDM* mythology in which an earlier rebellion of angels led by Sophia, known in *HDM* as Xaphania, preceded Asriel's rebellion. This means the *PL* allegory uses Xaphania as a symbol for Sophia, the ancient goddess of wisdom. One could quibble about whether Xaphania is a genuine symbol when what she represents is really an alter ego of Sophia, but she definitely participates in the allegory and serves the purposes of a symbol. Xaphania is Sophia, leader of the earlier rebellion and the personification of wisdom.

Kirjava and the Oxford Botanic Garden. Will has a late-arriving daemon, torn from inside him when he entered the land of the dead. His daemon's name is Kirjava. She is not a symbol in any of the allegories, but she deserves consideration because of her interesting name and her linkage with one of the story's two main characters. *Kirjava* is a Finnish word describing something that has many different colors, especially streaks, spots, or patches of different colors. When Serafina Pekkala bestows the name Kirjava on Will's daemon, Pantalaimon asks, "What does it mean?" "Soon you will see what it means," Serafina replies.[53] What the two daemons soon see is what Kirjava becomes when she "settles," that is, assumes her final, permanent form, signifying that Will has reached puberty. She becomes an extremely large cat with lustrous fur that displays "a thousand different glints and shades of ink black, shadow gray, the blue of a deep lake under a noon sky, mist-lavender-moonlight-fog . . ."[54]

Pullman may have chosen the name partly for a reason other than its literal meaning, using the literal meaning as a disguise. A second meaning can be read into *Kirjava*. This is probably a case of reading too much into a word, yet the second meaning's agreement with "you will soon see" is hard to ascribe to coincidence. *Kir* is an alcoholic beverage made from white wine or champagne and flavored with cassis, a type of currant; *java* is slang for coffee. Pullman might be using kir to represent sweetness: many wines, particularly white wines, are sweet (white grapes are sweeter than purple grapes). For its part, coffee represents bitterness. Combining *kir* and *java* in the name *Kirjava* thus gives us "bittersweet," said with "bitter" and "sweet" in reverse order. "Bittersweet" is an adjective describing something that is a mixture of pleasure and pain, happiness and sadness.

The parting of Lyra and Will is, like Kirjava's colors, something the two daemons "soon see." It is a bittersweet parting, an emotional blend of torment—knowing that they can never see each other again—and abiding love. Their love is sealed with an agreement that they will each come to their own world's Oxford Botanic Garden at midday on Midsummer Day (June 24) and sit on a certain bench as though sitting side by side. The two Botanic Gardens jointly symbolize the Garden of Eden. Each year Will and Lyra will return to Paradise to be with each other again.

PLACES, THINGS, AND EVENTS AS SYMBOLS

The three worlds and the characters are not the allegory's only symbols. Pullman's symbols also include other places (other than the three worlds), things, events, and the Johannine concept of being set free by the truth.

Svalbard. This chapter's earlier subsection on Baruch explained how Lucifer-Satan, in a huff over being demoted, takes one-third of the angels and departs. He goes to "the limits of the North," where he has a palace called his "quarters of the North."[55] There he plans his rebellion against God. The rebellion fails when Jesus uses his chariot to force the rebel leader and his followers over the edge of Heaven, from which they tumble down to a burning lake in Hell.

In *GC*, when Lord Asriel leaves Jordan he goes to "the North," capitalized as in *PL*.[56] There he takes up residence in Svalbard, the arctic island homeland of the armored bears. (Svalbard appears to be Lyra's world's counterpart of a cluster of Norwegian off-coast islands above the arctic circle.) Asriel has been captured and is being held in exile by the armored bears, who are being paid by Mrs. Coulter. But Asriel has mysterious powers, as well as the not-so-mysterious power to bribe, cajole, and flatter. His ability to get what he wants renders Asriel's captive status no more than a technicality. He is "a prisoner acting like a king."[57] He does what he pleases and plans his rebellion against the Authority. Without doubt, Asriel's trip to "the North" symbolizes Satan's trip to "the North," and Asriel's capacious residence at Svalbard is Satan's northern palace in Heaven.

Asriel's Fortress and Adamant Tower. In *Paradise Lost*, Satan and his companions waste little time getting their house in order after being cast out of Heaven. Hell, which began as a lake of fire, is soon converted to a place of luxury. Satan even builds a capital city. He names it Pandemonium.

In *The Amber Spyglass* (*AS*), Lord Asriel builds his own capital in the mountains of a world that is neither Lyra's nor Will's nor Cittàgazze's nor the *mulefas*'. We learn about Asriel's new world when the witch Ruta Skadi sees a flight of angels heading for the north pole in Cittàgazze's world. She joins the angels to gain information. Night comes, then day again, and then another night as they fly on. "And at some point the quality of the air changed, not for the worse or the better, but changed nonetheless, and Ruta Skadi knew that they'd passed out of that world [Cittàgazze's] and into another." Ruta learns from the angels that they have gone through one of many "invisible places in the air" that are "gateways into other worlds." The angels can see these gateways, but witches can't.[58]

This new world, conveniently free of Specters, is where Asriel builds his fortress. As they approach it, one of the angels says to Ruta, "Lord Asriel is in this world, and there is the fortress he's building."[59] The fortress Ruta sees is so huge—its basaltic rock walls are a half mile high—that its rectangular dimensions must be measured in flying time. We might call this gigantic fortress New Hell to distinguish it from Asriel's (and Lyra's) home world of Hell. New Hell's salient feature is the Adamant Tower, located on the highest part of the fortress. The Adamant Tower symbolizes Pandemonium.

How do we know that just the Adamant Tower and not the entire fortress symbolizes Pandemonium? Either interpretation is defensible. But Pullman's emphasis on the Tower strongly implies that the Tower, not the fortress, is Pandemonium. The emphasis takes the form of Pullman's decision to use the Tower's name as a chapter title: chapter 5 of *AS* bears the title "The Adamant Tower." Another consideration is that the Tower lies within and is part of Asriel's overall domain, the fortress, just as Pandemonium lies within and is part of Satan's overall domain, Hell. One more argument suggesting that the Tower, not the fortress, is Pandemonium is that Pandemonium is a towered structure. Its architect is Mulciber, the designer of many towered structures in Heaven: "His hand was known in Heav'n by many a towered structure high."[60]

Since the Tower is in a world other than Asriel's and Lyra's, it might seem that Pullman has misplaced his allegorical capital. Doesn't it belong in the world that symbolizes Hell, the world Asriel and Lyra come from? Not necessarily. Pullman's message is that we must build our own Heaven, a Republic of Heaven, where we live. Where we live, the new world in Asriel's case, is not where *PL* and theology put Heaven. It is not in the sky. And it is not under the ground or, as with Milton's Hell, below Earth. It is where living humans dwell.

The name *Adamant* could suggest any of several things. *Adamant* is derived from the Greek *adamas*, which means "unconquerable"—a good description of Asriel's fortress. The first four letters also spell Adam, which puts Adamant in a religious context that fits the allegory. Pullman might even be implying that Asriel is commemorating Adam, the first man to challenge God. Adam deliberately refused to obey one of God's arbitrary and unreasonable commands. But the main reason for Pullman's choice of "Adamant" for the name is probably that, in *PL*, Pandemonium has "adamantine gates."[61] Pandemonium's adamantine gates allow "Adamant Tower" to serve as a hint that Asriel's (Satan's) Adamant Tower symbolizes Pandemonium.

Leaving the Land of the Dead. The belief in a celestial Heaven as a place of salvation was not part of earliest Christianity, back when Christianity was still a sect within Judaism. To be sure, the earliest Christians, along with the rest of the Jews, believed Heaven existed. But Heaven was not a place where the souls of the righteous went after the mortal body died. Instead, it was a domed vault above a flat Earth. Heaven was where God, Jesus, the Holy Spirit, angels, a few saints, prophets (Elijah at any rate), and other overachievers (Noah, Moses, maybe Joshua) lived among stars and other heavenly bodies. As Christianity spread into the Hellenistic (culturally Greek) world, and as a promised Kingdom of God on Earth kept failing to materialize, a new religion gradually evolved. This new religion, Christianity, differed from Judaism in that, among other differences, the Christians had assimilated the Hellenistic idea of salvation—an afterlife in the celestial Heaven.[62]

The original Christian sect within Judaism began with the Jewish belief that existing society with its earthly kings and kingdoms would soon be replaced by God's Kingdom on Earth—the Kingdom of God, also called (in the New Testament Gospel of Matthew) the Kingdom of Heaven. A messiah would come and with him all sorts of tumult and destruction, marking the end of worldly kingdoms. Then God would literally reign *on Earth*. The Kingdom of God would be an earthly paradise, not a place in heaven—not a place in the sky. It would replace the multiple kingdoms of mortal, human kings.

Jesus believed that the end was near and that the Kingdom of God was just around the corner. His constant message was: "The time is fulfilled, and the kingdom of God is at hand; repent, and believe in the gospel."[63] Eventually, Jesus came to believe that he himself was the messiah and that, after first being taken up to Heaven, he would descend on a cloud, attended by angels, on Judgment Day.[64] Then, in accordance with the belief of many (not all) Jews, the dead would be resurrected and judged alongside the living. Jesus would be the judge. Righteous persons would be allowed to dwell with God in his kingdom on Earth; the wicked would be damned to eternal torture in a Hell of fire.

Matthew gives us Jesus's description of Judgment Day. After arriving on a cloud from Heaven with "all the angels," Jesus "will sit on his glorious throne" to judge the people of all nations. "He will separate them one from another as a shepherd separates the sheep from the goats, and he will place the sheep at his right hand, but the goats at the left. Then the King [Jesus] will say to those at his right hand; 'Come, O blessed of my Father, inherit the kingdom prepared for you.' . . . Then he will say to those at his left hand, 'Depart from me, you cursed, into the eternal fire prepared for the devil and his angels.' . . . And they will go away into eternal punishment, but the righteous into eternal life."[65]

Now we get to the point. It concerns the *resurrection* of the dead. Before Judgment Day, the dead would simply be dead, or else in Judaism's Sheol, a netherworld of mere existence, offering neither reward nor punishment. Then Jesus, the Christ (*Christos* is Greek for *messiah*), would come and restore the dead to life—soon to become life in either Hell or the Kingdom of God. Christianity's Apostles'

Creed incorporates this belief in the following words: "He descended into Hell. On the third day He arose from the dead. He ascended unto Heaven, where he sitteth at the right hand of God, the Father Almighty, from thence [sometimes "whence"] *he shall come* to judge the quick and the dead." The "quick" are the living; the "dead" are the arisen dead. Jesus, not God, "shall come to judge" both the living and the *resurrected dead*—the quick and the dead. Confirming that the "dead" are the resurrected dead, the creed continues, "I believe in . . . the resurrection of the body."

When Lyra and Will go to the land of the dead, they go not to Hell but to a place having characteristics of Sheol and Hades. It is an underground land where the dead live on as ghosts when mortal life ends. Both good people and bad people go to the land of the dead when they die. Judgment Day comes when Lyra leads them out past the harpies. The judge is not the Christ but the harpies, the overseers. They allow anyone who tells them a true story—truth—to exit. This judging represents Jesus's promised judging of the dead, notwithstanding Pullman's use of harpies as proxies for Jesus. Lyra's act of freeing the dead symbolizes Christianity's predicted Resurrection of the Dead, an event that many of today's Christians (mostly conservatives and fundamentalists) still believe will occur.[66] It will occur with a Second Coming of Jesus.

Judgment Day is a future event; it has not yet happened. Being a *future* event associated with the future Second Coming of the Christ, it should not be confused with the "harrowing of Hell," a *past* event. The harrowing of Hell occurred immediately after Jesus was crucified, two thousand years ago.[67] Pullman's "harrowing of Hell" symbolism lies elsewhere. It will be discussed shortly.

"The Truth Shall Make You Free." The harpies' act of judging the ghosts is another symbolic event. A famous quotation from John 8:32 (AV) reads, "Ye shall know the truth, and the truth shall make you free." This is one of John's many gnostic passages. Gnostic theology revolves around a struggle between light and darkness. The human soul originates in a remote realm of light, the home of the gnostic God.

The soul—a spark of light—falls to Earth, which is the creation of an evil god. Christian gnostics generally regarded Satan as the evil creator, but some gnostics actually viewed Yahweh (God) as the "evil one." On Earth the soul is imprisoned in the body under the watchful eye of the "ruler of this world" or "prince of darkness" (usually Satan) and his demons.

The soul can be redeemed and can return to the realm of light *if* given secret knowledge possessed only by gnostics. The secret knowledge includes magical passwords that give the initiate control over the archons, demonic spirits who guard a series of mysterious "aeons" that must be passed through to reach the remote god of light, who dwells in the highest aeon. The aeons are concentric time-space shells or heavens—think of them as barriers—that enclose "this aeon" (Earth). Usually there are seven aeons (whence "seventh Heaven") or twelve, representing either the seven planets of the ancients or the twelve signs of the zodiac, but some gnostic systems had more, sometimes 30 or even 365.

A divine redeemer—Jesus in the case of Christian gnosticism—from the remote realm of light comes to Earth and brings to men the secret knowledge they need to escape their earthly prison. This knowledge is called *gnosis* (Greek for *knowledge*). To fool the demons, the redeemer reveals himself guardedly, saying things like "I am the bread of life," "I am the door," "I am the good shepherd," and "I am the truth." In "the truth shall make you free," truth refers to *gnosis*, the esoteric knowledge that enables the souls of gnostic initiates to fool the archons and return from incarceration in our world of *darkness* to God's realm of *light*, where the presently imprisoned sparks of light, the souls of men, originated. Other gnostic passages besides 8:32 in John include 1:7–9, 2:20–21, 3:19–21, 5:35, 6:35, 8:12, 8:23, 9:5, 10:9, 10:14, 11:9–10, 12:31, 12:35–36, 12:46, 14:6, 14:30, 15:5, 16:11, and 26:18.

Professor R. M. Grant of the University of Chicago, a leading authority on gnosticism, summarized John's gnostic tendencies. "Even though the Gospel of John is not fully Gnostic, it remains a fact that in it we find a portrait of Jesus which is essentially mythological. . . . It is a story of the descent of the redeemer from the invisible, unknown God above. He descends from heaven, and his appearance on earth as Jesus produces the judgment of the world and the defeat of Satan, the prince of this world. He returns above, exalted on the cross, to the heavenly house of his Father, and thereby opens the way to his disciples."[68] This is the context in which "Ye shall know the truth, and the truth shall make you free" must be understood.

Lest there be doubt about whether Pullman would inject gnosticism into his allegory, a second gnostic reference in *HDM* should be noted. Lord Asriel has an alethiometer and an alethiometrist, Mr. Basilides, to read it.[69] The name *Basilides* is that of an early Christian gnostic who taught at Alexandria and whose most memorable ideas were that (*a*) there are 365 heavens that must be passed through to reach the god of light and (*b*) the evil god who created this world is not Satan but Yahweh, the Hebrew God.

When the Authority created the land of the dead, he empowered the harpies to see and feed on the worst in the ghosts who came down. Suddenly the harpies hear Lyra telling true stories about her life. They are enthralled. Asked why, the harpy leader, No-Name, replies: "Because it was true. . . . Because she spoke the truth. Because it was nourishing. Because it was feeding us. Because we couldn't help it. Because it was true."[70]

The harpies threaten to keep the ghosts where they are, but Lyra gets help from Tialys, a Gallivespian who has accompanied her. He negotiates a deal with the harpies. The harpies will have the assignment of guiding back to the surface all truth-telling ghosts who come to the land of the dead. In payment, the ghosts will tell them true stories from their lives. The harpies will *judge* these stories as truth or lies. By telling the truth to the harpies (the judges), a ghost will gain freedom. A ghost who lies will not be released. When the freed ghosts get to the surface, they will dissolve into atoms and become part of nature—the wind, the soil, rivers, plants, and animals.

This is how the harpies come to know the truth. The truth, in turn, sets the ghosts free. Giving truth and freedom to separate parties is not what John, the nominal writer of the Gospel bearing his name, had in mind, but the symbolism still depicts "the truth shall set you free." The ghosts finally reach the surface and are "alive again in a thousand blades of grass, and a million leaves; . . . falling in the raindrops and blowing in the fresh breeze; . . . glittering in the dew under the stars and the moon."[71]

Several new symbols pointing to gnostic concepts are visible in the land of the dead episode. The land of the dead itself becomes a secondary symbol for Earth. Earth's primary symbol remains the world of Cittàgazze, but for purposes of symbolizing gnosticism the secondary symbol takes over. Earth is where human souls, the sparks of light from the realm of the remote god of light, are imprisoned by the prince of darkness. The harpies symbolize the archons who guard the aeons the souls must pass through to escape to the remote realm of light. The inmates of the land of the dead who tell the truth to the harpies symbolize gnostics. This is again secondary symbolism, because the truth-telling inmates also symbolize the resurrected dead who on Christianity's Judgment Day will be admitted to Heaven. The truth the truth tellers tell symbolizes the *gnosis*—magical words—that allow the gnostics to get past the archons. Those inmates who lie to the harpies symbolize people who are not gnostics, people who lack the secret knowledge needed to escape this world. Outside the context of gnosticism, the liars also symbolize those among Judgment Day's resurrected dead who will be assigned to Hell when they are judged.

The Harrowing of Hell. The Apostles' Creed says that Jesus, after being crucified, dying, and being buried, "descended into Hell." Theologians tried to explain this potentially embarrassing event through several related interpretations that, collectively, have become known as "the harrowing of Hell." In some versions, Jesus merely preached to the dead; in others he really went only to Limbo, whose inmates he rescued because they didn't deserve punishment. But the most common interpretation holds that Jesus descended into Hell itself and rescued either a select few saints and Old Testament icons (e.g., Noah,

Moses) or else—this is the customary version—all the *righteous* inmates. He then ascended with the rescuees *directly to Heaven*. The harrowing, a past event associated with the crucifixion of Jesus, should not be confused with the resurrection of the dead on Judgment Day, a future event associated with the Second Coming of Jesus and marking the arrival on Earth of the Kingdom of God.

Some interpreters hold that Lyra's releasing the dead from the land of the dead is "harrowing of Hell" symbolism. Watkins writes, "the exit from the world of the dead echoes Christ's Harrowing of Hell."[72] Scott thinks that "the descent [of Lyra and Will] into the underworld . . . parallels the Harrowing of Hell."[73] And Pinsent argues that the release of the underworld's dead "recalls the 'harrowing of hell,' a key scene of the medieval Mystery plays, in which Christ, between his death and his resurrection, was able to release from limbo the souls of those who had died before his coming."[74]

These interpreters are wrong. The role of the harpies in judging the ghosts (giving passage to those who tell the truth) shows that Judgment Day is being symbolized: the ghosts are being judged. When the righteous ghosts—those who tell the truth—are led out of the world of the dead, the joyful return of their atoms to nature symbolizes the ascension to Heaven of those judged to be righteous on Judgment Day.

Pullman does symbolize the harrowing of Hell, but the symbolism describing the actual "harrowing"—the rescue of the dead—appears much earlier in the trilogy, in the first book, *GC*. That symbolism, discussed in connection with the *LWW* allegory, is really indirect. Pullman directly symbolizes an event from C. S. Lewis's *LWW*, and that event in turn symbolizes the harrowing of Hell; C. S. Lewis is the person *directly* symbolizing the harrowing. The directly symbolized event is Aslan's (Jesus's) act of restoring to life the many righteous creatures that the evil White Witch (Satan) had turned to stone statues. This act occurs right after Aslan's death and resurrection (the death and resurrection of Jesus). We saw that Iorek, the good armored bear, symbolizes Aslan and that Iorek's losing and regaining his armor symbolizes Aslan's death and resurrection. An armored bear's armor is his soul; the soul departs when a person dies. The stone creatures Aslan restores to life are symbolized by the intercised children, who have been separated from their daemons—their souls—and who are figuratively restored to life when they are reunited with their souls, with Iorek's help.

Some additional "harrowing of Hell" symbolism will be examined under the next subheading, which looks at two other facets of the harrowing myth.

Pullman's harrowing of Hell symbolism admittedly suffers from Iorek's having just a secondary role in reuniting the intercised children with their daemons (souls) and bringing about the children's escape. Lyra has the primary role, and the witch Serafina Pekkala even lends a hand. But Iorek does come to the rescue at a crucial moment. One other development confirms that the rescue of the children is *LWW* symbolism, which in turn involves harrowing of Hell symbolism. After Aslan restores the dead creatures to life, he seeks, finds, and kills the evil witch. Correspondingly, after Iorek helps restore the figuratively dead (intercised) children to life, he seeks, finds, and kills the evil armored bear, Iofur. Iofur symbolizes Lewis's White Witch in this scene. (In some other scenes, Mrs. Coulter is the White Witch.)

The Two Descents into Hell. Pullman evidently wanted some *direct* symbolization of the harrowing of Hell to supplement the indirect symbolization found in the *LWW* allegory. He also wanted to symbolize two other facets of the harrowing: (1) Jesus's descent into Hell—the "He descended into Hell" event from the Apostles' Creed—and (2) Jesus's fight with Satan. The descent into Hell occurs before Jesus rescues the incarcerated souls from Satan. And, according to some (not all) versions of the harrowing of Hell, Jesus had to fight Satan in order to rescue the worthy souls. Where did Jesus find Satan to fight him? In Hell, of course—under the Earth. That is why Jesus had to *descend* to reach Satan.

But wait. How did Satan get into Hell, ahead of Jesus? This part of the story comes not from the creed but from *PL*. On the second day of fighting between God's loyal angels and Satan's rebel angels, God gets tired of fooling around. He sends Jesus to attack the rebel forces, unassisted. Attacking with "the roar of ten thousand thunders," Jesus drives his mighty chariot at the rebels, herding them thunderstruck before him. The crystal wall of Heaven opens, creating a "spacious gap." Terrified, Satan and his cohorts throw themselves headlong through the breach. They cascade into Hell; they *descend* to Hell.[75] Satan is one of the descenders.

In chapter 30 of *AS*, while the Battle on the Plain is raging, Asriel learns about (*a*) the explosion of the hair bomb that the Church intended for Lyra, (*b*) the abyss created below the worlds, and (*c*) cracks and fissures leading to the underworld that have appeared. (He has his own alethiometer and a skilled reader, who provides this information.) Asriel orders Xaphania to take her angels and search for an opening. Before long they find a small crack in the mountain near Asriel's fortress. They enlarge it, creating a large opening. The opening symbolizes the "spacious gap" in the wall of Heaven through which Satan fell.

The angels notify Asriel. Soon he is "climbing down into a series of caverns and tunnels extending a long way below the fortress."[76] What does he have in mind? The plot gets confusing at this point. He has told King Ogunwe, "I'm going to destroy Metatron" by going "down to the edge of that abyss."[77] But how he intends to lure Metatron there is never explained. Mrs. Coulter isn't in on the plan. She apparently has overheard what is going on, though, and Asriel somehow (here is a big plot loophole) knows she will lure Metatron to the abyss. So Asriel descends. His descent, the act of going down, is the real point of the action: Pullman is symbolizing the scene from *PL* where Satan, forced back through the opening in Heaven's wall, falls into Hell. Asriel's descent into the caverns symbolizes Satan's fall from Heaven into Hell. The broader context of the event confirms this: Asriel descends shortly after Metatron (Jesus), riding in his "Chariot" (the alternate name of the Clouded Mountain), attacks Asriel (Satan) and his rebel forces.

As Asriel descends, a particular tunnel suddenly opens out into a huge cavern. It has no floor, only sloping sides that funnel down to the edge of the abyss created by the bomb that Lyra escaped. Asriel descends to a position not far from the edge of the abyss. Asriel is now where Satan belongs—deep under the Earth, in a cavern that symbolizes Hell. (Lyra's world also symbolizes Hell, but in this scene Hell has a different symbol.)

The symbolization of Jesus's descent into Hell then begins. Led by the insidious Mrs. Coulter (Judas), Metatron (Jesus) goes to the cavern, Hell. Seeing Asriel far below, Metatron and Coulter follow him down. Here Metatron *descends into Hell*, just as Jesus did, according to the Apostles' Creed. Mrs. Coulter tells Metatron to keep out of sight while she goes to Asriel to "lull him."[78] But instead of lulling Asriel, she plots with him—just as Judas, figuratively speaking, plotted with Satan to arrange the death of Jesus: Judas is plotting with Satan. (In the Bible Judas literally plots with the chief priests, but for literary purposes Pullman is treating them as agents of Satan.) Mrs. Coulter then calls softly to Metatron. As Metatron approaches he unexpectedly finds himself ambushed by the not-so-lulled Asriel, and by Mrs. Coulter too. A horrible fight ensues. Together, Asriel and Coulter manage to drag Metatron over the edge of the abyss. All three plunge to their deaths.

Here we have a reenactment of—symbolization of—Jesus's "harrowing of Hell" fight with Satan, the fight that precedes the rescue of the dead. In the Christian version, Jesus wins, although Satan doesn't die. In the upside-down Pullman version, Satan wins and dies, deliberately and heroically sacrificing his own life in order to bring Jesus's reign to an end. In both versions, Judas is on Satan's side, but only in Pullman's version does Judas die.

It seems likely that the specific way Satan dies is based loosely on an incident from the New Testament's book of Revelation. In Revelation 20 an angel comes down from Heaven and seizes "the dragon, that ancient serpent, who is the Devil and Satan." Well, Metatron is an angel; he comes down from the Clouded Mountain, which symbolizes Heaven; and he seizes (and is seized by) Asriel, who represents Satan. In Revelation, the angel throws Satan into a "bottomless pit," where

Satan remains sealed for a thousand years, presumably lying on the bottom that isn't there. After the thousand years are up, Satan will be released and thrown "into the lake of fire and brimstone," there to "be tormented day and night for ever and ever." (This is where Milton gets the idea of having Satan and his followers fall into a lake of fire when Jesus shoves them out of Heaven.) Pullman, being more merciful than God, makes his pit merely deep rather than bottomless and thereby implicitly lets Satan die when he hits bottom: Satan will not be tortured. We see that the details of Satan's demise are somewhat different in Pullman's story, but the basic facts remain the same: Satan (Asriel) is assaulted by an angel (Metatron) who is intent on throwing him into a pit and who more or less realizes his goal.

In *PL*'s passage where Jesus drives Satan over the edge of Heaven, Satan falls for nine days to "the bottomless pit," by which Milton means Hell, not just a part of Hell.[79] Milton clearly borrowed the phrase from Revelation, where he also found the "lake of fire." Pullman arguably is symbolizing Milton's pit rather than Revelation's; but the difference is not worth debating, since Milton's bottomless pit comes from Revelation. Pullman might well intend to symbolize both pits.

The Battle on the Plain. Under the "Leaving the Land of the Dead" subheading, the discussion referred to Christian doctrine concerning destructive earthly tumult followed by the Second Coming of Jesus, the resurrection of the dead, and Judgment Day. There the emphasis was on the resurrection of the dead (the ghosts in the land of the dead) and on Judgment Day (the harpies' judging whether particular ghosts were telling the truth). Now we need a closer look at the apocalyptic tumult that precedes the Second Coming and Judgment Day. The tumult eventually leads to the Kingdom of God on Earth, with God ruling in place of the former earthly kings. As said before, the earthly Kingdom of God was the salvation concept of the earliest Christians, before modern Christianity's idea of an afterlife in Heaven, a place in the sky, took over.

When Jesus preached, his basic message was that God's reign on

Earth, the Kingdom of God, was just around the corner. Jesus told how the world, as known to the people of his time and place, was about to come to an end. "For in those days there will be such tribulation as has not been from the beginning of the creation which God created until now."[80] Elaborating, Jesus said: "For nation will rise against nation, and kingdom against kingdom, and there will be famines and earthquakes in various places: all this is but the beginning of the sufferings."[81] Men will betray one another and hate one another. Then: "Immediately after the tribulation of those days the sun will be darkened, and the moon will not give its light, and the stars will fall from heaven, and the powers of the heavens will be shaken," after which people "will see the Son of man [Jesus] coming on clouds of heaven with power and great glory."[82]

The apocalyptic horror that will precede the Kingdom of God is described in far greater detail, and with considerably more imagination, in the last book of the New Testament, Revelation. There we read about the many horrible catastrophes that will constitute the apocalypse: war, human slaughter by the sword, famine, pestilence, men gnawing on their tongues, earthquakes, the blackening of the sun, a full moon looking like blood, hail and fire mixed with blood, plagues of stinging locusts with tails of scorpions, horses with serpent tails whose heads strike and wound, waters turned into blood, mountains and islands moved, raging fires that burn up a third of the earth, seas turned into blood, a horrible beast that ascends from a bottomless pit and makes war against men, every kind of plague, a dragon whose tail sweeps stars down from Heaven, and—finally some good news—Satan's getting thrown into a lake of fire. The "first Earth" will pass away and the holy city, new Jerusalem, will come down out of the sky. Thereafter the dwelling place of God, the Kingdom of God, shall be with men, on Earth, in new Jerusalem.

Pullman uses the great battle between Metatron's forces and Asriel's as his symbol of the apocalypse. This is the "Battle on the Plain" from chapter 29 of *AS*. Its participants include angels (on both sides, but mainly God's), witches (on both sides, but mainly Asriel's), humans (on both sides), ghosts (on Asriel's side), Specters (on God's side), Gallivespians (on Asriel's side), armored bears (on Asriel's side), the Swiss Guard (on God's side), Ogunwe's atheist army (on Asriel's side), and many other beings that aren't as prominently featured.[83] Some of the ghosts, which Lyra and Will have rescued from the land of the dead, attack the Specters; the Specters can't hurt the ghosts. And high above, witches with flaming torches set Metatron's angels aflame and clear them from the sky. Asriel and Mrs. Coulter attack Metatron, and all three die.

When Lyra and Will escape to the world of the *mulefa*, the battle is still going on; the outcome is uncertain. Or so it seems. But Asriel has really told us the outcome in earlier statements: "All of us, our Republic, the future of every conscious being—we all depend on my daughter's [Sin's] remaining alive, and on keeping her daemon and the boy's out of the hands of Metatron . . . so that she has a chance to find her way to a safer world—she and that boy, and their daemons."[84] He obviously knows about the witches' prophecy and realizes that what Lyra does will determine the outcome of the war. He thus continues: "We all know what we must do, and why we must do it: we have to protect Lyra until she has found her daemon and escaped. Our Republic might have come into being for the sole purpose of helping her do that."[85]

Lyra and Will do escape to another world, the *mulefa* world. When soon thereafter Lyra eats the Forbidden Fruit, thereby becoming sinful, Asriel's judgment is proven correct. Dust begins falling on her and Will and all the worlds. The witch's prophecy has come true: the Church's spell has been broken. We can easily guess what the battle's outcome will be. When Xaphania, commander of the rebel angels, later visits Lyra and Will, any lingering uncertainty about that outcome is dispelled. The fight is over; the apocalypse is over. Otherwise Xaphania wouldn't be free to leave her post as commander of the rebel angels. Asriel's side has won. As for the last of the Specters, Xaphania says, "We shall take care of the Specters."[86] That mopping-up operation marks the beginning of the post-apocalypse era, the Republic of Heaven, which replaces Christianity's Kingdom of God.

The Tree of Knowledge. The land of the *mulefa* (wheeled animals), where Mary now lives, has stands of unusual trees. These are the wheel-pod trees. They produce and occasionally drop the huge, ultrahard, three-foot-wide seedpods that the *mulefa* use on their single front and rear legs as wheels while their two side legs push the creatures along.

But the trees are dying. Why? Because they depend for fertilization on Dust that falls from the sky onto their upturned blossoms. For the last 300 years—ever since the knife was forged—the Dust has been flowing out of the world through windows opened by the knife. Hardly any Dust now falls on the blossoms. The trees are Dust-starved. Consequently, they face extinction. And if they disappear, the *mulefa* will disappear.

Then Lyra and Will arrive. They are the new Eve and new Adam, not literally (not the original Adam and Eve) but as figures of speech. Searching for their daemons, which have been hiding, they pause to eat. Mary, the new "serpent" (tempter), has packed them some lunch. It includes tempting little red fruits. These are the new Forbidden Fruit. Eating the fruit, the coming-of-age youths fall in love, reenacting "the Fall" and fulfilling the witches' prophecy. Once the prophecy is fulfilled, the Dust stops flowing out of the world and begins falling on the children and on the blossoms of the wheel-pod trees. The Dust saves the trees; they will now be healthy and will reproduce. Consequently, the *mulefa* will have the two things on which their survival depends: (1) the pod wheels, needed for mobility, and (2) the pod oil, from which they absorb knowledge. The *mulefa* race will endure.

The point about pod oil requires elaboration. Remember, the Dust symbolizes knowledge. The trees need knowledge to survive. So do the *mulefa*. And, as we shall see in more detail in *HDM*'s third hidden story, the trees transfer the Dust that falls on their blossoms to the oil in their seed pods. The oil—with the Dust—is then absorbed by the *mulefa* through the claws with which they grip the pod-wheels. The trees thereby deliver knowledge to the *mulefa*. Now we know what the wheel-pod trees really are. They are Trees of Knowledge. Collectively, they symbolize the Tree of Knowledge from Genesis.

(There is a small problem with the symbolism here. The Forbidden Fruit eaten by Lyra and Will should come from the Tree of Knowledge. But a tree can bear only one kind of fruit, be it seed pods, nuts, cones, or fleshy fruit like peaches and the little red fruits eaten by Lyra and Will. Either (*a*) the world of the *mulefa* has extraordinary bifruital trees unlike those of Earth or (*b*) Lyra's fruit came from another species of tree. Considering that the *mulefa* are unlike animals in our world—the *mulefa* lack spines and other features of Earth's quadrupeds—we should probably give Pullman the benefit of the doubt by assuming that the trees are likewise unlike their Earth counterparts: maybe he simply forgot to tell us that the Trees of Knowledge bear two kinds of fruit.)

THE THREE INSTRUMENTS OF THE TRILOGY

The American title of each book of Pullman's trilogy spotlights a tool or instrument introduced and featured in the book. The three instruments are the alethiometer in *The Golden Compass*; the window-opening, Specter-creating, Specter-killing knife in *The Subtle Knife*; and Mary's Dust-viewing telescope in *The Amber Spyglass*. Being named in the three book titles is not the only thing that links the three instruments.[87] Another common characteristic is that all three involve events that occurred 300 years ago. The alethiometer and the knife were both invented 300 years ago, and the spyglass is invented by Mary to investigate why it is that 300 years ago (*a*) the Dustfall declined precipitously, (*b*) the murderous white *tualapi* birds began multiplying rapidly, and (*c*) the wheel-pod trees, on which the *mulefa* depend for survival, began to sicken and die. These linkages make it especially important that we ask what the three instruments symbolize and how they are symbolically related.

The Alethiometer. The alethiometer is a truth-telling instrument, and Dust (knowledge) is what makes it operate. We cannot doubt that the alethiometer is a well-designed symbol of truth. Truth is what both sides are after in the war between religious superstition and knowledge. So the alethiometer points to Pullman's basic theme of warfare between religious superstition and knowledge. Both enemies, the advocates of superstition and the advocates of knowledge, are fighting for the right to declare what is true.

This conflict suggests that calling the alethiometer a symbol of truth oversimplifies. The instrument really symbolizes two *approaches* to truth—the religious approach and the rational or scientific approach. What is the point of Lyra's losing her intuitive, nonscientific ability to read the instrument after she falls in love? Her falling in love signifies that she has reached puberty and is becoming an adult. This means she has left the child's state of innocence and graduated to the adult's state of sin. Sin is, in the eyes of the Church, knowledge—the outcome of eating the Forbidden Fruit from the Tree of Knowledge. Innocence entails being told—by authority figures such as priests, teachers, and parents—what to think, what to believe, what to do. Children are too young to do their own thinking: they must be guided. Sin, in contrast, is a state of free will. It entails being free to think for yourself, to make your own decisions, to learn from experience, to acquire knowledge, and to become wise.

Immediately after Lyra learns she has lost her ability to read the alethiometer, the angel Xaphania, who personifies wisdom, appears and explains in cryptic language why this has happened: "You read it by grace," she says, "and you can regain it by work."[88] What does "by grace" mean? Grace in its religious meaning is an unearned (but not necessarily undeserved) gift, favor, or benefit freely given to a person or group by God. An example would be generous rainfall in a farming area during the growing season. The recipient acquires the benefit without hard work or special effort. By analogy, an innocent child lives in a state of grace, because the child need not think or work to learn what to do: the child is told what to believe and what to do by authority figures. The child is told all the answers. Told to wash her hands before coming to the table, the little girl does so. Told to believe in the tooth fairy and angels, the little boy believes.

Pullman thinks religious people behave like children in a state of innocence: they behave like the beneficiaries of grace. Instead of thinking for themselves they accept whatever beliefs and behavioral codes their pastors and priests and churches tell them they must accept, no matter how unsupported or imaginative or absurd those beliefs are. Tell the parishioners that they must have a priest smear ashes on their foreheads in order to please God and they will do just that. In the words of Will's father, these people "obey and [are] humble and submit."[89]

"You read it by grace" means that Lyra read the alethiometer without the special knowledge—adult knowledge—of how to read it that trained experts require. For surface story purposes, we can assume that angels within the alethiometer silently spoke the answers to Lyra, just as they wrote the answers to Mary's questions on the screen of her computer, "the Cave" (an allusion to Plato's cave). But for symbolic purposes, Pullman is saying that Lyra has progressed beyond the state of innocence and must now behave like an adult. Instead of freely receiving knowledge, she must use the adult method: she must work diligently to acquire it. She must develop a healthy skepticism toward the claims of authorities who would have her accept unsupported and irrational "truth" on the basis of faith. In Xaphania's words, Lyra must apply "thought and effort" and develop "conscious understanding" by "thinking" and "reflecting."[90]

We can now see more clearly how the alethiometer and the two ways by which it can be read represent the battle between religious superstition (acquired by blind faith) and knowledge (acquired by work and thought). Before Lyra falls in love, she is living in an era in which faith—belief in superstitions—has the upper hand in the war between faith and science. Lyra's ability to read the alethiometer intuitively during this era represents the religious approach to truth, the easy way of getting answers. The easy way is faith. Faith enables you to learn "truth" without thinking. Indeed, if you pause to think about the "truth" you learned through faith, you recognize that the "truth" is falsehood. Lyra's initial ability to read the alethiometer by grace symbolizes faith.

After Lyra falls in love—after she becomes sinful by acquiring knowledge—she is living in an era in which science has the upper hand and faith is in decline. (The Church is in chaos.) Her sudden loss of what amounts to psychic skill represents science's and skepticism's gaining control of her mind, and of society. From now on she must learn truth the hard way—by studying, observing, reasoning, experimenting, and building a foundation of experience and knowledge.

Pullman, we can see, is using the alethiometer to describe the importance of using science—hard work and *thinking*—as the road to truth. He is condemning the use of faith, the humble abdication of the responsibility to think. He is denying that by deferentially believing what you are told you must believe, no matter how ridiculous or cruel the belief, you can receive truth. He is asking you to take sides in the war between knowledge (Dust) and superstition (Specters).

To restate the point, the alethiometer symbolizes two conflicting approaches to truth: thinking and faith. It symbolizes the war between knowledge and religious superstition.

The Subtle Knife. Will's "subtle knife" opens windows to other worlds. It was invented by the philosophers' Guild of the Torre degli Angeli (Tower of the Angels) for that very purpose. The Guild amounted to a "Guild of thieves," which is why Cittàgazze's name means City of Magpies.[91] Magpies steal. Drop an earring on the ground and a magpie will swoop down, pick it up, and fly off with it— hence the title and plot of Rossini's opera *The Thieving Magpie*. The Guild used the knife to enter other worlds and steal from them. Guild members brought back gold, jewels, and other valuable items. What they didn't know, however, is that each time they cut a new window they created a Specter. Soon their world was flooded with Specters. The Specters turned the adults into zombies, mindless no-longer-humans who symbolize people who are devoid of knowledge (free from sin) and are totally under the control of superstition.

What does the knife symbolize? The windows, we have seen, symbolize churches and sects. That means the knife is an instrument for creating new religions, new sects. So, at first glance, the knife would seem to symbolize religiosity. Religiosity is the belief that "truth" must be learned from churches, must be accepted on faith, and consists of what atheists, agnostics, and other people who reject organized religion regard as superstition. In a word, the knife *seems* to symbolize faith, which is what creates churches.

But things are really more complicated. For the knife is double-edged. One edge opens windows, creating churches and Specters in the process; the other cuts through any material from the hardest metal to the spiritlike Specters, which it kills. Consider the irony: one edge creates Specters, the other destroys them. This schizophrenic character of the knife is what makes interpretation difficult. The knife can be used for both evil purposes (making Specters) and good purposes (killing Specters), depending on which edge is doing the cutting. So the knife can't represent faith: faith doesn't destroy Specters—doesn't destroy superstitions. Only the edge that opens windows symbolizes faith.

The next question is: what does the other edge symbolize? Whatever it is, it is something that can get out of control if the knife gets in the wrong hands. That "something" is the impulse to kill. Recall that the young man who stole the knife from its rightful owner, Tullio, tried to use it to kill Will. Tullio actually succeeded in slicing off two of Will's fingers. The edge that cuts anything can be used—misused—to kill and maim good people, not just Specters.

Viewed as an agent of death, the knife's second edge could be interpreted as a way of suggesting some of the homicidal excesses of religion: Moses's slaughter by the sword of three thousand worshippers of the golden calf, Joshua's slaughter by the sword of all the residents (men, women, children, and infants) of Jericho and many other non-Jewish towns, the Christian crusades, the Spanish Inquisition (and others), Christianity's burning of witches and heretics, religious wars, assassinations of abortion doctors and other perceived enemies of a zealot's religion, and car bombings and suicide-vest bombings by Muslim fanatics. Does this list of atrocities impute to Pullman ideas that he would not really endorse? Hardly. It is time to repeat part of a longer statement by Pullman that was quoted in this book's introduction: "Churches and priesthoods have . . . in the name of some invisible god . . . burned, hanged, tortured, maimed, robbed, violated, and enslaved millions of their fellow-creatures, and done so with the happy conviction that they were doing the will of God, and they would go to Heaven for it."[92]

Now we can understand why Iorek, a wise bear with remarkable insight, expressed grave reservations about mending the knife: "I don't like that knife, . . . I fear what it can do. . . . It would have been infinitely better if it had never been made."[93] Translation: It would be infinitely better if no religions, no churches, and no religious superstitions had ever been created and no innocent people had ever been tortured and killed because of religion.

We return to the original question: what does the knife symbolize—the knife as a whole, both edges combined? The knife seems intended as another symbol of the war between knowledge and religious superstition. Like the alethiometer, which can be *read* in two ways (by grace and by the application of scientific rules), the knife can be *used* in two ways. The edge that opens windows and, in the process, creates Specters—superstitions—can be used in the cause of superstition. This edge can be labeled "faith": faith creates superstitions. The edge that kills can be used to kill Specters—kill superstitions. This edge might be labeled "reason" or, more broadly, "the scientific method" (a combination of observation, experiment, and reason): reason and science kill superstitions. If this interpretation is correct, both the alethiometer and the subtle knife symbolize in slightly different ways the struggle between the two forces fighting for control of our minds. Each instrument can be used in two ways—the way of faith ("truth" received by grace and accepted on faith) and the way of reason or science (truth received through hard work, empiricism, and reason and accepted through understanding). Both the alethiometer and the subtle knife are symbols of the warfare between knowledge and religious superstition.

The Amber Spyglass. The spyglass is counterpoint to the knife's Specter-creating edge. The knife's chief use has been to create churches and their knowledge-destroying superstitions (Specters). In contrast, Mary Malone uses the spyglass to see Dust, which represents knowledge. The spyglass, in turn, represents scientific instruments in general. Mary's work with the *mulefa* therefore represents using the tools of science (the spyglass) to gain or "see" knowledge (Dust). So we might say that, just as the knife's anti-knowledge edge represents faith, or the religious approach to truth, the spyglass represents the scientific approach to truth—insistence that truth be based on observation and reason. Alternatively, we could say that the spyglass symbolizes the scientific method, contrasted with the religious method of humble submission to religious authority.

The interrelationship of the symbolism displayed by the three instruments can now be seen. Although (1) reading the alethiometer by grace and (2) the knife's window-cutting, Specter-creating edge do not directly symbolize superstition—Specters are the precise symbol— both enumerated symbols to point to superstition's chief weapon in its war with knowledge: faith. And although (1) reading the alethiometer by thought and effort, (2) the knife's Specter-killing edge, and (3) the spyglass do not directly symbolize knowledge—Dust is the precise symbol—all three enumerated symbols point to knowledge's chief weapon in its war with superstition: thinking. In short, each instrument exploits one or both of the two conflicting concepts of truth—superstition (acquired by faith) and knowledge (acquired by hard work, observation, experience, experimentation, and reason).

At the end of the story we learn which approach is winning. The Authority and Metatron are dead, the knife is destroyed, the windows are being closed, the last of the Specters are being eradicated by Xaphania's angels, the Church is in disarray, and Dust is falling on everyone. The war isn't won, but knowledge is on the attack. Superstition is in full retreat.

REVIEW OF THE SYMBOLS

The preceding discussion of the *PL* allegory has brought to light 108 symbols. Thirty-one of these use surface story characters to symbolize hidden story characters or other entities. The surface story characters and their hidden story antecedents are the following:

1. The Authority = God
2. Metatron = Jesus
3. Lord Asriel = Satan
4. The Master of Jordan = the angel Michael
5. Lyra Belacqua = Sin, as personified by Milton
6. Pantalaimon (Lyra's daemon) = Death, as personified by Milton
7. Roger Parslow = Chaos, as personified by Milton
8. Salcilia (Roger's daemon) = Night, as personified by Milton
9. Will Parry = Cain, son of Adam and murderer of Abel
10. John Parry = Adam, from Genesis and the Garden of Eden
11. Mrs. (Elaine) Parry = Eve, Adam's mate
12. Stanislaus Grumman = Prester John, a priest-king in Christian legend
13. The upstairs intruder slain by Will = Abel, brother of Cain
14. Pullman's Lapland witches = Milton's "Lapland witches"
15. Mrs. (Marisa) Coulter = Judas, betrayer of Jesus
16. The Gallivespians = Satan's demons
17. The angel Baruch = Abdiel, God's loyal angel
18. King Ogunwe = Beelzebub, Satan's second in command
19. Xaphania = Sophia, the goddess of wisdom, wisdom personified
20. The intercised children at Bolvangar = children who have been brainwashed—inculcated with religious superstition—by priests, Sunday school teachers, and parents; also indirect (via *LWW*) symbols of Satan's prisoners in Hell from the "harrowing of Hell" myth
21. The zombies of Cittàgazze's world, adults overcome by

Specters = faith personified, or people in the grip of religious superstition, which deprives them of the ability or willingness to think

22. The dead persons being rowed across the lake to the land of the dead = souls being ferried across the river Styx to Hades

23. The aged boatman who rows the dead across = Charon, the boatman of Greek mythology

24. Lyra's "death" spirit that gets her into the land of the dead = the obol coin demanded by Charon for ferrying the dead to Hades

25. Father MacPhail ("Make Fail") = a fanatical Muslim suicide bomber

26. Metatron, in a second role = the angel who, in Revelation 20, comes down from Heaven, seizes Satan, and tosses him into the bottomless pit

27. The harpies = gnosticism's archons, who guard the aeons and prevent passage to the realm of light of any soul that lacks *gnosis*, the secret knowledge (in effect, passwords) needed to get past the archons

28. The land of the dead's dwellers who tell the truth, first meaning = the righteous dead who on Christianity's Judgment Day will be judged worthy of Heaven

29. The land of the dead's dwellers who tell the truth, second meaning = the gnostics, Earth dwellers who have *gnosis*, the secret knowledge needed to get past the archons

30. The land of the dead's dwellers who lie, first meaning = the wicked dead who on Christianity's Judgment Day will be thrown into the "eternal fire" by Jesus

31. The land of the dead's dwellers who lie, second meaning = Earth dwellers who are not gnostics and who therefore lack the secret knowledge needed to get past the archons

Seventy-seven additional symbols represent places, things, and events. These symbols and their antecedents are the following:

1. Lyra's and Asriel's world = Hell, located below Earth in *PL*
2. Cittàgazze's world = Earth, located above Hell and below Heaven in *PL*
3. The aurora borealis = the dark, chaotic void separating Hell and Earth and crossed by Satan, Sin, and Death in *PL*
4. The Cittàgazze world's status as a passageway from Lyra's world to Will's = Earth's intermediate position between Heaven and Hell in *PL*
5. The Clouded Mountain = Heaven, located above Earth in *PL*
6. Will's world = Eden-Paradise-Bliss, where Adam first lived and where Lyra longs to go (she wants to live in Bliss with Will)
7. Dust = knowledge
8. Specters = religious superstitions
9. The Authority's claim to be the creator of the universe = God's claim to be the creator of the universe
10. The Master of Jordan's unsuccessful attempt to poison Asriel = the archangel Michael's unsuccessful attempt to kill Satan
11. The poison the Master of Jordan puts into the decanter of Tokay = Michael's sword
12. Asriel's being the leading adversary of the Authority and Metatron = Satan's being the leading adversary of God and Jesus
13. Asriel's trip to "the North" = Lucifer's trip to his palace in "the North" of Heaven (the original name of Satan in *PL* is Lucifer)
14. Lyra's being the daughter of Asriel = Sin's being the daughter of Satan
15. Lyra's leading the undead ghosts to their joyful deaths in the outside world = Sin's being the mother of Death
16. The death of humans when their daemons die = death of humans as a concomitant, in Christian mythology, of the departure of their souls
17. The death of daemons when their humans die = Pullman's message that there is no supernatural soul that lives on in Heaven or Hell after a human dies

18. Mrs. Coulter's Gobblers (kidnappers) = the goblins who, in Irish folklore, kidnap the souls of children who die in the night and who thereby cause the children's deaths

19. The "Ratter" daemon-coin Lyra places in Tony's mouth before his cremation-style "burial" = the coin that, in Greek mythology, must be placed in a dead person's mouth at burial as a condition (i.e., passage money) for the soul's being ferried to Hades

20. The children's rescue from Bolvangar = the harrowing of Hell, or Jesus's rescue of inmates from Hell when he "descended into Hell"

21. Asriel's estate at Svalbard = Lucifer's palace in "the North"

22. Asriel's "Bridge to the Stars" = Satan's bridge from Hell to Earth

23. Asriel's crossing his "bridge" from his world to the world of Cittàgazze = Satan's crossing his bridge from Hell to Earth

24. Lyra's and Pantalaimon's following Asriel across his bridge = Sin's and Death's following Satan up to Earth over *PL*'s "bridge of wondrous length"

25. Will's being the son of John and Elaine Parry = Cain's being the son of Adam and Eve

26. Will's ramming the upstairs intruder in the belly = Cain's smiting Abel in the belly

27. Will's killing the intruder = Cain's killing Abel

28. Will's condition of "guilt," or his assuming the post-innocence adult role vis-à-vis his childlike mother = Cain's guilt as the slayer of Abel (a highly questionable symbol)

29. Will's going to the Cittàgazze world after killing the intruder = Cain's being exiled to Nod after killing Abel

30. Windows opened by the knife = churches (religions, denominations, sects, etc.)

31. John Parry's walking through a window from his world to Cittàgazze's = Adam's departure from Eden

32. John Parry's becoming ultra-mortal, subject to death within

ten years in the new world = Adam's becoming mortal as part of his punishment for eating the Forbidden Fruit

33. Asriel's Adamant Tower = Pandemonium, Satan's capital

34. The towered design of the Adamant Tower = the towered designs of Mulciber's previous architectural creations in Heaven

35. Baruch's report to Asriel = Abdiel's report to God

36. Father MacPhail's Consistorial Court of Discipline = John Calvin's Consistatorial Court of Discipline

37. Father MacPhail's deliberately killing himself to explode a bomb intended to kill Lyra, an enemy of his religion = a Muslim suicide bomber's deliberately killing himself to explode a bomb intended to kill enemies of his religion

38. The lake that isolates the island gateway to the land of the dead = the river Styx, which isolates Hades in Greek mythology

39. The boatman's refusal to take Lyra until she is properly separated from her daemon = the boatman Charon's refusal to ferry souls who have not been properly buried

40. The land of the dead, first meaning = Hades

41. The land of the dead, second meaning = Earth, in the context of gnostic theology (Earth is where human souls, sparks of light from the realm of the remote God of light, are imprisoned by the evil "Prince of this World")

42. The ghosts' telling true or false stories to the harpies, first meaning = Judgment Day

43. The ghosts' telling true or false stories to the harpies, second meaning = efforts by gnosticism's imprisoned souls to get past the archons who guard the aeons

44. The truth told by the ghosts to the harpies = *gnosis*, the secret knowledge of the ancient gnostics that allowed their souls to escape their earthly prison

45. The ghosts' being set free by the harpies when the ghosts tell the truth = John 8:32, or "Ye shall know the truth, and the truth shall make you free"

46. The ghosts' leaving the land of the dead = the resurrection of the dead on Judgment Day

47. The ghosts' joyfully dissolving into atoms upon reaching the outside world = the ascension to heaven of the resurrected dead on Judgment Day

48. Metatron's "Chariot" = Jesus's chariot (in *PL*)

49. Metatron's using "the Chariot" to attack Asriel's fortress = Jesus's using his chariot to attack Satan and his rebel angels

50. Mrs. Coulter's betrayal of Metatron = Judas's betrayal of Jesus

51. The cavern with the abyss, deep below Asriel's fortress = Hell, here symbolized with an alternate symbol (the original symbol is Lyra's world; another symbol is Mrs. Coulter's Experimental Station at Bolvangar; still another is Asriel's fortress)

52. The crack in the mountainside near Asriel's fortress = the breach in the wall of Heaven through which Satan and the rebel angels fell when shoved out by Jesus, driving his chariot, in *PL*

53. Asriel's descent through the crack into the caverns under the mountain = Satan's fall from Heaven to Hell in *PL*

54. Asriel's waiting for Metatron in a cavern deep below the Earth = Satan's presence in Hell, deep below the Earth, when Jesus descends into Hell (in the Apostles' Creed)

55. Metatron's coming down from the Clouded Mountain in the sky before attacking Asriel = the angel's coming down from Heaven to seize Satan in Revelation 20:1

56. Metatron's descent into the cavern = Jesus's descent into Hell, as stated by the words "he descended into Hell" in the Apostles' Creed

57. Metatron's attack on Asriel = the angel's attack on Satan in Revelation 20:2–3

58. Metatron's fight with Asriel = Jesus's fight with Satan during the "harrowing of Hell"

59. Asriel's fall into the abyss = Satan's fall into the pit in Revelation 20:3

60. The battle on the plain, primary meaning = the *PL* battle in Heaven between Jesus and Satan's forces in *PL*

61. The battle on the plain, secondary meaning = the apocalypse foretold by Jesus in the Gospels and by the book of Revelation

62. Mary's telling Lyra about the marzipan and how it helped her fall in love = the serpent's tempting Eve to eat the Forbidden Fruit in the Garden of Eden

63. The wheel-pod trees of the *mulefa* = the Tree of Knowledge in the Garden of Eden

64. The little red fruits = the Forbidden Fruit from the Tree of Knowledge

65. Lyra's eating the little red fruits = Original Sin, or Eve's eating the Forbidden Fruit

66. Lyra's status before eating the fruit = innocence

67. Lyra's status after eating the fruit = sin, viewed as adulthood, or the state of having received knowledge; also a basis for her symbolizing Sin, as personified in *PL*

68. Lyra's and Will's becoming covered with Dust after eating the fruit = the acquisition of knowledge, which is also the loss of innocence

69. Lyra's ability to read the alethiometer "by grace" while still innocent = faith, or humbly receiving "truth" from religious authorities without thinking and without questioning the alleged truth's validity

70. Lyra's need to read the alethiometer by thought and effort after losing her innocence = reason, or the method that must be used to acquire genuine, reliable truth

71. Lyra's inability to go to another world, Will's world, and live in Bliss with him = our inability to enjoy an afterlife in another world, a world of bliss

72. The Botanic Gardens at Lyra's Oxford and Will's Oxford = the Garden of Eden, or Paradise

73. The alethiometer = the warfare between knowledge (truth reached by thought and effort) and religious superstition

("truth" received by grace = faith, truth received without thought or effort)

74. The subtle knife's edge that opens windows, creating churches and Specters = faith, or the religious approach to truth, the approach that yields superstitions

75. The subtle knife's edge that kills Specters = reason or, more broadly, the scientific method (observation, experiment, and reason), the nonreligious approach to truth, the approach that yields knowledge

76. The knife as a whole = another symbol of the warfare between knowledge (the edge that kills Specters) and religious superstition (the edge that creates Specters)

77. The amber spyglass = science, or the rational-scientific approach to truth, contrasted with faith, the religious approach to truth

CHAPTER 7

MISSIONARIES, DARWIN, AND CONCLUSION

I n his third hidden story, Pullman returns to the task of his surface story and the *Paradise Lost* (*PL*) allegory: attacking Christianity. He also returns to the *PL* allegory's theme of warfare between religious superstition and knowledge. Whereas superstition and knowledge are directly symbolized (by Specters and Dust) in the *PL* allegory, they are indirectly symbolized in this allegory. Pullman directly symbolizes Christian missionaries, and the missionaries in turn symbolize superstition. Similarly, Pullman directly symbolizes evolution theorist Charles Darwin, and Darwin in turn symbolizes science or knowledge.

This last narrative has relatively few symbols, just nineteen. And the symbols are widely scattered, lacking in continuity. So the label "allegory" isn't warranted; "allegorical tendency" is the applicable term. The new story could be regarded as a sort of subplot within the *PL* allegory, since both hidden stories feature the clash between superstition and knowledge. But because the characters and setting include nothing from Milton's *PL*, other biblical material, or theology, the new story is essentially separate. Instead of using characters and events from fiction and mythology, the new story bases its details on actual history. Because this story uses missionaries and Darwin as its central characters, I will call it the missionaries-and-Darwin story.

To the extent that this story has a narrative, that narrative concerns developments over the last 300 years or so. We have seen that 300 years ago is when (*a*) the alethiometer was invented in Lyra's world, (*b*) the subtle knife was invented in the world of Cittàgazze, (*c*) the Dustfall declined sharply in the *mulefa* world, (*d*) the *tualapi,* whose numbers had previously been small and constant, began to multiply rapidly, and (*e*) the Dust-starved wheel-pod trees began to sicken. Three hundred years ago is also when something else happened, something not mentioned in the surface story. Christian missionary activity in faraway lands expanded under the aegis of ocean transportation. Subsequently, this period witnessed the rise of science, and eventually scientific knowledge of evolution. Evolution, in turn, pushed atheism and agnosticism into prominence. Although the missionaries-and-Darwin story emphasizes events of the last 300 years, its renewed theme of warfare between religious superstition and knowledge involves a struggle as old as religion.

THE HIDDEN STORY'S SETTING

The surface story setting for the hidden story is the land of the *mulefa,* the wheeled animals. The *mulefa* live in a fifth world, a world other than Lyra's, Will's, Cittàgazze's, and the Adamant Tower's. How do we know they don't live in some remote corner of one of the first four worlds? Near the end of the trilogy, "the people of three worlds" have dinner together at the *mulefa* village.[1] The three worlds represented are those of the three sets of participants: (1) Lyra and the gyptians, (2) Will and Mary, and (3) the *mulefa.* This means the *mulefa* world cannot also be Lyra's or Will's. The Cittàgazze world can also be ruled out. Mary, after first going from her world, which is also Will's, to Cittàgazze, "stepped through [a window] into the new world" of the *mulefa.*[2] Mary's world—our world—does not have fantasy creatures such as *mulefa* and *tualapi,* so we know Mary didn't step back into her own world. The *mulefa* world and the Cittàgazze world must be separate worlds. Asriel's Adamant Tower world, the fourth world, can likewise be eliminated: Lyra and Will, in their escape from the battlefield in Asriel's world, go through another window to the world of the *mulefa*, a different world. Conclusion: the *mulefa* live in a fifth world.

(Near the end of *The Amber Spyglass*, John Faa and his gyptians arrive by sea to take Lyra home to Oxford. This event does seem to suggest that the *mulefa* live in Lyra's world. The gyptians travel by water in their world, which is also Lyra's. How could they have gotten into another world, and how could they expect to sail home to Lyra's Oxford from a location in that other world? This question seems to reveal a plot loophole. But there is an implied answer. The witch Serafina Pekkala, who arrives ahead of the gyptians to provide friendly advice, tells the daemons of Lyra and Will, "I came with the gyptians, all the way from our world."[3] We must assume that Serafina has guided the gyptians to a sea window leading from one world's ocean to another's. She could have learned about this window from the angels the same way that Ruta Skadi learned from angels the location of the sky window to Asriel's new world.)

Besides being in a fifth world, the land of the *mulefa* has another noteworthy characteristic. The *mulefa* are primitive people with a primitive culture. The missionary allegory's setting symbolizes places here on Earth, our planet, where missionaries ply their trade.

THE SYMBOLIC CHARACTERS

The third hidden story's symbolic characters are the *mulefa* and the *tualapi* (coordinate symbols), Dr. Mary Malone, the Africans (blacks), and the witches.

The *Mulefa* and Their Wheel-Pods. The *mulefa* are intelligent but primitive wheeled animals. (Pullman apparently borrowed the concept from chapter 6 of L. Frank Baum's *Ozma of Oz*, which features wheeled creatures called Wheelers.)[4] Evolution produced their higher intelligence about 33 thousand years ago, or at roughly the same time humans acquired it (35 thousand thousand years ago, according to the story). The *mulefa* are strange creatures: quadrupeds with one front leg, one rear leg, and two side legs. These legs are attached to a diamond-shaped frame (as viewed from above); the *mulefa* have no spines. An axle-like claw on each front and rear leg hooks through a huge, hard seedpod, which becomes a wheel. The two side legs provide propulsion. The *mulefa* world has smooth, straight, ribbonlike roads over which the creatures usually travel, although they can also move more slowly over paths. The roads apparently were created by ancient lava flows. The wheel-pods come from wheel-pod trees, which are fertilized by Dust. The Dust falls from the sky onto their upturned blossoms.

Besides having front and rear legs with wheels, the *mulefa* have horns and short but powerful trunks with two fingerlike projections at the trunk's tip. When meat is needed, the *mulefa* separate a grazing animal from its herd, then break its neck with a wrench of a trunk. The projections on the trunks can apply enormous force in tasks requiring strength yet are superbly gentle when used for delicate tasks. Additionally, the skin texture on the projections' "fingertips" adapts to the task, becoming velvet soft for activities like milking grazing animals and becoming hard for forceful activities like tearing branches. By working cooperatively to tie knots—it takes two *mulefa* to tie a knot—the wheeled creatures can make nets and catch fish.

A symbiotic relationship exists between the *mulefa* and the wheel-pod trees. The *mulefa* cannot live without pods from the trees, and the trees cannot reproduce without pod opening and tree tending by the *mulefa*. The pods that fall from the trees are too hard to open naturally for seed dispersal. They can open only by being used as wheels, undergoing constant pounding on the lava-flow roads until the pods eventually crack. When a pod cracks, the *mulefa* replace it with one of the spares they always carry. The *mulefa* pry open each cracked pod, remove the seeds, and plant them. The seeds don't germinate easily, so constant tending is needed for sprouts to appear.

The trees return the favor, completing the symbiotic relationship. Not only do the trees provide wheels, they provide pod oil that both lubricates the wheels and gets absorbed by the foot claws the *mulefa* use as wheel axles. The absorbed oil delivers knowledge and wisdom to adult *mulefa*. How can the oil convey knowledge to the adults? It contains *sraf*, which is the *mulefa* word for Dust. The *mulefa* don't realize how the *sraf* enters the oil, but in fact it falls from the sky onto wheel-pod tree blossoms. After fertilization occurs, the blossoms deliver the *sraf*—Dust, knowledge—to the seed pods that form and to the oil within the pods. Whereas Dust falls directly on humans, it enters the *mulefa* indirectly, via the oil. This fact is vitally important in Pullman's symbolism. Because the trees transfer knowledge (Dust) to the *mulefa*, the trees collectively symbolize the Tree of Knowledge from Genesis.

The *mulefa* children lack the wisdom of adults, because they can't use the pod-wheels: they can't absorb pod oil through their claws. This inability to absorb oil creates an obvious similarity between the *mulefa* children and the children of Lyra's world. When Dust falls in Lyra's world, it accumulates largely on adults. Before reaching puberty, human children accumulate very little Dust. Both the *mulefa* children and the human children display innocence until they are old enough to absorb knowledge, which is sin (as the Church of Lyra's world sees things) and which destroys their innocence.

By the time Mary arrives in this new world, things are going badly. A crisis looms. The very existence of the *mulefa* is threatened by the gradual disappearance of Dust, starting about 300 year ago. Instead of falling, most of the Dust is flowing out of the world. The trees have become sick. Some have died; others are dying. And if the trees die (i.e., if the *mulefa* source of knowledge vanishes), the *mulefa* will die too.

One more detail about the *mulefa* leads us to their symbolic meaning. The *mulefa* have a partly agricultural, partly hunter-gatherer society: they eat sweet grass, grain, fruit, meat and milk from domesticated grazing animals, and fish they catch with nets. They live in villages in thatched huts with wooden beams. It isn't hard to see that the *mulefa* are ideal symbols for primitive humans. Their village symbolizes native villages in underdeveloped countries on earth.

The derivation of the word *mulefa* is uncertain. Conceivably, its meaning comes from the word *mule*. A mule is a hybrid, a cross between a horse and a donkey. In appearance, one of the *mulefa* is also a hybrid, a cross between an elephant (the trunk) and perhaps a bison or an antelope (the horns).

The *Tualapi*. Periodically, great white flightless birds called *tualapi* attack the *mulefa* settlements. The *tualapi* are water birds. They are huge, the size of rowboats. Their heads and beaks resemble those of swans, but the beaks have fearsome incurved teeth. And their wings are most unswanlike: one is in front of the other. The *tualapi* arrive from the sea and cruise up rivers, sailing by using their huge wings as sails. They hold their wings upright in seemingly awkward positions that mimic the fore and aft sails of sailing ships. Once ashore at a village, the *tualapi* kill any *mulefa* they can catch, eat all the food, try to destroy the pods (which contain knowledge), demolish every- thing else they can see, and defecate all over the place. Then they sail away to wherever they came from.

Before air transportation came into widespread use after World War II, missionaries had to travel by water to reach the faraway lands where unchurched natives lived—places similar to the *mulefa* villages. Once at their destinations, the missionaries would destroy the knowl- edge necessary for human advancement by replacing knowledge with superstition. (This may be an overstatement, but it fairly reflects what the symbolism depicts.) In view of Pullman's antireligious themes, it's hard to doubt that the *tualapi* symbolize missionaries, enemies of knowledge. Like missionaries, the *tualapi* sail to their destinations. Those destinations are the villages of primitive beings with human ways and human intelligence.

Consider what the *tualapi* do. They first try to destroy the pod wheels. Failing in that effort, they next push the pods into the river to float away. Symbolically, the birds are getting rid of Dust (knowl- edge), which the pod wheels deliver to the *mulefa* in the pod oil. And when the *tualapi* defecate all over the *mulefa* villages, missionaries are depositing their superstitions on primitive cultures—replacing knowl- edge with superstition.

Lest uncertainty remain about who the *tualapi* symbolize, Pullman throws in the scene where Father Gomez learns he can make the birds "do exactly as he said."[5] Pullman's point: the *tualapi*, like missionaries, are working for the Church. Father Gomez represents the Church.

The *tualapi* were around but weren't much of a threat—they weren't multiplying—until Dustfall began declining 300 years ago. Why not? Because knowledge militates against superstition. And the Dust represents knowledge. The weakening of knowledge allowed superstition—the *tualapi*, representing missionaries—to multiply.

The 300-years-ago dating of the decline in Dustfall and the attendant sickening of the wheel-pod trees ties in nicely with the rise of Christian missionaries. Missionary work didn't suddenly materialize. (The *tualapi* always existed.) Any starting date is therefore arbitrary. But when sea travel to distant lands became practical, missionary expeditions gradually escalated. Three hundred years ago, counting backward from the 1995 publication date of *The Golden Compass* (*GC*), puts us in 1695. That's a good approximation of the time when missionary work was gathering steam. In North America, the French-Canadian explorer Louis Joliet and the Jesuit priest Jacques Marquette began a joint exploration of the area between the Great Lakes and the Mississippi River in 1673, and in 1675 Marquette began preaching among the Indians. The first Spanish mission in Texas was established at San Antonio de Senecu in 1682; the former San Antonio mission now known as the Alamo was established at San Antonio de Valero in 1718. The first Spanish mission on the Baja Peninsula came in 1697. This period, centering close to 1695, was when Christian superstition began displacing knowledge among native populations. The Spanish missions, incidentally, tie in nicely with Father Gomez's nationality: he is Spanish.

Pullman's likely derivation of the name *tualapi* provides additional evidence that the *tualapi* are missionaries. Tual is a town on Ewab, a small island southwest of New Guinea in Indonesia—just the sort of place missionaries visit to spread their doctrines. Visitors to

286   PHILIP PULLMAN'S *HIS DARK MATERIALS*

Tual could be called *tualapi*, a plural word for which *tualapan* is the singular form. That much is fact. Beyond established fact, a highly speculative secondary derivation that in all probability is dead wrong provides food for thought. *Tualapan* is an anagram for "Paul at An," where "An" could stand for Antioch. Paul of Tarsus, Christianity's St. Paul, was the first Christian missionary. He made three missionary journeys. All three began at Antioch.

Name anagrams often arise accidentally. At the very end of the trilogy, back at Oxford, Lyra is introduced to Dame Hannah Relf, usually referred to as Dame Hannah. "Dame Hannah" is an anagram for "ham and a hen." Since a hen can represent eggs, that anagram amounts to "ham and eggs." Just a coincidence. The best test of intent is how accurately the anagram describes the character or a plot feature related to the character. "Paul at Antioch" is a good description of a missionary, but "An" for Antioch is not terribly convincing. Still, the possibility that *tualapan* is a deliberate anagram is reinforced by the "a dark suit" anagram found in the name of the witch Ruta Skadi, who is dressed entirely in black. If "a dark suit" is intentional—a big if— "Paul at An" is probably intentional too.

Dr. Mary Malone. Dr. Mary Malone is from Oxford in Will's world, our world. She began her career as a religious person, a Roman Catholic nun. (Mary is easily the most popular English language name for Catholic girls; Malone is a stereotypical Irish Catholic name.) Along the way Mary lost her faith and became an atheist. She is now a research-oriented scholar. Her research focuses on Dust, which in her world is called dark matter or Shadows. Blocked in her work by religious interests, she flees to another world where the *mulefa* live. She learns to speak their language. The wheel-pod trees are dying, so the *mulefa* ask Mary for help. She agrees to help them and launches new research in this faraway land, remote from her home in Oxford.

Sounds a lot like Charles Darwin, doesn't it? Like Mary, Darwin began as a religious person. He was a Unitarian at a time when Unitarians were reasonably orthodox Christians. He even contemplated becoming a minister. But he became interested in science and, before long, sailed away to remote places in his famous voyage on the *Beagle*. On this trip he conducted the research that led to his earth-shaking 1859 book, *The Origin of Species by Means of Natural Selection*. This is the book that introduced what is now known as the theory of evolution, a scientific advance that produced momentous changes in society and in religion. "He had given up his belief in the Old Testament, then in the New, and finally in Christianity as a divine revelation, only to discover without distress, without surprise even, that he was completely lacking in faith."[6] Darwin's book marked (*a*) the beginning of the decline of religion and (*b*) the emergence of atheism and agnosticism as at least marginally acceptable viewpoints within Christian society.

Both Mary and Darwin (1) began as religious people, (2) became atheists, (3) traveled to faraway lands located near the sea and populated by primitive people, and (4) conducted research in faraway places. When we also consider the importance of Darwin's work to the religious issues Pullman is debating, we have a strong case for the proposition that Mary Malone symbolizes Charles Darwin. A reinforcing consideration is that Mary's representing Darwin provides a historical context in which atheists and agnostics—their symbols are just around the corner—can be symbolized. No other famous atheist (e.g., Karl Marx, Thomas Huxley, Robert Ingersoll, Samuel Clemens [Mark Twain], Friedrich Nietzsche, Sigmund Freud, George Bernard Shaw, George Santayana, Bertrand Russell, H. L. Mencken, Isaac Asimov) comes even close to matching Mary's characteristics and thereby offering an alternative antecedent for Mary.

One more similarity between Darwin and Mary, a crucial one, demands notice: both persons brought crucial knowledge to the world. Not since Copernicus, whose theory that the planets revolve around the sun revolutionized the way we think about the universe, had there been anything even approaching Darwin's contribution to *knowledge*. Darwin's theory of evolution, moreover, dealt a far more devastating blow to religion than did Copernicus's theory.

Mary's contribution to knowledge is comparable to Darwin's.

Mary gives to Lyra and Will the knowledge of love. She does this by telling them the story of her experience with marzipan and how the sugary almond confection led to her falling in love when she was twelve. Mary's tale of sexual awakening leaves Lyra primed for love: "Lyra felt something strange happen to her body. She felt as if she had been handed the key to a great house she hadn't known was there, a house that was somehow inside her, and as she turned the key, she felt other doors opening deep in the darkness, and lights coming on. She sat trembling as Mary went on."[7] The next day, Lyra and Will eat the red fruit, the analog of the Forbidden Fruit from Genesis. They are now flushed with knowledge; their innocence is gone, and with it the evil spell of the Church that was causing knowledge to flow out of the world. The witches' prophecy has been fulfilled.

Mary's marzipan story, appropriately highlighted in an *AS* chapter title ("Marzipan"), symbolizes Darwin's theory of evolution. Just as Darwin's theory enlightened society and had prodigious socioreligious effects, Mary's story enlightens Lyra and Will and has prodigious socioreligious effects. Newly acquired knowledge magically breaks the spell of the Church, causing the Dust to stop flowing out of the worlds and to start raining down from above. It settles on the young lovers and on the upturned blossoms of the wheel-pod trees. The trees, and the *mulefa* too, will survive.

Just as important, the *tualapi* will languish; they will no longer be a serious threat to the *mulefa*. Pullman doesn't make this explicit, but it is definitely implicit in the situation. Until 300 years ago, when the Dustfall suddenly declined, the *tualapi* were not a serious problem. Sattamax, a *mulefa* elder, tells Mary that "even if once in a while the *tualapi* came, our numbers and theirs remained constant."[8] The Dust was apparently keeping them in check. Symbolically speaking, knowledge was resisting superstition. Now that Dust is again falling, the *tualapi* will again be held in check.

The Dust begins to fall again in Lyra's world too. This development is a staggering blow to religion. The Church experiences chaos, confusion, and decline—which is what the Christian Church experienced when Darwin's knowledge settled on our own society. The impact of the spell's end symbolizes the impact of Darwin's breaking the spell of religion on nineteenth-century society in our world.

Still another argument supports the thesis that Mary symbolizes Darwin. We can see that the missionaries-and-Darwin hidden story is a resymbolization of the superstition versus knowledge hidden story of Pullman's main allegory, the *PL* allegory. In the *PL* allegory, the Specters symbolize superstition and Dust symbolizes knowledge. In the missionaries-and-Darwin hidden story, the missionaries symbolize superstition and Darwin symbolizes knowledge. Just as the Specters and Dust are complementary symbols, the missionaries and Darwin are complementary symbols. The evidence that the *tualapi* directly symbolize missionaries and thereby indirectly symbolize superstition is compelling. But if Mary isn't a direct symbol for Darwin and an indirect symbol for knowledge, the *tualapi* lack their complement. Superstition has nothing to clash with.

In addition to the above evidence that Mary symbolizes Darwin, a series of hints from Pullman direct our attention to Darwin. All involve Pullman's mentioning the name Parslow. Roger's last name, once again, is Parslow. But he isn't the only Parslow in the story. The name Parslow comes up no less than seven times in chapter 3 of *GC*—once in reference to Roger; twice in reference to a family of Jordan College "masons and scaffolders"; four times in reference to Simon Parslow, a friend of Lyra and Roger (why a "friend" and not a cousin of Roger's?); and once in reference to the Housekeeper, Mrs. Lonsdale, who is a second cousin of Roger's father.[9] Parslow, we saw, was the name of Darwin's butler and friend. Why is Pullman giving his name to so many characters and mentioning it so many times? Pullman seems to be hinting. He is apparently calling Darwin to our minds so that, when the Darwin symbol comes up, we will think of Darwin and see the symbolic connection.

The evidence that Mary symbolizes Darwin is convincing. But someone is bound to ask: how can a woman symbolize a man? That question was answered in the preceding chapter when we examined

Mrs. Coulter. She symbolizes Judas, a man. Several other examples of superficially inappropriate symbols that nevertheless are genuine were given. One of these was Iofur, from Pullman's *The Lion, the Witch and the Wardrobe* (*LWW*) allegory. Iofur, who is male and a bear, symbolizes C. S. Lewis's White Witch, who is female and resembles a human. The witch, in turn, symbolizes Satan in Lewis's own allegory: female symbolizes male. It was also pointed out that the Master of Jordan's three male servants symbolize the three female servants of *LWW*'s kindly old Professor.

Minor objections to the Mary = Darwin interpretation remain. Darwin was not an ex-Catholic. He did not seek to help primitive people encountered on his voyage. His voyage took him nowhere near Tual (if that is the root word for *tualapi*). The leg of Darwin's journey nearest to Ewab, the island where Tual is located, took Darwin northwest from the southwest corner of Australia to Keeling Island, also called Cocos Island, which is southwest of Sumatra. Both Ewab and Keeling Island are, however, in the Indian Ocean. And the other differences between Mary and Darwin don't invalidate the symbolism: one good analogy remains all it takes to establish a symbol. The Darwin symbolism rests on more than one good analogy. Mary = Darwin looks like a safe bet.

The Africans. Lord Asriel has three main groups in his army, not counting the independently operating witches and armored bears. The three groups are the rebel angels, led by Xaphania; the Gallivespians, led by Lord Roke; and the Africans, led by King Ogunwe. Asriel's angels are simply angels, nonsymbolic persons (except for Xaphania, who symbolizes Sophia), and the Gallivespians are marvelous symbols for demons. We have an ironic alliance of angels and demons. Those two groups are supernatural beings. But what about the non-supernatural, human part of Asriel's army—the Africans? Are they symbolic?

They surely are. They probably symbolize atheists. In English vernacular, Africans are called blacks. Black is the traditional color of badness or evil. Black magic is magic used for evil purposes. A black sheep is a disreputable member of a group. A blacklist is a list of people marked for censure, exclusion, or reprisal. A black mass is a perverted form of the Roman Catholic mass, conducted by Satan worshippers. A blackguard is a scoundrel. In the western film genre, the villain wears a black hat (contrasted with the hero's white hat) or even an entirely black outfit, as with Wilson (Jack Palance) in the western classic *Shane*. In *Star Wars*, the evil Darth Vader is dressed in black. So what could be more logical than having blacks symbolize atheists, who are viewed by most conservative and fundamentalist Christians— even many moderate Christians—as the epitome of evil?

In this connection, Ogunwe's Africans battle Metatron's Swiss Guard when Lyra is rescued from Mrs. Coulter at the cave; the Swiss Guard is trying to kill Lyra. In real life, the Swiss Guard is a long-standing papal institution, founded in 1505. The pope's private army, the Swiss Guard, now consists of about one hundred men. They are the pope's bodyguards and are responsible for maintaining security at the Apostolic Palace. They guard the main entrances to the Vatican. They also protect the pope when he travels. Recruits must be Roman Catholic, Swiss, former trainees of the Swiss armed forces, and unmarried. Where could you find a more appropriate opponent of Metatron's symbolically Catholic army of Swiss Guards than an army of atheists? Besides, what humans if not atheists are going to take up arms against religion in the war against God? And why else, if not to symbolize atheists, would Pullman bother to make the human army all black?

The Witches. The witch symbolism may not end with the *LWW* and *PL* allegories, where the witches respectively symbolize Britain's Royal Air Force (RAF) and the "Lapland witches" from Milton's epic poem. In the missionary story, the *tualapi* (missionaries) and the Africans (atheists) are the two religious extremes: zealous belief and total disbelief. Most likely, the witches symbolize the in-between viewpoint, that of the undecided people who say that maybe there is a God and maybe there isn't. The witches are on neither side, at least not at first, in Lord Asriel's war against the Authority and Metatron. Lyra asks Serafina Pekkala's daemon, Kaisa, "Are they [the witches] on his side or against him [Lord Asriel]?" Kaisa replies: "That is a question with too complicated an answer. Firstly, the witches are not united. There are differences of opinion among us. . . . Thirdly, Serafina Pekkala's clan—my clan—is not yet part of any alliance, though great pressure is being put on us to declare for one side or another."[10]

Serafina's witch clan does help Lyra, but this help involves (*a*) the rescue of the intercised children at Bolvangar and, later, (*b*) the escape of Will and Lyra from the belvedere temple in Cittàgazze when armed children attack them. The witches at this point aren't trying to help Asriel. Much later several clans of witches, including Ruta Skadi's, do attack Metatron's angels, but some other witch clans support Metatron. A witch helps Father MacPhail when he is struggling with Mrs. Coulter, who has turned against the Authority and is trying to prevent MacPhail from exploding the hair bomb intended for Lyra. In *Lyra's Oxford*, the short story sequel to the trilogy, a witch tries to kill Lyra. The witch killed her own son while her clan was fighting *against* Asriel. She blames Lyra because she thinks, mistakenly, that the war was being fought over Lyra.

We see that the witches can't decide which side they're on. That indecision makes them an ideal symbol for agnostics. Another similarity is that agnostics almost always lean toward atheism. In general, they either avoid religion altogether or become Unitarians or Quakers. Many are really atheists who, lacking the courage of their convictions, call themselves agnostics to avoid the social stigma that goes with atheism. This leaning toward atheism would explain why most of the witches, Serafina's clan and Ruta Skadi's in particular, come around to Lord Asriel's side.

Review of the Symbolism. The missionaries-and-Darwin hidden story has nineteen symbols, not enough to constitute allegory but enough to establish allegorical tendency. The symbols are these:

1. The *mulefa* = primitive humans, the targets favored by missionaries
2. The *mulefa* world = primitive societies, collectively

3. The *tualapi*, direct meaning = old-style missionaries, who arrive by sailing ship

4. The *tualapi*, indirect meaning = religious superstition, represented by missionaries

5. The fore and aft wings (as held in their sailing position) of the *tualapi* = the fore and aft sails of sailing ships bringing missionaries to primitive societies

6. The existence of *tualapi* before they began multiplying 300 years ago = the existence of missionaries before they began multiplying 300 years ago

7. The increase in *tualapi* numbers and activity over the last 300 years = the increase in missionary numbers and activity over the last 300 years

8. The loss of pod wheels through *tualapi* vandalism = the loss of knowledge, when missionaries replace knowledge with superstition

9. The excrement deposited by the *tualapi* = superstitions deposited by missionaries

10. Mary Malone, direct meaning = Charles Darwin

11. Mary Malone, indirect meaning = scientific knowledge brought to society by Darwin

12. Mary's becoming an atheist = Darwin's becoming an atheist

13. Mary's trip to *mulefa* country = Darwin's voyage on the *Beagle*

14. Mary's marzipan story = Darwin's *Origin of Species*, the story of evolution

15. The indirect impact on the *tualapi* of Lyra's and Will's acquisition of knowledge of love = the impact on society of its acquisition of knowledge of evolution

16. King Ogunwe's Africans = atheists

17. The black skin of Ogunwe's Africans = the evil character (black as a symbol of evil) of atheists, as viewed by most Christians (particularly evangelical Christians), Jews, and Muslims

18. The witches = agnostics
19. The witches' indecision on whether to side with Asriel or the Authority = an agnostic's indecision about whether God exists

THE HIDDEN STORY AND WHERE SOCIETY IS TODAY

The hidden Darwin story amounts to a review of the religious history of the last three centuries. Three hundred years ago was a time when nobody dared admit being an atheist or even an agnostic. Pantheism (Spinoza) and deism (Pope, Voltaire) were then the only acceptable forms of non-Christian skepticism in the Christian world. During this era missionary work among natives living in remote places accelerated. The growth of sea travel from short-range or exploration-oriented voyages to long-range and commerce-oriented voyages made long missionary trips feasible. The missionaries brought new superstitions to the primitive settlements they visited. That definitely was not what these people needed. They were already overburdened with superstition. They needed knowledge.

Barely more than half way through this 300-year period, Charles Darwin presented his theory of evolution. This theory and its extensive supporting documentation, documentation that rapidly expanded in subsequent years, demolished religion's claim that God created the world in six days and that humanity suddenly burst into existence about six thousand years ago with a couple of biblical characters named Adam and Eve. The more intelligent and enlightened members of society gradually—sometimes quickly—accepted Darwin's theory. In the process, atheism and agnosticism took hold. Darwin's influence has been trenchantly summarized by Homer Smith:

> The *Origin* shattered the complacency of the Victorian world and initiated what may be called the Darwinian revolution. . . . The theory of evolution was but one of many factors contributing to the

destruction of the ancient beliefs; it only toppled over what had already been weakened by centuries of decay, rendered suspect by the assaults of many intellectual disciplines; but it marked the beginning of the end of the era of faith.[11]

Religion is now fighting a losing battle with science. In Gallup polls taken regularly since World War II, around 94 percent of Americans have always said they "believe in God or a universal spirit." But the Gallup figures exaggerate by (a) including people who actually have a degree of doubt and (b) also including people to whom "universal spirit" does not mean the personal god of Judeo-Christian and Islamic religion. A 1998 poll by the International Social Survey Program (ISSP), a cooperative endeavor of the University of Chicago in the United States and other leading universities in other countries, produced findings remarkably different from Gallup's. People were asked if they agreed or disagreed with the statement, "I know God really exists *and I have no doubts about it.*" Only 63 percent of Americans, or less than two-thirds, agreed.[12]

The shift toward irreligion was even more evident in other advanced, non-Catholic, Christian nations, where US-style fundamentalism is virtually unknown and church attendance is weak. Except for Canada (33 percent Catholic), none of these other countries had even half the American percentage of free-from-any-doubt believers. Only 39 percent of Canadians, 31 percent of New Zealanders, 29 percent of Australians, 23 percent of Britons, 26 percent of the Dutch, 20 percent of the French (France is 49 percent Catholic), 18 percent of Norwegians, 16 percent of Germans (average of East and West Germany), and 12 percent of Swedes believed in God and had no doubts about his existence.[13]

As you would expect, Hell was on even shakier footing than God in the ISSP survey. Only 55 percent of Americans responded, "Yes, definitely," when asked if they believed in Hell. The comparative findings for the other advanced, non-Catholic, Christian countries were Canada, 26 percent; New Zealand, 23 percent; Australia, 15 percent;

Great Britain, 14 percent; the Netherlands, 13 percent; France, 10 percent; Norway, 10 percent; Germany, 8 percent; and Sweden, 7 percent.[14] Hell's decline is even more severe than the poll results suggest, because the concept of torture is vanishing. Heaven and Hell have become "states" rather than places in some denominations and to many of the individual Christians who struggle to rationalize an obligatory belief in Hell.

Not only that, the devil who formerly presided over Hell has fallen on hard times. The ISSP survey had no question about the devil. But in a poll undertaken in the early 1960s by the Research Program in the Sociology of Religion, University of California, Berkeley, the devil performed even more poorly than Hell did in the ISSP survey. The California survey measured the beliefs of three thousand *church members*. Church membership naturally inflates the percentage of devil believers. Nonetheless, only 38 percent of Protestants and 66 percent of Catholics said it is "completely true" that "the Devil actually exists." (Only 6 percent of the Congregationalists, 13 percent of the Methodists, and 17 percent of the Episcopalians, but 77 percent of the Missouri Synod Lutherans and 92 percent of the Southern Baptists said "completely true.")[15]

Church attendance is also weakening. Respondents in the ISSP survey were asked, "How often do you attend religious services?" Surprisingly high percentages replied either (1) "Never" or (2) "Less frequently" than (a) "several times a year" in most countries, (b) 1–2 times a year or less in Australia, New Zealand, and France, or (c) once a year in Great Britain. The "never" and "less frequently than . . ." responses totaled 41 percent in the United States, 53 percent in Canada, 64 percent in New Zealand, 67 percent in Australia, 59 percent in Great Britain, 60 percent in the Netherlands, 73 percent in France, 80 percent in Norway, 55 percent in Germany, and 53 percent in Sweden.[16]

Another remarkable development is the widespread abandonment of religion by the most highly educated members of society. Harvard and Stanford universities are among the schools with the highest admission standards in the United States. A 1986 survey of a stratified sample consisting of 3,600 Harvard and Stanford graduates found that only 73 percent believed in "God or a supreme being."[17] Since the survey used a Gallup-style question without the "and have no doubts about it" add-on of the ISSP survey's question, that 73 percent compares with the Gallup poll's 94 percent for the general population. Only 24 percent of the Harvard and Stanford graduates considered religion an important part of their lives; the comparable figure for the general population, taken from benchmark data, is 53 percent, or more than double the Harvard-Stanford figure.[18] Nowadays many people profess to be "spiritual"—they implicitly believe in God—but reject organized religion with its multifarious superstitions and medieval ritual. These people rarely attend church.

Arthur Bellinzoni, a retired professor of religion, has aptly described where Christianity stands today:

> Among developed countries, the United States is an anomaly. Although about 5 percent of French adults attend church once a week, more than 30 percent of Americans claim to do so. Even former Communist countries, which experienced a brief religious resurgence following their liberation, have settled back into religious indifference. . . .
>
> Although fewer and fewer Christians regularly attend church, sizable majorities say that they still believe in something they continue to call God. There is, however, among Christians a disconnection between believing and attending church. Studies show that as people grow wealthier and are better educated, they gradually fall away from their ancestral faiths. Once again, Americans, or at least evangelical American Christians, may be the anomaly, the exception to the rule.[19]

"Dust" is falling on society. Knowledge is gradually superseding religious superstition.

CONCLUSION

Fully 230 allegorical symbols have come to light in this analysis of Pullman's trilogy. A few may rest on invalid interpretations, but other symbols undoubtedly have been overlooked. Pullman's achievement is nothing short of astonishing. *His Dark Materials* is possibly the most imaginative, complex, thorough, symbol-laden allegory ever written, and certainly among the most readable and entertaining.

Imaginative? Pullman gives Boreal-Latrom two social identities, complete with two names, to symbolize C. S. Lewis's two-physical-identities (human-goat) faun. He invents Specters to symbolize religious superstition and Dust to symbolize superstition's enemy, knowledge. He invents daemons so he can symbolize the Milton personifications that come in pairs—Sin and Death, Chaos and Night—and so he can also symbolize the White Witch's dwarf. He treats both daemons and the armored bears' armor as souls in order to symbolize the death (departure of the soul) and resurrection (regaining of the soul) of both Aslan and the intercised children; the latter are revived in the symbolized "harrowing of Hell." He uses witches with flaming torches who dive on angels, set their wings afire, and send them screaming to earth to symbolize Spitfires and Hurricanes with flaming machine guns that dive on German Heinkel bombers, set their wing engines afire, and send them screaming to earth. The scene where witches tow Lee Scoresby's balloon—reindeer are towing Santa's sleigh—is a gem. Pullman even manages to symbolize the famous biblical passage "Ye shall know the truth, and the truth shall make you free."

Complex? This is no standard one-hidden-story allegory. Three hidden stories, two of them fully allegorical, have been artfully interwoven into one surface story tapestry, apparently for the first time in the history of literature. The tapestry is all the grander in that it displays bold patterns depicting the evils of religion, patterns that warn of the seductive allure of religious superstition and the horrible damage it can inflict on society.

Thorough and symbol laden? Nothing of consequence in either

The Lion, the Witch and the Wardrobe or *Paradise Lost*, the literary sources of the two principal hidden stories, has been left unsymbolized. Even many minor details and, in the *Paradise Lost* allegory, items from the Bible and other religious sources have been additionally symbolized. On top of all this, the literary works to be allegorized have been superbly chosen: the two symbolically retold stories are two of the best-known works of children's literature and epic poetry in existence, and both literary antecedents have Christian themes that make them perfect foils for Pullman's antireligious themes.

His Dark Materials is destined to become a literary classic, not only literature's first (and so far only) multiple allegory but the post-Darwin era's anti-Christian, antireligious counterpart of—and answer to—one of the most famous allegories ever written, John Bunyan's pro-Christian allegory, *The Pilgrim's Progress*.

NOTES

CHAPTER 1

1. Theodore M. Bernstein, *The Careful Writer: A Modern Guide to English Usage* (New York: Atheneum, 1985), p. 393.

2. H. W. Fowler, *Fowler's Modern English Usage*, 2nd ed., rev. Sir Ernest Gowers (Oxford: Oxford University Press, 1983), p. 559.

3. Leonard F. Wheat, *Kubrick's* 2001: *A Triple Allegory* (Lanham, MD: Scarecrow Press, 2000), pp. 88–89, 91, 100–105, 109–11.

4. George Orwell, *Animal Farm* (New York: New American Library, 1956), p. 123.

5. Norman Friedman, "Allegory," in *Princeton Encyclopedia of Poetry and Poetics*, ed. Alex Preminger, Frank J. Warnke, and O. B. Hardison Jr., 12 (Princeton, NJ: Princeton University Press, 1974).

6. Susan Roberts, "A Dark Agenda?" interview with Philip Pullman, November 2002, p. 3, http://www.surefish.co.uk/culture/features/pullman_interview.htm

7. Tony Watkins, *Dark Matter: A Thinking Fan's Guide to Philip Pullman* (Damaris: Southampton, 2004), p. 247.

8. Philip Pullman, "The Darkside of Narnia," *Guardian*, October 1, 1998, p. 2. Available at *The Cumberland River Lamp Post*, http://www.crlamppost.org/darkside.htm.

9. Ibid.

10. Ibid. (italics added).

11. Ibid., p. 3.

12. Ibid.

13. Roberts, "Dark Agenda?" p. 3.

14. Ibid.

15. Philip Pullman and Rowan Williams, "The Dark Materials Debate: Life, God, and the Universe . . . ," recorded conversation at London's National Theatre, November 7, 2004, p. 10, http://www.telegraph.co.uk/arts/main.jhtml?xml=/arts/2004/03/17/bodark.xml.

16. Ibid., p. 9 (italics added).

17. Watkins, "Interview with Philip Pullman" (part two), 2004, p. 7, http://damaris.org/content/content.php?type=5&id=369.

18. BBC Newsround, chat with Phillip Pullman, January 23, 2002, p. 5, http://news.bbc.co.uk/cbbcnews/hi/chat/hotseat/newsid_1777000/1777895. stm.

19. Pullman, http://www.philip-pullman.com/about_the_writing.asp (FAQ page).

20. Roberts, "Dark Agenda?" p. 2.

21. Pullman, http://www.philip-pullman.com/pages/content/index.asp ?Page ID=12.

22. Philip Pullman, "Republic of Heaven" speech (time and place not given), *His Dark Materials* Web site, p. 1, http://www.hisdarkmaterials.org/content-22.html.

23. Ibid.

24. Roberts, "Dark Agenda?" p. 2.

25. Philip Pullman, "Philip Pullman in His Own Words . . . ," Random House Web site, "Author Q & A," p. 2, http://www.randomhouse.com/features/pullman/philippullman/qanda.html.

26. Pullman, "Heat and Dust," interview with Huw Spanner, *Thirdway* Web site, p. 2, http://www.thirdway.org.uk/past/showpage.asp?page =3349.

27. Ibid., "Philip Pullman in Readerville: 02.05.01–02.09.01" (discussion), p. 1.

28. John Milton, *Paradise Lost*, ed., introduction, and notes by John Leonard (London: Penguin Books, 2000), bk. VII, lines 225–32.

29. Ibid., bk. II, line 916.

30. Philip Pullman, *The Golden Compass* (New York: Knopf, 1996), pp. 73, 78; Philip Pullman, *The Subtle Knife* (New York: Knopf, 1997), pp. 90, 238.

31. An excellent description of "The Novel's Reception," with extensive quotations from reviews and commentaries, can be found in Claire Squires, *Philip Pullman's* His Dark Materials *Trilogy: A Reader's Guide* (New York: Continuum, 2003), pp. 66–75.

32. The eight books are John Houghton, *A Closer Look at* His Dark Materials (Colorado Springs: Victor, 2004); Watkins, *Dark Matter* (Southampton: Damaris, 2004); Millicent Lenz, ed., with Carole Scott, His Dark Materials *Illuminated: Critical Essays on Philip Pullman's Trilogy* (Detroit: Wayne State University Press, 2005); Glenn Yeffeth, ed., *Navi-*

gating the Golden Compass: Religion, Science and Daemonology in Philip Pullman's His Dark Materials (Dallas: Benbella Books, 2005); Claire Squires, *Philip Pullman's* His Dark Materials *Trilogy: A Reader's Guide* (New York: Continuum, 2003); Nicholas Tucker, *Darkness Visible: Inside the World of Philip Pullman* (Cambridge: Wizard Books, 2003); Lance Parkin and Mark Jones, *An Unofficial and Unauthorized Guide to Philip Pullman's Internationally Bestselling* His Dark Materials *Trilogy* (London: Virgin Books, 2005); and Laurie Frost, *The Elements of* His Dark Materials: *A Guide to Philip Pullman's Trilogy* (Buffalo Grove, IL: Fell Press, 2006). The first two books are from religious publishing houses. The next two are collections of, respectively, scholarly essays and popular essays about the trilogy. Four of the books include Philip Pullman biographical material, plot summaries, or both. Unfortunately, none of the authors and essayists realizes that the trilogy is allegory or even recognizes and correctly interprets more than a few of the trilogy's hundreds of symbols.

33. Michael Chabon, "Dust & Daemons," review of *His Dark Materials* trilogy, *New York Review of Books*, March 25, 2004.

34. An example is Lili Ladaga, "Philip Pullman Weaves Spell with '*His Dark Materials*': Author Combines Adventure with Allegory," *CNN.com Book News*, November 10, 2000, http://archives.cnn.com/2000/books/news/11/10/philip.pullman/. The article's only support for the word *allegory* in the subtitle is an inaccurate statement that the trilogy "can be viewed as . . . a sophisticated, allegorical retelling of man's beginnings" (p. 3). That statement alludes to, but does not even explicitly recognize, Pullman's depiction of five things from the Adam and Eve myth: "Eve," "Adam," "the serpent" (in Eden), "little red fruits" (the Forbidden Fruit), and "the Fall." These five things neither establish the presence of allegory nor recognize either of Pullman's two allegories. Why not? First, Pullman has no Adam and Eve allegory: his main allegory is instead a retelling of Milton's *PL*, and his material depicting the new "Fall" takes up only 21 of 1,243 pages of the trilogy, or less than 2 percent of the story. Second, neither does Pullman retell "man's beginnings": nothing in the trilogy depicts the beginning of the human race. Third, Eve, Adam, and the serpent are not actually symbolized; they are metaphors used to compare what Lyra, Will, and Mary do with what the Genesis characters do. Fourth, two symbols (the little red fruits and Lyra's and Will's falling in love), or even five, don't create an allegory. Fifth, the material Ladaga refers to is entirely in the third book of the trilogy, a fact that

leaves her without even a semblance of an argument that the trilogy as a whole (the *"His Dark Materials"* she refers to) is an allegory.

NOTES FOR CHAPTER 3

1. Leland Ryken and Marjorie Lamp Mead, *A Reader's Guide through the Wardrobe: Exploring C. S. Lewis's Classic Story* (Downers Grove, IL: InterVarsity Press, 2005), p. 172.

2. Ibid.

3. C. S. Lewis, *The Lion, the Witch and the Wardrobe* (New York: HarperCollins, 2000), pp. 79, 141.

4. Ibid., p. 82.

5. Ibid., pp. 134–35.

6. Pullman's surface story has a curious allusion to the name Cair Paravel. The Church's Consistorial Court has an alethiometrist named Fra Pavel. The resemblance between "Paravel" and "Pavel" is too obvious to miss. It becomes even more obvious when we take the letters *ra* from F*ra* and insert them after the *a* in Pavel to get "F. Pa*ra*vel." Pullman might be using this letter play as a hint that his surface story has something to do with *LWW*.

7. Lewis, *The Lion, the Witch and the Wardrobe*, p. 104.

8. Edmund's betrayal of his siblings has raised the issue of whether Edmund symbolizes Judas, who betrayed Jesus (William Booth, "The Roar over C. S. Lewis's Otherworldly Lion," *Washington Post*, December 8, 2005). But the betrayal-of-Jesus analogy doesn't fit Edmund. Edmund doesn't betray Aslan, who symbolizes Jesus; he betrays his siblings. When Edmund also tells the witch that Aslan has returned, this isn't betrayal. Unlike Judas, who was a friend and disciple of Jesus, Edmund has never met and doesn't know Aslan. Furthermore, whereas Judas never repented his "sin" and never received forgiveness, Edmund later repents and is forgiven. Yes, Edmund is a symbol, but what he symbolizes is a sinner, and later a repentant sinner who achieves salvation.

9. Marvin D. Hinten, *The Keys to the Chronicles: Unlocking the Symbols of C. S. Lewis's Narnia* (Nashville: Broadman & Holman, 2005), p. 16.

10. C. S. Lewis, *The Lion, the Witch and the Wardrobe*, p. 136.

11. Mk. 27:50. Cf. Jn. 19:30.

12. Mt. 26:36–37 Revised Standard Version (RSV).

13. Lewis, *The Lion, the Witch and the Wardrobe*, pp. 146, 150.

14. Lk. 8:49–56.

15. Jn. 11:1–44.

16. Rev. 6:8.

17. Mk. 14:53–62. Cf. Mk. 8:38, 13:26; Mt. 10:23, 24:3, 24:30; Lk. 21:27 RSV.

18. Rev. 21:2 RSV.

19. Rev. 21:3 RSV.

20. Rev. 21:23 RSV.

21. Colin Duriez, *A Field Guide to Narnia* (Downers Grove, IL: Inter-Varsity Press, 2004), p. 96. Also quoted in Paul F. Ford, *Companion to Narnia* (San Francisco: HarperSanFrancisco, 1994), p. xxv, note 2, with the word *an* added in front of *allegory*.

22. Ford, *Companion to Narnia*, p. xxv.

23. Duriez, *Field Guide*, p. 96.

24. Ibid., p. 44.

25. Ibid., p. 45.

26. Ibid., p. 96.

27. Ibid.

28. Ford, *Companion to Narnia*, p. xxv, note 2.

29. Ibid., pp. xxv–xxvi, note 2.

30. Ibid., p. xxv, note 2, and Duriez, *Field Guide*, p. 96.

31. Ford, *Companion to Narnia*, p. xxvi, note.

32. Ibid.

33. Duriez, *Field Guide*, p. 97.

34. Ibid.

35. Bruce Edwards, *Further Up & Further In: Understanding C. S. Lewis's* The Lion, the Witch and the Wardrobe (Nashville: Broadman & Holman, 2005), p. 75.

36. Richard Wagner, *C. S. Lewis & Narnia for Dummies* (Hoboken, NJ: Wiley, 2005), p. 98.

37. Ibid., p. 99.

38. Devin Brown, *Inside Narnia: A Guide to Exploring* The Lion, the Witch and the Wardrobe (Grand Rapids, MI: BakerBooks, 2005), p. 195.

39. Ibid., p. 217.

40. David C. Downing, *Into the Wardrobe: C. S. Lewis and the Narnia Chronicles* (San Francisco: Jossey-Bass, 2005), p. 64.

41. Ibid., p. 70.

42. Ryken and Mead, *Through the Wardrobe*, p. 63.

43. Ibid.

44. Ibid., p. 172.

45. Ibid., p. 71.

46. The authors think they also recognize what they seem to construe as a Last Supper symbol—"an affecting and somber evening meal" (ibid., p. 98). But this meal is merely one of seven mentioned in *LWW* (two with Tumnus, two with the Beavers, two with Aslan, one at a "merry party" quashed by the witch), and it has not even one feature that is analogous to one the distinctive features of the Last Supper: the twelve disciples (surely not Aslan's army of supernatural creatures and three recent human converts), the bread and wine, Judas, and a prediction of betrayal. I don't consider the evening meal a Last Supper symbol.

47. Peter J. Schakel, *The Way into Narnia: A Reader's Guide* (Grand Rapids, MI: William B. Eerdmans, 2005), p. 37.

48. Ibid., p. 44.

49. Schakel actually denies that the White Witch is Satan. Ibid., p. 124.

50. The comma after "Witch"—not found in Lewis's title—was inserted by Veith.

51. Gene Veith, *The Soul of* The Lion, the Witch, & the Wardrobe (Victor: Colorado Springs, 2005), p. 66.

52. Ibid.

53. Ibid., p. 40.

54. Ibid., p. 104.

55. Mt. 27:50. Cf. Jn. 19:30.

56. Lk. 8:53–55.

57. Mt. 1:18–20, Lk. 1:26–36.

58. Acts 1:8, 5:12–16.

59. Acts 2:4, 10:44–46, 19:6.

60. Acts 19:6.

61. Hinten, *Keys to the Chronicles*, pp. 106–107.

62. Ibid., p. 108.

63. Ryken and Mead, *Through the Wardrobe*, p. 64.

64. Schakel, *Way into Narnia*, p. 44.

65. Hinten, *Keys to the Chronicles*, pp. 11, 102.

NOTES FOR CHAPTER 4

1. Philip Pullman, *The Amber Spyglass* (New York: Knopf, 2000), p. 392.

2. The image of Spitfires and Hurricanes diving with flaming machine guns evokes a line from World War II's US Army Air Corps (now the US Air Force) song: "*Down we dive*, spouting our *flame* from under."

3. Tony Watkins, *Dark Matter: A Thinking Fan's Guide to Philip Pullman* (Damaris: Southampton, 2004), pp. 29, 30.

4. Bridgetothestars.net, "Chris Weitz Interview," 2004, p. 4, http://www .bridgetothestars.net/index.php?p=weitzinterview.

5. C. S. Lewis, *The Lion, the Witch and the Wardrobe* (New York: HarperCollins, 2000), p. 3.

6. Philip Pullman, *The Golden Compass* (New York: Knopf, 1996), p. 301 (italics added).

7. Ibid.

8. Take *Lyra* as the name being compared with other four-letter names. The computation assumes that the last three letters of the second name (the name being compared with *Lyra*) are different from each other but not necessarily different from the initial letter. Assume that the second name is Lois. Since the alphabet has 26 letters, there is 1 chance in 26 that the second name's (*Lois's*) first letter will match the initial *L* in *Lyra*. The second name has three "last three" letters (the *ois* in *Lois*), so there are 3 chances in 26 that the second letter of the first name (the *y* in *Lyra*) will match one of the last three letters of the second name. If the second letter provides no match, the second letter of *Lyra* (*y*) cannot be among the last three letters of the second name: they now belong to a group of 26 − 1 = 25. Hence there are 3 chances in 25 that the third letter of the first name (the *r* in *Lyra*) will match one of the last three letters of the second name. If the third letter still provides no match, neither the second nor the third letter of the first name can be among the last three letters of the second name: those three letters now belong to a group of 26 − 2 = 24. So there are 3 chances in 24 that the last letter of the first name (the *a* in *Lyra*) will match one of the three last letters of the second name (the *ois* in *Lois*).

9. Two-letter female names, most of them Chinese, include Di, Jo, Li, Lu, On, Vi, Yi, Yu, Zi, and Zo. The names with more than nine letters include

Annamathilda, Antoinette, Bernadette, Christiana, Clementine, Desdemonia, Eufrosiina, Evangeline, Floramaria, Georgianna, Gwendoline, Hildegarde, Jacqueline, Juandalynn, Konstantian, Margaretha, Marguerite, Persephone, Petronella, Sagittarious, Tranquilla, and Wilhelmina.

10. Pullman, *Golden Compass*, p. 214.

11. Ibid., p. 50.

12. Ibid., p. 86.

13. Ibid., p. 273.

14. Philip Pullman, "Philip Pullman in Readerville: 02.05.01–02.09.01" (discussion), p. 15.

15. Philip Pullman, "There Has to Be a Lot of Ignorance in Me When I Start a Story," *Guardian Unlimited*, February 18, 2002, p. 5, http://www.guardian.co .uk/books/departments/childrenandteens/story/0,6000,650988,00 .html.

16. Place names featuring trolls are not unheard of in Norway. The home of composer Edvard Grieg near Bergen, Norway, was (and still is) named Troldhaugen. Troldhaugen means "troll hill" or "hill of the trolls." A road near Andalsnes, Norway, is named Trollstigen, which means "troll's road" or "the troll road."

17. Philip Pullman, "Philip Pullman in His Own Words . . . ," Random House Web site, "Author Q & A," p. 3.

18. Pullman, *Golden Compass*, p. 302.

19. Pullman, *Amber Spyglass*, pp. 71, 69.

20. Ibid., p. 370.

21. Pullman, *Golden Compass*, p. 155.

22. Ibid., pp. 196, 202, 224, 316, 349.

23. In Christian belief and in Bible stories, a person's soul or spirit leaves the body when the person dies and returns to a person if the person comes back to life. Jesus's spirit departed when he died (Mt. 27:50, Jn. 19:30). When Jesus brought a dead girl back to life, "her spirit returned" (Lk. 8:55).

24. Iorek's *descending* into the cellar and then *arising* from it also provides some nonallegorical symbolism depicting events from Christianity's Apostles' Creed. The creed says that Jesus, after dying, "*descended* into Hell" and then, on the third day, "*arose* from the dead." Although the descent and climb at the priest's house do depict the creedal events, Iorek's actions are not symbols in either allegory. In the *LWW* allegory Iorek symbolizes Aslan, not Jesus. And in the *PL* allegory, someone other than Iorek symbol-

izes Jesus; Iorek fights on the side of Asriel, the enemy of the character symbolizing Jesus. The *PL* allegory does have symbolization of Jesus's descent into Hell, but Iorek is not the character who descends.

25. Pullman, *Golden Compass*, p. 198.

26. Leonard F. Wheat, *Kubrick's* 2001: *A Triple Allegory* (Lanham, MD: Scarecrow Press, 2000), pp. 100–105, 109–11, 119–22.

27. Lewis, *The Lion, the Witch and the Wardrobe,* p. 81.

28. Ibid.

29. Pullman, *Golden Compass*, p. 27.

30. Ibid., p. 333.

31. Ibid., p. 336.

32. Ibid., p. 353.

33. Pullman, *Amber Spyglass*, p. 456.

34. Ibid., p. 479.

35. Ibid., p. 32.

36. Ibid.

37. Ibid., p. 491.

38. Ibid., p. 479.

39. Tony Watkins, "Interview with Philip Pullman" (part two), 2004, p. 1, http://news.bbc.co.uk/cbbcnews/hi/chat/hotseat/newsid_1777000/1777895.stm.

40. Ibid.

41. Pullman, *Amber Spyglass*, p. 32.

42. Ibid., p. 490 (italics added).

43. Pullman, *Golden Compass*, p. 176.

44. Ibid., p. 310.

45. Pullman, *Amber Spyglass*, pp. 362–63, 485.

46. Pullman, *Golden Compass*, pp. 301–302.

47. Pullman, *Amber Spyglass*, p. 191.

48. Ibid., pp. 409, 417.

49. Michael Dirda, review of "*The Amber Spyglass*: *His Dark Materials*, Book III," *Washington Post*, October 29, 2000.

NOTES FOR CHAPTER 5

1. John Milton, *Paradise Lost*, ed., introduction, and notes by John Leonard (London: Penguin Books, 2000), bk. V, line 605.

2. Ibid., line 689.

3. Ibid., bk. II, line 1028.

4. Ibid., bk. V, line 70.

5. Ibid., bk. X, line 208.

6. Ibid., bk. XI, lines 444–47.

7. Ibid., bk. XI, line 397.

8. Ibid., bk. XII, lines 386–465.

9. Philip Pullman, *The Golden Compass* (New York: Knopf, 1996), pp. 48–50, 66–67.

10. William Butler Yeats, "The Stolen Child," in *William Butler Yeats: Selected Poems and Four Plays*, 4th ed., ed. and introduction by M. L. Rosenthal (New York: Scribner Paperback Poetry, 1966), pp. 2–4.

11. William Blake, *The Marriage of Heaven and Hell* (New York: Dover, 1994), pp. 6, 30.

12. Blake, "Milton," in *William Blake: The Complete Poems*, ed. Alicia Ostriker, 513–607 (London: Penguin, 1977).

13. *Superstition* is sometimes used loosely or metaphorically to describe any irrational or false belief, whether or not it relies on the assumed reality of something supernatural. The loose meaning is not used in this study. To be properly called a superstition in the strict sense of the word, a belief must incorporate the assumed existence of something supernatural—a being (e.g., an angel or a demon), a place (e.g., Heaven), a supernatural "cause" that is actually unrelated to the effect it supposedly produces (e.g., a broken mirror's causing bad luck), a law or command supposedly emanating from a god or other divine power, communications from the dead, things people can do to make the gods friendly, clairvoyance or psychic powers, something of that sort.

14. Philip Pullman, *The Amber Spyglass* (New York: Knopf, 2000), p. 479.

15. Ibid., p. 441.

16, Philip Pullman, *The Subtle Knife* (New York: Knopf, 1997), p. 320.

17. Pullman, *Amber Spyglass*, p. 486.

18. Ibid.

19. Ibid., p. 381.

20. Ibid., p. 479.

21. Ibid., *Subtle Knife*, p. 250; *Amber Spyglass*, p. 80.

22. Pullman, *Amber Spyglass*, pp. 76, 79.

23. Ibid., p. 68.

24. Ibid., pp. 67, 71.

25. Ibid., p. 314.

26. Pullman, *Golden Compass*, p. 371.

27. Ibid., p. 370.

28. Pullman, *Amber Spyglass*, p. 60.

29. Pullman, *Subtle Knife*, p. 84.

30. Ibid., p. 238. Will's father, John Parry, dates the origin of human beings slightly earlier when he says to Lee Scoresby that Asriel's task is "the greatest in thirty-five thousand years of human history." Ibid., pp. 214–15.

31. Pullman's 33,000 years ago timing for the evolution of *Homo sapiens* ties in nicely with research findings published in 2005, or five years after *HDM* was completed. The new research is reported in the article "Genes Tied to Recent Brain Evolution," published in the September 24, 2005, *Science News*, p. 204. A team led by Bruce T. Lahn of the University of Chicago found that a variant of the gene *microcephalin*, previously found to influence brain size, evolved about 37,000 years ago. It is now found in seven of ten people and seems to increase survival rates. A reasonable inference is that the higher survival rates result from higher intelligence, the most distinctive characteristic of *Homo sapiens*. (The Latin *sapiens* denotes wisdom.) Cf. Pullman, *Subtle Knife*, p. 89.

32. Pullman, *Amber Spyglass*, pp. 223–24.

33. Pullman, *Golden Compass*, pp. 89, 370.

34. Philip Pullman and Rowan Williams, "The Dark Materials Debate: Life, God, and the Universe . . . ," recorded conversation at London's National Theatre, November 7, 2004, p. 4.

35. Tony Watkins, "Interview with Philip Pullman," part two, p. 9, http://news.bbc.co.uk/cbbcnews/hi/chat/hotseat/newsid_1777000/1777895.stm.

36. Pullman, *Amber Spyglass*, p. 491.

37. Ibid., p. 483.

38. Pullman, *Subtle Knife*, p. 280.

39. Pullman, *Amber Spyglass*, p. 121.

40. Pullman, *Subtle Knife*, p. 280.

41. Gen. 1:27, 2:7.

42. Gen. 13:10–13, 19:24–25.

43. Mt. 8:28–33, Lk. 8:26–33.

44. Pullman, *Golden Compass*, p. 370.

45. Watkins, "Interview with Philip Pullman," part two, p. 1.

46. Pullman, *Golden Compass*, p. 390.

47. As part of his "borrowed-ideas" approach, Pullman could easily be consciously borrowing potential-becomes-actual from Hegel. Hegel's pantheistic philosophy revolves around dialectics. A dialectic is a movement from (1) a *thesis*, a concept or idea, to (2) its *antithesis*, something that is the opposite of the thesis, to (3) their *synthesis*, a sort of compromise that combines part of the thesis with part of the antithesis. In a typical Hegelian dialectic (but not in all of them), both the thesis and the antithesis have two parts. The synthesis takes one part from the thesis and one part from the antithesis. Hegel's most basic dialectic thus progresses from (1) the thesis, potential *unity*, to (2) the antithesis, *actual* separation ("estrangement"), to (3) their synthesis, *actual unity*. The synthesis combines "actual" from the antithesis with "unity" from the thesis. Hegel writes about a metaphysical Spirit that is the invisible, nonmaterial, spiritual essence of everything that exists. Unlike God, who the Spirit replaces, the Spirit has no mind or consciousness apart from the minds of individual humans. The Spirit is (1) potentially *one*, one Spirit that comprises everything in the universe, but is (2) *actually* many, estranged from itself, because individual humans don't realize that the many external "objects" they see, including other humans, are essentially the same thing as themselves, Spirit. The Spirit achieves "self-realization"—it overcomes self-estrangement and becomes self-conscious—when the world's smartest man, Hegel, finally realizes that he and everyone and everything else in the universe are essentially Spirit. The Spirit, which is the essence of Hegel and of his mind, recognizes itself (Spirit) in all external objects. Through this act of self-realization, Spirit becomes *actually one*. Hegel's dialectical synthesis combines "actually" from the antithesis ("*actually* many") with "one" from the thesis ("potentially *one*"). This synthesis is the culmination of a movement from potentially one to actually one—analogous to Pullman's Dust's movement from potential knowledge to actual knowledge.

48. Milton, *Paradise Lost*, bk. II, lines 910–20.

49. Pullman, *Amber Spyglass*, p. 381.

50. Nicholas Tucker, *Darkness Visible: Inside the World of Philip Pullman* (Cambridge: Wizard Books, 2003), pp. 157–58.

51. Political institutions exist in Lyra's world—there is a prime minister with a cabinet council—but the Church is in control of society. See Pullman, *Golden Compass*, p. 10.

52. Tucker, *Darkness Visible*, p. 173.

53. Leonard F. Wheat, *Kubrick's* 2001: *A Triple Allegory* (Lanham, MD: Scarecrow Press, 2000), pp. 41–62, 96–99, 113–116.

54. Pullman, *Subtle Knife*, p. 224 (italics added).

55. Ex. 22:18 Authorized Version (AV).

56. H. L. Mencken, *Treatise on the Gods* (New York: Vintage, 1963), p. x.

57. Ex. 20:13 RSV.

58. Ex. 21–17 RSV.

59. Lev. 20:10 RSV.

60. Lev. 20:12 RSV.

61. Jesus. Mt. 5:32 RSV.

62. Ibid.

63. Deut. 22:13–21, 22:23–24 RSV.

64. Lev. 21:9 RSV.

65. Ex. 22:19 RSV.

66. Lev. 20:13 RSV.

67. Lev. 19:26 RSV.

68. Ex. 22:18 RSV.

69. Deut. 13:6–10 RSV.

70. Deut. 13:1–5.

71. Ex. 31:15, 35:2; Num. 15:32–36 RSV.

72. "Headmaster Is Decapitated by Extremists in Afghanistan," *Washington Post*, January 5, 2006, home edition, p. A11.

73. Ibid.

74. Ex. 20:3 RSV.

75. Roman Catholic doctrine.

76. Roman Catholic and Protestant fundamentalist doctrine.

77. Roman Catholic and Protestant fundamentalist doctrine, accepted also by some moderates. Cf. Deut. 23.2.

78. 1 Cor. 7:29 RSV.

79. Jesus. Mk. 10:9, Mt. 19:6 RSV.

80. Gen. 3:16 RSV, Eph. 5:22–24 RSV.

81. Deut. 25:11 RSV.

82. Deut. 23:2 RSV.

83. Deut. 23:1 RSV.

84. 1 Tim. 5:9–12 RSV.

85. Deut. 12:2–3 RSV.

86. Deut. 20:10–14 RSV.

87. Ex. 21:2 RSV.

88. Ex. 21:4–6 RSV.

89. Col. 3:22 RSV.

90. Divine law preached by many fundamentalist, conservative, and moderate Protestant ministers.

91. Divine law observed by Mormons and assorted other Protestant congregations.

92. Ex. 35:3 RSV.

93. Ex. 20:10 RSV.

94. Ex. 20:7 RSV.

95. Jesus. Mt. 5:22, 23:17 RSV.

96. Lev. 19:28 RSV.

97. Lev. 18:22, 1 Cor. 6:9–10, Rom. 1:18, 26–27.

98. Ex. 20:17 RSV.

99. Jesus. Mt. 6:19 RSV.

100. Deut. 23:19 RSV.

101. Lev. 19:19 RSV.

102. Ex. 20:24 RSV.

103. Ex. 22:29 RSV.

104. This law nowadays is observed mainly by conservative Muslims, Amish, and Mennonites but was firmly endorsed by Christians in the nineteenth century and earlier.

105. Deut. 25:5–9 RSV.

106. Lev. 19:19 RSV.

107. Deut. 22:5 RSV.

108. Lev. 11:1–19 RSV.

109. Jewish religious law, observed by Orthodox and conservative Jews.

110. Some early theologians relied on the Apostles' Creed to explain why the crucifixion was necessary for man's salvation. After dying, Jesus supposedly "descended into Hell," fought and defeated Satan, and thereby destroyed Satan's ability to thwart God's desire to bring deserving souls into Heaven. Only then did God become truly omnipotent, able to do what he wanted. Some Christians argue that God was always omnipotent but was *unwilling* to admit people to Heaven until mankind was punished for its manifold sins, or else for the Original Sin of Adam and Eve. These people tacitly

concede that Jesus's suffering was *not really necessary* for man's salvation. His suffering becomes an irrational act by a sadistic, irrational deity who regarded torture as an appropriate form of punishment (God did, after all, create Hell and its "eternal fire") and who foolishly believed that by torturing his own son he could thereby deliver anguish—punishment—to the real sinners. It never occurred to God that most of those sinners were already dead (unable to experience anguish), or would never hear of Jesus, or approved of his death, or were not concerned about Jesus, or admired him but were no more pained by his suffering than they were when they read about Aslan's suffering or that of the innocent Salem "witches."

111. Lev. 16:5–10, 20–22.
112. Gen. 1:1–2:7 RSV.
113. Gen. 2:21–23 RSV.
114. Gen. 1:3–5, 14–19.
115. Gen. 3:1–5, 3:13 RSV.
116. Gen. 19:15–26 RSV.
117. Ez. 37:1–14 RSV.
118. Dan. 3:13–27 RSV.
119. Dan. 5:5–28 RSV.
120. 1 Sam. 28:3–20 AV.
121. Ex. 3:1–4:17 RSV.
122. Ex. 7–8 RSV.
123. Ex. 14:15–29 RSV.
124. Mt. 1:18–25, Lk. 1:26–45 RSV.
125. Mt. 17:1–3; Mk. 9:2–4; Lk. 9:28–30 RSV.
126. Mk. 6:45–51, Mt. 14:22–33, Jn. 6:16–21 RSV.
127. Mt. 21:18–19 RSV.
128. Mk. 1:29–34, 5:1–13, 7:24–30, Mt. 8:14–16, 8:28–32, 15:21–28, Lk. 4:38–41, 8:26–36 RSV.
129. Jn. 9:6–7, Mk. 8:22–25, 10:46–52 RSV.
130. Lk. 8:49–56, Jn. 11:1–44 RSV.
131. Mk. 16, Mt. 28, Lk. 24, Jn. 20–21 RSV.
132. Jn. 20:19, 26 RSV.
133. Acts 1:3, 9 RSV.
134. Mk. 8:38, 13:26–30, Mt. 10:23, Lk. 9:26–27, Rev. 21, 22:6–7 RSV.
135. Mt. 22:23–30, Jn. 5:28–29, 1 Cor. 15:52, 1 Thes. 4:15–17, Tim. 4:1, Rev. 20:5–6 RSV.

136. Acts 3:1–8. Cf. 5:12–16 RSV.

137. In 1437 and 1445, Pope Eugene IV issued papal bulls that called for reprisals against the witches responsible for bad weather.

138. Mt. 22:14. Cf. Mt. 7:13–14, Lk. 13:23–24 RSV.

139. Mt. 8:12, 13:42, 13:50, 24:51, Lk. 13:28 RSV.

140. Pullman, *Subtle Knife*, p. 20.

141. Pullman, *Amber Spyglass*, p. 33.

142. Ibid., p. 298.

143. Ibid., p. 33.

144. Ibid., p. 320.

145. Ibid., p. 319.

146. Ibid., p. 363.

147. Ibid., p. 518 (italics added).

NOTES FOR CHAPTER 6

1. John Milton, *Paradise Lost*, ed., introduction, and notes by John Leonard (London: Penguin Books, 2000), bk. II, line 1028.

2. Philip Pullman, *The Golden Compass* (New York: Knopf, 1996), p. 389.

3. Milton, *Paradise Lost*, bk. II, lines 1024–25.

4. Pullman, *Golden Compass*, p. 188.

5. Philip Pullman, *The Amber Spyglass* (New York: Knopf, 2000), p. 31.

6. The hymn's words are borrowed from Revelation 4:8: "Holy, holy, holy, is the Lord God Almighty."

7. Ex. 6:3n RSV. Also see Theophile James Meek, *Hebrew Origins* (New York: Harper Torchbooks, 1960), pp. 92–118.

8. Joseph Gaer, *The Lore of the Old Testament* (Boston: Little, Brown, 1951), p. 264.

9. Milton, *Paradise Lost*, bk. VI, lines 8–15, 749–50, 829, 835–66.

10. Philip Pullman, *The Subtle Knife* (New York: Knopf, 1997), pp. 28, 32, 373.

11. Ibid., p. 373.

12. Milton, *Paradise Lost*, bk. X, lines 11–13. Cf. 301–302, 314–16, and bk. II, lines 1024–27.

13. Pullman, *Subtle Knife*, pp. 39, 314.

14. Pullman, *Amber Spyglass*, pp. 67, 71, 205.

15. Pullman, *Subtle Knife*, pp. 250.

16. Pullman, *Amber Spyglass*, pp. 76, 80.

17. Death's dart might have been adapted by Milton from 1 Corinthians 15:55: "O death, where is thy sting?"

18. Pullman, *Golden Compass*, pp. 121, 124, 175, 367.

19. Pullman, *Amber Spyglass*, p. 364.

20. Ibid., p. 68.

21. Ibid., p. 71.

22. Ibid.

23. Pullman, *Subtle Knife*, p. 103. For an extended discussion of Lyra's penchant for lying, see Tony Watkins, *Dark Matter: A Thinking Fan's Guide to Philip Pullman* (Damaris: Southampton, 2004), pp. 205–208, 212–16.

24. Pullman, *Amber Spyglass*, p. 281.

25. Ibid., p. 282.

26. See, for example, Nicholas Tucker, *Darkness Visible: Inside the World of Philip Pullman* (Cambridge: Wizard Books, 2003), p. 141.

27. Milton, *Paradise Lost*, bk. II, lines 575–78.

28. Edith Hamilton, *Mythology: Timeless Tales of Gods and Heroes* (New York: Mentor, 1953), pp. 39, 227–28.

29. Milton, *Paradise Lost*, bk. II, lines 970–80.

30. Pullman, *Golden Compass*, p. 392.

31. The wire leading up through the aurora borealis toward Cittàgazze might be intended as a symbol of the path along which Satan struggles to traverse the dark, chaotic void between Hell and Earth. But there is too much uncertainty about this interpretation for it to count as a symbol.

32. Pullman, *Golden Compass*, p. 393.

33. Milton, *Paradise Lost*, bk. XI, line 383.

34. Michael Chabon, "Dust & Daemons, " review of *His Dark Materials* trilogy, *New York Review of Books*, March 25, 2004.

35. Pullman, "Philip Pullman in Readerville: 02.05.01–02.09.01" (discussion), p. 12, http://www.readerville.com/webx?14@285.RLH1axXov9M .1@ef6c70e/41.

36. Gen. 2:7, 3:19.

37. Milton, *Paradise Lost*, bk. X, lines 206–208.

38. Pullman, *Amber Spyglass*, p. 141. The name *Elaine* has no special

significance other than, possibly, an intent to give the name the same first and
last letters as *Eve*.

39. Milton, *Paradise Lost*, bk. X, lines 431–33.

40. Milton, *Paradise Lost*, bk. X1, lines 384, 396–97.

41. Mt. 26:14–15.

42. Milton, *Paradise Lost*, bk. II, lines 662–65.

43. Pullman, *Golden Compass*, p. 163.

44. Pullman, *Amber Spyglass*, p. 209.

45. Milton, *Paradise Lost*, bk. V, lines 606–608.

46. Ibid., line 662.

47. Ibid., bk. VI, lines 31–33.

48. Pullman, *Amber Spyglass*, p. 61.

49. Ibid., p. 334.

50. Ibid., p. 66.

51. Milton, *Paradise Lost*, bk. I, lines 79–81.

52. Pullman, *Amber Spyglass*, p. 490.

53. Ibid., p. 473.

54. Ibid., p. 498.

55. Milton, *Paradise Lost*, bk. V, lines 755, 689.

56. Pullman, *Golden Compass*, p. 28.

57. Ibid., p. 362.

58. Pullman, *Subtle Knife*, p. 142.

59. Ibid.

60. Milton, *Paradise Lost*, bk. I, lines 732–33.

61. Ibid., bk. II, line 853. In Greek mythology, Hades also has an
adamantine gate, the name of which Milton presumably borrowed for his
gates of Hell (Hamilton, *Mythology*, p. 39).

62. The idea of salvation in a celestial realm was prominent in the Hellenistic world, both in the gnostic religions and in the many so-called mystery religions. A Persian mystery religion, Mithraism, was widespread in the
Roman Empire, was carried back to Rome by Roman soldiers, and had the
most influence on Christianity. Mithraism's principal deity was Mithras.
Like the Christ of Christian mythology, Mithras was the son of a higher
god, Zoroastrianism's Ahura Mazdah. Mithras was identified with the sun.
His birthday was December 25, which on the old Julian calendar was the
winter solstice, the day the sun is reborn (December 21 or 22, depending on
leap year proximity, on our Gregorian calendar, established in 1582). He

was worshiped on Sun-day. Mithraism featured (*a*) baptism by immersion, (*b*) sacramental eating of the god and drinking of his blood in bread and wine ceremonies, (*c*) initiates who were "reborn" into the service of Mithras, and (*d*) "mysteries"—secret procedures—that would enable initiates to pass through seven heavens to salvation in the realm of the remote god. Borrowing from Mithraism, the Christians decided that Jesus was born on December 25, changed their day of worship from the Jewish Sabbath (Saturday) to Sunday, adopted the bread and wine Communion sacrament, and refashioned their Christ as a redeemer who could bring them salvation in a celestial Heaven. The celestial Heaven largely replaced Judaism's earthly, not-yet-in-existence Kingdom of God, although even today the Kingdom of God survives in the background as a secondary form of salvation that will materialize with the Second Coming of Jesus.

63. Mk 1:15, 13:30; Mt. 3:2, 4:17, 10:7, 16:28; Lk. 21:32 RSV.

64. Mk. 13:26; Mt. 24:30; Lk. 9:27, 21:27 RSV.

65. Mt. 25:31–46 RSV.

66. The fundamentalist Protestant denominations are the Southern Baptists, the Missouri Synod Lutherans (second largest of the three main Lutheran bodies in the United States), the Jehovah's Witnesses, the Seventh-Day Adventists, the Pentecostals, the various Bible Churches and Churches of God and Gospel Tabernacles, the Amish and Mennonites, and assorted other minor sects, including the snake-handling cults. The conservative denominations are the nonsouthern Baptists and non-Missouri-Synod Lutherans (Evangelical Lutheran Church in America, Wisconsin Synod, and many smaller branches). The moderate denominations, whose members tend not to believe in the Second Coming, are the Presbyterians and the Disciples of Christ (Christian Church). The liberal denominations are the Quakers, Congregationalists (United Church of Christ), Methodists, and Episcopalians. Even more liberal are the Unitarians, many of whom still regard themselves as Christians but whose religion has really evolved into a new, ultraliberal, non-Christian religion, just as Christianity evolved from a sect within Judaism into a separate religion. The Roman Catholic and Eastern Orthodox Churches are fundamentalist in their theology, but individual members tend to range from conservative to very conservative and are occasionally moderate or liberal. The Mormons (Latter-day Saints) must be classified as a third branch of Christianity. (The same could be said of the Quaker religion, which could be treated as a fourth branch.) The Christian Scientists are

also in a class by themselves, despite some doctrinal overlap with the Jehovah's Witnesses and the snake cultists.

67. Watkins errs in writing that "the exit from the world of the dead echoes Christ's Harrowing of Hell" (Watkins, *Dark Matter*, p. 64). He is confusing an event that occurred two thousand years ago (the "harrowing") with the Judgment Day that will occur in the future—mythologically speaking, of course.

68. R. M. Grant, *Gnosticism and Early Christianity* (New York: Columbia University Press, 1959), pp. 173–74.

69. Pullman, *Amber Spyglass*, pp. 63–64, 371–72, 377–79.

70. Ibid., p. 317.

71. Ibid., p. 320.

72. Watkins, *Dark Matter*, p. 64.

73. Carol Scott, "Pullman's Enigmatic Ontology: Revamping Old Traditions in *His Dark Materials*," in His Dark Material *Illuminated*, ed. Millicent Lenz with Carole Scott (Detroit: Wayne State University Press, 2005), p. 104.

74. Pat Pinsent, "Unexpected Allies? Pullman and the Feminist Theologians," in Lenz and Scott, His Dark Materials *Illuminated*, p. 204.

75. Milton, *Paradise Lost*, bk. VI, lines 817–66.

76. Pullman, *Amber Spyglass*, p. 400.

77. Ibid., p. 379.

78. Ibid., p. 404.

79. Milton, *Paradise Lost*, bk. VI, lines 865–71.

80. Mk. 13:19 RSV.

81. Mt. 24:7–8 RSV.

82. Mt. 24:29–30 RSV.

83. The identity of Ogunwe's Africans as atheists is explained in chapter 7.

84. Pullman, *Amber Spyglass*, pp. 378, 379.

85. Ibid., p. 379.

86. Ibid., p. 494.

87. As explained in chapter 1, the first book's title, *The Golden Compass*, does not actually refer to the alethiometer. It refers to compasses, the kind used to make circles and referred to in *Paradise Lost*. But most people assume that the title refers to the alethiometer.

88. Pullman, *Amber Spyglass*, p. 491.

89. Pullman, *Subtle Knife*, p. 320.

90. Pullman, *Amber Spyglass*, p. 491.

91. Pullman, *Subtle Knife*, pp. 135, 136.

92. Philip Pullman, http://www.philip-pullman.com/pages/content/index.asp?PageID=12.

93. Pullman, *Amber Spyglass*, pp. 180–81, cf. 191.

NOTES FOR CHAPTER 7

1. Philip Pullman, *The Amber Spyglass* (New York: Knopf, 2000) p. 501.

2. Ibid., p. 82.

3. Ibid., p. 475.

4. Michael Dirda was the first to recognize the Oz wheelers as the source of Pullman's wheeled animals concept. See Dirda, review of *"The Amber Spyglass: His Dark Materials*, Book III," *Washington Post*, October 29, 2000.

5. Pullman, *Amber Spyglass*, p. 370.

6. Homer W. Smith, *Man and His Gods* (New York: Grosset's Universal Library, 1952), p. 364.

7. Philip Pullman, *Amber Spyglass*, p. 444.

8. Ibid., p. 233.

9. Pullman, *The Golden Compass* (New York: Knopf, 1996), pp. 33, 35, 53, 55, 58, 64.

10. Ibid., p. 189.

11. Smith, *Man and His Gods*, p. 3.

12. Carlton University Survey Center (Ottawa, Canada), 1998 ISSP Religion II survey, http://www.carleton.ca/~ssdata/issp-1998.pdf, p. 52. Also see International Social Survey Program, http://www.issp.org (click on "Archive and Data," then on "1998 Religion II").

13. Ibid., pp. 52–53.

14. Ibid., pp. 59–60, 145.

15. Charles Y. Glock and Rodney Stark, *Religion and Society in Tension* (Chicago: Rand McNally, 1965), p. 98.

16. Carlton University, 1998 survey, pp. 182–83.

17. Florence Skelly, "To the Beat of a Different Drum," *Harvard Magazine*, March–April 1986, pp. 23–24.

18. Ibid., p. 23.

19. Arthur J. Bellinzoni, *The Future of Christianity* (Amherst, NY: Prometheus Books, 2006), p. 169.

INDEX